BEFORE THE BADGE

Growing up Alaska–In Short Stories

By A.W. "Andy" Anderson

PO Box 221974 Anchorage, Alaska 99522-1974
books@publicationconsultants.com—www.publicationconsultants.com

ISBN: 978-1-59433-839-7
eISBN: 978-1-59433-840-3

Library of Congress Catalog Card Number: 2018962724

Manufactured in the United States of America.

Dedication

In loving memory of my wife, Ann, and
to my daughter,
Donica, and Grandson, Westin.

Recognition

I want to thank Conny and Kevin Vandegriff for all their support and their visions for this book. I also want to thank Dianne Gruber and Mary Jo Stanley for their support and for all their hours of proof reading and editing this book for me. I also can't forget George Short, my Texas buddy, for his support and his suggestion for the title.

TABLE OF CONTENTS

BEFORE THE BADGE

A.W. (Andy) Anderson was born on a farm in Southern Illinois, the youngest of six boys. As a teenager he left home and traveled to Seldovia, Alaska, where he planned to spend the summer visiting a brother before returning home in the fall. He met a girl and, instead of leaving, he stayed in Alaska and made it his home and later married the love of his life.

Finding himself having to survive as a teenager in Alaska, he realized he had to work very hard and put in long hours to make ends meet. Hard work was not foreign to him having been raised on a farm. His understanding of equipment, and its maintenance, opened many doors for this young man. He found himself working in many different types of jobs. He attributes his being able to survive in a man's world to his upbringing. His parents taught him to build and maintain a good reputation, to be of good character, to always deal honestly with everyone and to give a man eight hours of work for eight hours pay. Andy was soon to find working hard and being honest in his dealings, paid great dividends.

Andy first worked in a king crab processing plant and later ran heavy equipment in the woods as a logger. He worked on construction jobs, running heavy equipment in different locations all around Alaska. At one point he hired on as an operator on a drill barge and traveled to

Good News Bay where they sample core drilled for platinum. Andy also spent a number of years commercially fishing for king crab and snow crab in Kachemak Bay, Lower Cook Inlet, Kamashak Bay, Port Lock Banks, around Augustine Island, all around Kodiak Island and in the Bering Sea. The larger king crab fishing vessels that stayed out for two weeks at a time became a second home to the young man. At one point he took a job as engineer on board an older bell system military tug. The tug worked in the winter, pushing through heavy ice flows in Cook Inlet as they assisted two large landing crafts hauling freight for an oil installation being constructed. He ran tugs and diving boats all around Cook Inlet in oil related contracts and he towed a barge to Valdez and Juneau for a company who was based on the waterfront in Anchorage. He later ran a tug boat out of Prudhoe Bay for one summer, after he had worked on the North Slope running heavy equipment for a two- and one-half years building roads and drill pads for oil companies.

In the fall of 1979 Andy was sworn in as the Chief of Police for the City of Seldovia, Alaska, the community he called home. He held that position for nearly 32 years, setting an all-time record for the longest serving Police Chief for one City in Alaska's history.

This book of short stories outlines many of Andy's adventures, which were both exciting and, at times, dangerous to the point of being life threatening. The seven short stories in this book occurred during the 15-year period of time between 1964, when Andy arrived in Alaska, up until the fall of 1979, when he was sworn in as Chief of Police.

All the events and adventures, outlined in these seven stories, are factual and took place before Andy started his lengthy Police career. His Police career generated its own stories, excitement and adventures and, at times, its own dangers, but it was very interesting and exciting, as well. Because the short stories preceded his Police career, the title, "Before the Badge", seemed to be very appropriate.

Andy hopes to have another book, which will cover his Police career, in the bookstores by the spring of 2019. Watch for that publication, which will be entitled "Alaska Bush Cop".

SAMPLE CORE DRILLING
FOR PLATINUM

I met Ann Wilson in 1964 and we dated for a couple years and then married in February of 1967. Ann's sister, Gladys, was married to Harry Yuth. Harry and I became close friends even before he became my brother-in-law. We often fished together and hunted together and even worked on construction jobs together. In 1967 Harry had taken a job on a tugboat out of Anchorage. He was the engineer on the tug Lumpier VI. Harry had worked for the owner of the tug on and off for a couple years, when they would be awarded contracts on jobs that dealt with construction, salvage and/or drilling exploration. In the spring of 1967 Harry called me from Anchorage and asked if I was working. I had just gotten off a local king crab boat after the season ended and was between jobs at the time. Harry told me they were hiring men to work a man-barge that would be going to Good News Bay, off the Bering Sea, to take core samples for platinum. He said they were looking for crane operators, pump operators, laborers, riggers, a couple cooks and a couple bull-cooks. The crew would live aboard the man-barge and take core samples from the ocean floor in Good News Bay. The job was to last for a couple months and the crew would be expected to live aboard the barge and stay until the job was completed. He said they would be working 12-hour shifts, six days a week, and would have Sunday's off. The job would pay very well, with the overtime we would be putting in, and room and board would be supplied. There would be two shifts; a night and a day shift, to insure the exploration could be completed before winter set in, a fact which often comes early in the northern part of Alaska.

I decided I would take the job offer and arrangements were made for me, and the rest of the crew, to be flown out to the town of Platinum. We had to wait until the tug and barge arrived in Good News Bay from their Anchorage base. The Good News Bay area was known for its platinum deposits. A family owned dredge operation had been mining for platinum, on shore, in the area for a number of years before finally shutting their operation down. Their huge on-shore bucket dredge was still on site in its pond outside of the town of Platinum. Platinum sprung up as a result of the family dredging operations. After arrival in Platinum, we were told our crew would be given a tour of the dredge at a later date.

I, along with ten other men, arrived at the airport in Platinum and Harry was there to meet us. We were transported to the beach where we boarded a large work skiff and, with our duffle bags in tow, were transported to the barge, which had already been spudded in out in the middle of Good News Bay.

Being spudded in refers to being able to hold the barge in position with large pipes being driven in the ocean floor instead of having to anchor with conventional anchors and have difficulty staying on location. The spuds can be utilized when working in shallow waters. The deepest water in Good News Bay was around 30 feet deep at extreme high tide. A spud consists of a steel, heavy 24-inch schedule 80 pipe, approximately 80 feet long with a point welded on one end and a picking eye affixed to the other. The spud would be housed vertically in stationary tubes welded to the starboard bow and the port stern of the barge. The spuds are lifted into place with a crane and are held in place with pipe clamps. When on location, the pipe clamps are loosened and the spuds are lowered to the bottom of the Bay thus anchoring the barge in position. This enables the barge to be held directly over the location where the drilling, or, in our case, the collection of core samples, would take place. The barge would stay in place without any variance, which resulted in the drill pipe and core sample to easily re-enter the existing hole time after time. This is vitally important when taking repeated core samples from the same location, as would be the case in our operation.

In the center of the barge was a round hole approximately three feet across. The hole went completely through the deck of the barge to the barge's hull. Most drilling barges are built with, what is referred to as, a moon pool which is utilized for all drilling purposes. This access is used to drill or take samples from the ocean floor and enabled the crew to have 360-degree access around the hole and erased many hazards that exist when working off the side of a barge. For safety purposes a steel plate was placed over the moon pool when no drilling or core sampling was taking place.

The barge was also affixed with two engines on the stern, one on the port and the other on the starboard. The engines were mounted on the fantail deck of the barge and were utilized to move the barge into location. The engines were 671 GMC diesels and each had a large outdrive affixed to it. Each outdrive had a three-blade propeller, approximately 2 feet across. The engines were operated Independent of one another so each engine had to have an operator when the barge was being moved under its own power. The engines relieved the need for the tugboat having to be available for the moves between sample core locations. The tug was anchored near the West beach of Good News Bay during drilling operations.

A 60-ton, double drum, American cable crane, on tracks, with approximately 120 feet of boom, was aboard the barge as was a motor driven, 8-inch, water pump, mounted on wheels. The water pump would be used for dredging sand and gravel after the 20' to 40' of silt, mud and, hopefully, platinum was removed through the hole the sample core tube would create in the ocean floor. This silt or mud, extracted from the ocean floor, would be bagged and stored. The sand and gravel, which was also thought to house platinum, and other precious metals, would then be dredged in to a hopper located on the deck of the barge. A large air compressor was also aboard and was located on the starboard side on the deck. The large metal hopper was in place just to the stern of the moon pool. The hopper would be utilized for storing dredged gravel, which hopefully contained platinum and other precious minerals, after the mud and silt were removed. The hopper had four legs that were welded to the deck, as well as chained to pad eyes, to keep the unit in place in rough weather. It could hold approximately 25 yards of material.

The barge was capable of sleeping 32 men and had an engine room with two generators and an enclosed water and sewage system. There were 18 staterooms, for housing the crew, and a galley with all the necessities to feed the crew. Showers and toilet facilities were also aboard and all the accommodations were in excellent condition. A stairwell, approximately 30 feet from the stern of the barge, led below deck to the living quarters. Directly at the bottom of the steps was the barge engineer's stateroom. A hallway, on the port side of the barge, led forward to the galley, the bathroom/shower facilities, and then to the crew's staterooms. The engine room was between the engineer's stateroom and the galley. Harry was the engineer for the barge so he had the stateroom at the bottom of the stairway. Since I was his brother-in-law I was told I would share the stateroom with him and I was given the top bunk. Harry worked nights and I worked the day shift so we each basically had the stateroom to ourselves on our off-shift.

The duties were assigned and the work began the following morning after our arrival. A Texas firm was contracted to explore the floor of Good News Bay to ascertain whether mining platinum in Good News Bay would be cost effective. Three representatives of the Texas based firm were aboard the barge and their responsibility was to bag each silt and/or mud sample, after the barge crew had extracted the core samples and made them available.

The core sampler we used was a round metal tube, made out of thick-walled pipe, approximately sixteen inches in diameter and five feet long. The top of the sampler was reduced to 6 inches and a flange was welded to it so 6-inch heavy walled drill steel could be threaded onto it. The drill steel that was threaded onto the core sampler came in 12-foot sections and the crane was utilized to lift the core sampler, with the drill steel attached, and lower it through the moon pool and down to the ocean floor. Additional drill steel was added as and when the core sampler was setting on the bottom of the ocean, the crane, utilizing a drop hammer, would drive the sampler into the ocean floor five feet at a time. After driving the core sampler five feet the hammer would be set aside and the core sample would be lifted up to the deck of the barge by the crane and unscrewed from the drill steel. An air hose would then be affixed to the core sampler and the air introduced would force the sample out of the tube and onto the deck of the barge. The Texas crew would then cut the sample into smaller chunks with shovels and place the chunks in burlap bags. The bags were secured at the top and tagged with sample numbers, location where they were taken, the depth they were taken from and other pertinent information. The bags were then stored below deck in a room adjacent to the engine room.

Bud, the foreman, and I had met through Harry prior to this job and we had become friends. Bud told me he was the crane operator, but due to other duties, he wanted me to operate the crane on the day shift. He said it was really a job he was supposed to do but other his other duties made it difficult, if not impossible at times, for him to commit to it for a full shift. Bud was aware I had operated cranes and other equipment in the past and I felt confident I could do the job so I became the crane operator on the day shift.

As the job progressed, and we got better acquainted with the procedures, we all became more proficient and production was going very well. We would drive the core sampler five feet at a time and then pull it and blow it out of the tube onto the deck of the barge. This became routine and, in turn, became somewhat automatic and also somewhat mundane. To lighten the mood, following the sample being removed from the tube, one of the crew would occasionally reach down and pretend he had put something in his pocket. The Texas crew was very serious about their work and became very upset thinking the guy had picked up some mineral of value they felt belonged to them. The Texas crew never disappointed us in their reactions. This happened on a number of occasions and was always a good way to keep a light-hearted atmosphere. Even the Texas crew caught on after a while and everyone had a good laugh.

When we finished a hole, by removing all the silt and mud and, after we had dredged the sand and gravel material, we would have to move to our next location. One of the duties of the Texas crew was to position a buoy in place on the next location so we could move the barge onto that location. After a couple moves we found it was almost impossible to place the barge on location with an operator on each engine, each attempting to steer the barge independent of the another. I approached Jim and told him I thought it would be much easier if one engine was kept in the center position. The operator running that engine could place the port engine in forward or reverse and could advance the RPM's as needed without any steering. An operator on the starboard engine should call all the shots and direct the port side operator, hopefully making it possible to control the barge's movements. Any steering would be done by the starboard engine. Without doing this the two operators were overriding one another and all control of the barge was lost. Jim agreed and told me I was in charge of moving the bare onto location in all future moves. I told him I'd do my best but felt nervous even though I thought I could handle it. Jim said we had to try something different in that it was taking forever to get on location by doing what we had been doing. Two hand held radios would be used for communication between the port engine operator and myself. After a couple location moves, we found we could better control the barge using this method. My plan had worked and we were able to get on location much easier and much quicker than we had previously.

When we would have to change locations in the middle of the night I would be awakened and given the responsibility of the move. I found it much more difficult to get the barge on location on the night moves, when we couldn't see very well. Even though it doesn't get totally dark in Alaska's summers, the heavy cloud cover and the late hours did make it necessary to light the buoy that we were trying to set up on. The first time I moved the barge at night, I found it very difficult, if not impossible, to ascertain if the barge was completely stopped before dropping the spud into place. When we got on location we would spud in the bow spud first, utilizing the crane to lower the spud very slowly. Even though we thought the barge was totally stopped, when Bud lowered the spud, we found the barge was still moving a little and the heavy barge moving ahead put a bend in the spud. It did stop the barges forward movement but not without creating a lot of work for the crew. Since the spud was bent below its housing pipe, it had to be cut off just below the bottom of that pipe.

This meant the top of the spud had to be clamped off at the deck level and the whip line on the crane had to be connected to the lower part of the spud that was to be cut off. This cost us a number of hours of production due to the spud having to be repaired. The bend had to be cut out, thus making a cut above and below the bend, after which the two straight pieces of the pipe had to be welded back together. The repaired spud was then put in place to hold the barge on location. Sadly, this same scenario occurred on two more occasions before we completed the job. We found it nearly impossible to insure the barge was completely stopped when attempting to get on location at night. After this happened three times Jim made the decision we would make no more moves at night. He felt production would suffer more with our having to repair the spuds than if we shut down operations until we could have enough visibility to make sure the barge was completely stopped before spudding in.

By being spudded in on location we were able to repeatedly return to the same hole where we were removing the core samples.

The eight-inch water pump was utilized for the dredging operation. By lowering a pipe into the hole left after removing the mud and silt, and pumping water into the void, we created a vacuum, or a venturi, which forced the gravel and sand up the pipe and into the hopper. Jim, the boss on the job, and the owner of the tug and barge, was somewhat of a meteorologist and would climb into the hopper with his gold pan, and would sort out precious metals keeping his findings in a deck bucket. When he'd completed his exploration for the day, he would set the bucket by the leg of the hopper. He gave strict instructions that the bucket was not to be touched. No one ever questioned his authority and we all knew we'd best stay clear of that bucket.

We had been on the job approximately five weeks when Lowell Chapple, a longtime friend of Jim's, flew to Good News Bay and joined the crew. He had been finishing up another contract for the company and would take over the foreman's job on the day crew. The second day he was on deck he needed a bucket to wash some slick mud off the deck of the barge and he grabbed the deck bucket containing the precious metals and he dumped its contents overboard. He then tied a line to the bucket and used the bucket to get some salt water from over the side of the barge and he washed the mud off the deck. Everyone was busy and hadn't witnessed this and only realized what had happened when he was observed washing the deck with Jim's bucket. Lowell had not been informed of the bucket's contents and had no way of knowing about Jim's directives. Jim, to say the least, was very upset when it was discovered what had happened but he said he couldn't very well blame Lowell since he had no knowledge of Jim's prospecting or his previous directives. Lowell felt terrible but said he really didn't see anything in the bucket that he felt was worth saving. Jim jokingly told Lowell he'd think differently after the loss was reflected in Lowell's salary.

A couple days following his dumping the deck bucket overboard, Lowell was aboard the Lumpier VI and they were using the tow wince to pull the tug's anchor. The anchor winch had lost a hydraulic motor and was off line. The tow winch wire, located on the stern of the vessel, was threaded through a block and then taken around the port side of the boat, around the cabin and over the bow cleat. When they started to pull the anchor the cable became taught, and jumped off the bow cleat. Lowell, being in the wrong location at the time, was hit in the forearm by the tow wire and it fractured his forearm. His injury had to be splinted and he then had to be transported to Platinum in the skiff so he could catch an airplane to Anchorage for treatment. When we were loading Lowell into the skiff Jim jovially told the crew, "See what happens to people who mess with my bucket?" Everyone got a chuckle out of the humor, including Lowell, but we all knew it was said as a joke. Lowell's injuries were the only injuries sustained on the Good News Bay job and, in time, Lowell fully recovered without any loss of function in his arm.

About 4 weeks into the job we had just reached the gravel in one hole and set up to dredge. Since the crane wasn't needed for dredging I was given the job of running the 8-inch pump. Everything was set up and we were ready to dredge so I started the pump and then quickly increased the throttle. When the throttle was nearly wide open the 90-degree elbow, which the hose was attached to, blew at the elbow connection, and the force of the water hit Jim in the chest. He was knocked completely across the deck. I immediately shut down the pump and we hurriedly ran to Jim, fearing he had sustained serious injuries. Outside of his being soaking wet, he was unhurt. After finding he wasn't injured, Bud mentioned something to the effect that Jim needed a shower anyway. Jim chuckled about that and smiled at Bud then walked away shaking his head muttering something about his clothes weren't so dirty as to go to this extreme.

Throughout the entire time we were in Good News Bay the crew got along well and no arguments or altercations ever occurred. This is a rare event in that personality conflicts and disagreements often take place when this size crew are housed in such close quarters. Jim was a very likeable man who was very knowledgeable and picked his crew carefully. Everyone knew their job and did it to the best of their ability and their respect for Jim certainly was a factor in everyone's getting along. When mechanical problems did arise they were dealt with, corrected in a timely manner and production was again returned to normal.

On Sunday of the 6th week we were on the job, nine of us took the skiff to Platinum and asked if we could get a tour of the bucket dredge. The owner of the Platinum grocery store, Harold, told us he would transport us to the dredge and would give us a personal tour. We had been buying supplies from his store since we'd reached Good News Bay and he had become acquainted with many in the crew and had come to enjoy our presence. Jim had previously arranged the tour with Harold and we all jumped into his van and headed for the dredge.

Upon reaching the dredge Harold told us the operation was a family business and was totally owned by one family. The town of Platinum had come into existence due to the platinum dredging operation. The dredge consisted of a two-story building built on a barge. The barge was probably 120 – 140 feet long and approximately 60 feet wide. It was floating in a pond it carried with it during the dredging operations. The dredging operation had shut down a number of years ago and it was evident no maintenance had been done on the dredge since its dredging days. Harold said when the dredge was in operation anchors were placed ahead and behind the pond with cables attached from the dredge's winches. The anchors were still in place and were still anchoring the barge in the pond. The dredge was held in place by the stern anchor while dredging and then pulled ahead with the bow anchor when being re-positioned. The dredge was always attempting to move ahead when the dredging operation was underway due to the large buckets digging the material and continually pulling on the dredge. A walkway, which was hinged to the dredge's deck, was lifted up and down with winches and was the only access for the workers when they boarded or exited the dredge.

After the preliminaries, including some safety instructions and after each of us being given a hard hat, we boarded the dredge via the walkway. On the first level, or the deck of the barge, were a number of different items for extracting minerals from the soil. A couple of round drums, positioned on an angle, with slits and holes in them were observed. Harold said the material would enter the drums via a conveyor belt, as the drums rotated, and would then be washed downward by water pressure. This allowed the smaller material to fall through the holes and slits in the drum. The larger rocks would fall on through the drum and into another conveyor belt while the smaller material would fall through the slits and holes in the drum and would be caught in rug type material. Large wooden boxes, with screens in the bottom, were also fed by a conveyor belt and were affixed with a motor that would shake them back and forth, separating the smaller rocks from the larger ones, Harold explained. The boxes were also positioned on an angle, so gravity would assist in the disposal of the larger material. The excess material would be dumped into another conveyor to be disposed of out the back of the barge. The excess material was dumped into a conveyor belt that reached out past the stern of the barge approximately 75 feet. The conveyor belt was held in the air by a winch cable and the excess material, when deposited off the stern, built what appeared to be levies behind the barge. Harold told us maintenance of the dredge was never ending when it was in operation. All the vibration from the shakers and drums would loosen the tightest bolts and nuts and the crew continually had to tighten them to keep the operation going. He also said the oiling and greasing of the many chains and bearings for all the conveyor belts and drive chains was a never-ending task.

After being shown the deck of the barge with all the separating sluice boxes, drums and the other machinery, Harold led us up the steps to what he referred to as the wheelhouse. This is where the operator ran the dredging operation and dug the material utilizing large buckets for the digging, thus the name "Bucket Dredge". The buckets were affixed to a metal chain that ran along a rail on a boom out the front of the barge. The buckets could dig up to a depth of 50 feet. The material collected in the buckets would be dumped onto a large conveyor belt which would carry the material into the bowels of the barge and disperse the material onto the different conveyor belts. The conveyor belts would, in turn, carry the material into the bowels of the barge and would deposit it into the different sections of the sorting deck. The bow anchors would position the barge so it could move left and right, keeping the pond wider with the barge at all times. This also would swing the conveyor on the stern of the barge left and right, creating the levies that the excess material made when disposed of out the back of the barge.

It was a very interesting operation and we were all amazed at the amount of machinery that was utilized in the dredging operation. We all concluded it was no easy task extracting the platinum, and other precious metals, by using the dredge. The fact that it was utilized for so many years as a family operation, we found somewhat amazing. The levies, which were numerous, were evidence of the operation being in place for many years. It was quite an operation and, in such a remote location, made it even more spectacular.

Harold took us back to the skiff and we thanked him for the tour telling him how enjoyable it had been and that we'd always remember the time spent with him aboard the dredge. Now it was time to get back to the sample core barge and prepare for the next day of work.

Sundays had been set aside for maintenance on the barge. The equipment aboard was checked and serviced every Sunday. Since Harry was the engineer aboard the barge, he never took Sundays off, so while we were on a tour of the dredge, Harry had been changing oil in the engines and pulling maintenance on the crane, the pumps, the air compressor, the light plants, the hydraulic system, and any other equipment needing maintenance. Without this continuous maintenance the job would certainly have experienced many more problems and production could have suffered. Harry was a great engineer, very knowledgeable and a very loyal employee. He kept very busy during his night shift with maintenance of all the equipment aboard and, when not pulling maintenance, he would assist in the core drilling operations. Harry was a quiet man who was liked by everyone and fit in perfectly as one of the crew.

With the barge having been moved onto a new location, we started the sample core operation early Monday morning in a new hole. The day was very productive and we were abler to move to another location before the day shift ended. This set the night crew up for a good night of production, as well.

Everything went very well for the next week and a half even though the weather was becoming a factor. The fall weather brought on more wind and rain than we had experienced since we'd arrived in Good News Bay. We had two days when the wind was so strong it made it impossible to continue the sample core drilling. The barge was moving a lot, even being spudded in. We were afraid we could bend some drill steel if it got caught in the moon pool due to the movement of the barge. With the strong wind being spudded in didn't secure the barge over the location well enough to stop all movement in a storm and the barge would lurch back and forth. After Jim observed the problems we were having he decided to shut the operation down until the wind subsided somewhat. We were nearing completion of the job and he didn't feel it was worth taking the chance of getting someone injured or damaging some equipment just to acquire limited production. Everyone agreed it was a good call. In a couple days the wind did die down enough so we could continue operations but the rain was relentless. Even with the rain gear we were soaked at the end of our shifts. However, we did complete the job, drilling in every location the Texas Company had planned to drill.

Half the crew was told to pack their bags and they would be flown home the next morning. Five of us, including the tug crew, were kept on site to ready the barge for being towed back to Anchorage. We tied everything down on deck and readied the barge for travel. Being the fall of the year, it was likely they would hit some bad weather on their trip back to Anchorage so everything had to be secured. The last thing to be battened down was the crane. Its boom had to be set in a cradle and then cross-tied to deck pad eyes. The counterweight also had to be cross-tied with turnbuckles and chains to insure it didn't move. The spuds were set in cradles on the barge and then chained down. The Lumpier VI had been brought alongside and was anchored to hold the barge in place since the spuds could no longer be utilized. Everything we'd tied down and secured was double-checked and any corrections were made. It would be too late to correct any problems in the middle of a storm so extra precautions were taken.

The following morning Harry took myself and the rest of the crew to Platinum where we caught an airplane to Anchorage.

I have been on a number of bush type jobs since Good News Bay but I can honestly say I've never worked with a better crew or people who had more respect for the boss and for each other. Everyone on the job went out of their way to fulfill the contract due to the respect and admiration for each other and for Jim.

I'll never forget the days I spent in Good News Bay with a bunch of great men doing a job that few men have ever experienced. However, I must be honest. The core samples all looked like mud to me. I've always wondered what they decided. I can only guess we did not find enough platinum to make it cost effective to mine the Bay. I have never heard of any mining operations ever taking place in Good News Bay.

THE TUG BOAT SOUTHLAAND

My first introduction to Cook Inlet took place in 1966 when I hired on as engineer on a tugboat for a couple months during the wintertime. Cook Inlet can be a very dangerous body of water due to its fast tides, its winter icing conditions and the silt and mud conditions that are always shifting and changing bottom configurations.

In late October, in 1966, an old military, steel hulled, 86-foot army tugs boat, the Southland, pulled into the harbor in Seldovia. The captain of the vessel contacted the Harbormaster telling him they were looking for a crew to man the tug for a job they had in Cook Inlet. He said the job would last for a couple months and that they needed two people. I had been fishing king crab out of Seldovia on a local day boat but, with cold weather and windy conditions, we had not been able to go out fishing too often. A day boat was a local boat that fished king crab on a daily basis, if weather permitted, and delivered their catch the same day it was caught. The day boats did not have holding tanks, which circulated salt water to keep the crab alive, so it was imperative the daily deliveries were made. King crab has to be alive when processed so the canneries refused to buy them if they were not kept alive. Since we weren't going out fishing very often, and my wages were a percentage of the catch, I was making very little money.

After hearing about the job offers on the tug I contacted my skipper on the crab boat and told him about the possible job opportunity and, since fishing was so slow, I was thinking about applying for one of the positions. He told me it would probably be in my best interest to take the job if it was available. He said the weather was unpredictable in the winter and the crab fishing was hit and miss so there were no guarantees. He told me if I did get the job on the tug, and it didn't work out, to come back and see him and he'd put me back to work if he had an opening.

After meeting with him I walked down the float to where the Southland was moored and climbed aboard. I found the skipper in the wheelhouse and he introduced himself as Allen. He said he was looking for a couple people, a deckhand and an engineer. He told me the tug's owners had a contract with an oil company who was building an installation at Granite Point, on the west side of Cook Inlet. Two large military landing crafts, or LCU's, the Mr. Bill and the Chilkoot, were hired to deliver much needed supplies to the Granite Point location. The oil companies wanted the freight and supplies delivered before the end of the year. Due to icing conditions in Cook Inlet, the Southland had been hired to assist the landing crafts in navigating their way through the ice flows from the Nikiski Terminal, on the east side of Cook Inlet, to the Granite Point installation, located on the west side of the Inlet. The steel hulled tug would be utilized to break up ice jams for the landing crafts, to find leads of open water where they could have unrestricted navigation and also push them through the brash ice and some ice flows. Allen also said anyone hiring on will be expected to work long hours and to stick with the job until it was completed.

He asked me what experience I'd had on the water and I told him I'd been crab fishing on local boats on and off for the last couple years but I also told him I was a fair hand with machinery, having been raised on a farm. He said he'd give me a tour of the tug and, if I was interested following the tour, we would talk more about the position. He said he might be interested in bringing me on as engineer if things worked out.

Allen said getting acquainted with the operation of the tug would take a little time since it was an older vessel and was operated using the "bell system". He showed me the engine room and explained the operating systems to me. As we descended into the engine room, down the staircase from the rear of the galley, Allen pointed out a day tank hanging on the bullhead and said the tank held the fresh water for the main engine cooling and had to be refilled from time to time. He said the tank must never be allowed to run dry and he pointed out a valve at the top of the tank used to fill it. This tank had a glass gauge which showed the depth of the water in the tank. Allen then pointed out a lube oil tank, on the starboard side of the engine room, aft of the main engine, where all the lube oil on board was stored. Two water holding tanks and two fuel holding tanks, located on opposite sides on the boats bulkheads, were also brought to my attention. Each tank had a glass tube visible reaching from the bottom of the tank to the top which acted as gauges indicating how much fuel or water remained in each tank, the same type gauge I had observed on the engine cooling water holding tank.

I was then shown the two twin cylinder Lister diesel engines. The engines, located behind the man engine and on both sides of the engine room, each powered a four-kilowatt generator. These units produced the electricity aboard the tug. Allen said one of the generators was kept on line at all times and then switched out every 24 hours so the oil could be checked and the engine could be serviced. The Lister engine that was running was comparatively quiet and a conversation could be held in the engine room without too much of a problem.

After showing me around the engine room, Allen took me to the front of the engine where the main engine controls were located. He then explained the "Bell System" to me. He said all control of the engine was undertaken by the engineer. He then pointed out the controls, which were located on the front starboard side of the engine. He said all forwarding, reversing and the RPM's were activated using these controls. The bells and whistles, activated from the wheelhouse, would indicate what action was to be taken by the engineer. The "Bell System" is a system used on most of the older vessels before remote controls, or cable systems, were brought on line. In short, it is a system of bells and whistles, which, when activated from the wheelhouse, signaled the engineer, who is at the controls in the engine room. Bells indicated the direction of the rotation of the engine, either forward or reverse, and whistles indicated the RPM's needed. One bell called for the engine to be started in forward rotation while two bells called for the engine to be started in reverse rotation. When the engine was in forward or reverse, another single bell called for the engineer to shut down the engine. One whistle called for 100 RPM's, two whistles called for 200 RPM's and three called for 300 RPM's. Four or more whistles called for full throttle and were only used in an emergency situation. For example, if the skipper rang two bells and two whistles the engineer is expected to reverse the engine and advance the RPM's to 200. When the skipper would want to stop the boats movement, he would ring one bell, which signaled the engineer to shut down the engine. It was a simple system that was easily learned. Allen did caution me that anytime the engine was running, and you received a signal to stop the engine, you must first reduce the engine RPM's to the idle position before, or at the same time, you shut down the engine. He said it was imperative, when going from forward to reverse, or vice versa, you first insure the engine has totally stopped its rotation. He explained if the engine is idled down at the same time it is brought offline, you will not have any problems but it cannot be rotating when being started in an opposite rotation.

One six-cylinder Enterprise diesel engine powered the tug. The engine is referred to as an in-line, direct-reversible engine indicating the engines six cylinders are positioned one behind the other and the engine will run in both right- and left-hand rotations. When the engine is started in forward it's turning in a right-hand rotation. When it's started in reverse the engine is running in a left hand rotation. The propeller shaft, which drives the propeller, also turns in the same rotation as the engine so in reverse it would be turning in a left hand rotation and in forward the shaft would be turning in a right hand rotation. There was no transmission or gear reduction between the engine and the propeller shaft. It was direct drive and the rotation of the engine dictated the direction the propeller shaft turned. There was a lever at the back of the engine which could be thrown which disengaged the propeller shaft from the flywheel. The engine could then be started at an idle without the propeller shaft turning.

This was used for bringing the engine up to temperature when reading if for use or when working on it and having a need to start it without the propeller shaft turning. The engine was affixed with an air starter and a large air compressor was located on the starboard side of the engine room, just ahead of the main engine. The engine room control gauges were positioned directly above the engine controls so the engineer could easily scan them. The air pressure gauge was also located on the panel and Allen told me I should always keep a minimum of 60 pounds of air pressure. This would insure the engine would have enough air to start it upon demand. He said the unit built up air pressure quickly so, barring any major problems, that should not be an issue even when doing a lot of maneuvering. He also said a smaller compressor was stowed in a locker on deck, in the event the main compressor did break down.

Before leaving the engine room Allen pointed out the engine room log book which he said had to be kept up daily. It was a log of all maintenance that took place including the main engine hours. An hour meter on the main engine was then pointed out. I observed a column in the logbook for recording departing times and destination arrival times, which I observed had been kept up to date. Allen said it was the responsibility of the engineer to keep the log up to date and it could not be overlooked or put off. All oil changes, the adding of oil to any of the engines, any maintenance done on any equipment aboard, whether above or below deck, the amount of fuel, water and lube oils taken on board and any notes the engineer thought should be added, were also to be included on a daily basis. The logbook was kept on a small shelf at the bottom of the staircase.

Following the tour, Allen told me they would be staying in Seldovia for a couple more days while they attempted to hire a crew. He then introduced me to Tony, the other crewmember aboard. We shook hands and Tony said he had been hired on in Seward as a combination cook/deckhand. He was in his mid-thirties and said he had spent most of his life on Alaskan waters fishing salmon during the summer months with his family. He was acquainted with navigation and the operation of a boat but said he didn't have too much engineer experience and really didn't have a lot of interest in being an engineer.

Allen then showed me the engineer's stateroom. The stateroom was accessed from the deck with the entry door located on the port side of the vessel just aft of the galley. The stateroom consisted of a bed, built into the inner wall, with three drawers below it and a couple shelves above it, a small built in closet on the wall toward the bow, and a small desk with a chair pushed under it in the port aft corner of the room.

Allen told me if I wanted the engineer's position I could move aboard anytime within the next day or so. I told him the only problem I had was that I was engaged to be married and I would have to leave the boat at the end of December because January 7th had been set for our wedding day. Allen said he hoped to have the job completed by then and said he didn't see it as being a problem. We discussed what the wages would be and we reached an agreement so I was hired as the engineer for the tugboat, Southland. Following the meeting and the tour I left the tug to go to the crab boat I'd been fishing on, and get my gear. I picked up what gear I had aboard the crab boat, said goodbye to my old skipper and then went home to pack in preparation for my move aboard the tug.

Around mid-morning the next day I moved my gear aboard the tug. I again looked around to better acquaint myself with the operation of the boat. I wanted to be well acquainted with the boat before we left the Seldovia harbor.

I found Allen in the wheelhouse and he told me they had not had any luck finding another deckhand and feared we would have to go without one if they couldn't locate someone by the next day. I told him I'd look around town too but I didn't know of anyone who was looking for work right now. Very few people wanted to sail into Cook Inlet in the wintertime with the ice conditions being what they were. I was not really aware of the hazards of Cook Inlet when I took the job but, regardless, I needed to start making some money. I possibly would have been more hesitant to hire on if I had known what lay ahead. My only sailing experience, at this point in my life, was fishing on the local king crab day boats out of Seldovia. I was what was commonly referred to, in the nautical world, as a greenie.

When the next day passed without finding a deckhand, Allen said we would be pulling out on the next morning's tide. We would be leaving shorthanded but the tug had to get to the job site at the Nikiski Terminal. He said we could possibly pick up a deckhand when we reached the Terminal. He said he wanted to get under way just after low tide, at around 0930 hours. This would enable us to catch and ride the tide up the Inlet so we would hopefully reach Nikiski late in the day. The amount of time it would take depended on the ice conditions in Cook Inlet. Allen said the two LCU's we would be tending were already at the Nikiski Terminal and were being loaded with gear for the Granit Point installation. The landing crafts would not leave the Nikiski Terminal without a tug to break ice and assist them in reaching Granite Point. This made it imperative we get underway as soon as possible.

Cook Inlet stretches approximately 180 miles from the Gulf of Alaska to Anchorage in south-central Alaska. The Inlet then branches into the Knik Arm, to the northwest, and Turnagain Arm, to the east.

Cook Inlet and its tributaries are very dangerous bodies of water with extreme tides that reach upwards from -4.0 to 35 feet in approximately six hours. Due to the narrowing of Cook Inlet, off the Gulf of Alaska, the amount of water filling the Inlet creates a tide that runs like a river and at times, on the extreme tides, reaches speeds upwards of 12-15 mph. When the tide flows into Turnagin Arm, just south of Anchorage, a wall of water 2–6 foot high is often created on the extreme high tides. This wall of water is known as a bore tide and occurs due to the large amount of water flowing into the Turnagin Arm form Cook Inlet. The shallowing up and the narrowing of Turnagin Arm from Cook Inlet creates this phenomenon. The boar tide only occurs on extreme tides when the tide is coming in, or flooding, into Turnagin Arm. No bore tide is created when the tide is going out, or ebbing, because the fast water is flowing into the wider and deeper Cook Inlet. Whether flooding or ebbing, the tide runs the fastest at mid-tide, or half way into the flood or the ebb. Turnagin Arm is said to have the third fastest tide in the world.

Because we were leaving the next morning, I spent the day going over the engine room and learning the "Bell System" and the workings of the controls. I observed a 3-inch plastic pipe routed from the engine room to the wheelhouse. It was attached to an upright support pipe at the front of the engine near the engine controls. I found it to be a pipe that was used for verbal communications between the engine room and the wheelhouse. Even though modern day systems were available for this purpose, no one had installed one on this tug. Surprisingly I found a person could speak into the pipe from the engine room, or from the wheelhouse, and be heard very clearly on the other end regardless of the engine noise or other noises. A wooden plug had been carved and stuck in the end of the pipe in the engine room to muffle any noise in the wheelhouse until an audible signal from the wheelhouse was activated. A buzzer had been installed which, when activated from either the engine room or the wheelhouse, would signal communications were requested from either location. I would find this system to come in very handy in the next couple months.

I had moved aboard the tug and would spend my first night aboard but I told Allen I had to go see my fiancé before I left and say goodbye. If I failed to do that I probably wouldn't have any reason to leave the boat at the end of December. He laughed and told me to have a good evening.

I left the tug and picked up my fiancé and we went out to dinner. We discussed my new job and were both encouraged by the fact I would be getting a steady paycheck and we could quit worrying about having enough money to cover the expenses of the wedding. After having a nice dinner I walked her back home and we said our goodbyes. I then walked down to the tug and climbed aboard. Even though somewhat comprehensive, I was happy with the decision I had made to join the Southland crew.

At approximately 0830 hours, the next morning, Allen told me to ready the engine room for travel. No deckhand could be found in Seldovia so we were leaving shorthanded in hopes of finding and hiring someone in Nikiski.

Because the "Bell System" operates the tugboat someone had to be in the engine room at all times when the tug was underway. If something happened that called for shutting down the engine, for any reason, someone had to be present at the controls. A tall stool was supplied so the engineer could set at the controls instead of having to stand all the time.

In readying the tug for travel, I threw the lever to disengage the propeller shaft and then started the engine and ran it at an idle. I received my first "Bell System" experience when we were pulling out of Seldovia and getting underway to Nikiski. I found the signals from the wheelhouse to be very clear and responding to them was found to be very simple. I quickly realized I would be spending almost all of my waking hours in the engine room of this tug.

We got underway out of Seldovia Bay and were cruising along at 300 RPM's. I would find this was pretty much commonplace when running in open or unrestricted waters. After pulling out of Seldovia Bay and settling into a heading, Allen buzzed the engine room and I pulled the plug on the voice pipe. He told me we'd be heading up the Inlet and would probably not be hitting any ice until we passed the Anchor Point area. He said signals would not be too frequent but I should not get too far from the engine controls in the event we did have to shut down for any reason. I told him I'd be standing by ready for any signals.

We had been underway for a couple hours without any maneuvers needed when I started hearing scraping sounds going down the length of the hull of the boat. Allen buzzed me on the voice pipe. He told me we were getting into some ice in lower Cook Inlet and I should stand ready in the event we would have to maneuver around some ice flows. I told him I was standing by and would be ready when signaled.

The ambient temperatures had been hovering in the mid 20's during the day and had gotten down in the teens at night, and in some places, to single digits. In Cook Inlet there is a lot of fresh water flowing from the rivers and creeks that empty into the Inlet and, in these temperatures, the fresh water would freeze quickly and would freeze rather hard. Salt water also freezes, creating ice flows, but it is usually colder weather when the salt water freezes hard enough to create any major problems. It had been cold enough to make salt water ice but it hadn't frozen so hard that we couldn't push through it with the tug. We did have to change course a few times to avoid the larger ice flows, and we had to reduce the speed on a few occasions, but we did reach the Nikiski Terminal at approximately 1825 hours that evening, even with the detours we were forced to make.

On my first day as engineer it really hit home that 99% of my time would be spent below deck in this job and I would not be enjoying much of the Alaskan scenery, a situation that, after a time, would become somewhat monotonous. Tony had delivered a couple of meals to me in the engine room consisting of a sandwich and a drink and he had relieved me on a couple occasions when I had to use the bathroom. Other than those two bathroom breaks, I had been in the engine room since leaving Seldovia. I would come to accept the fact that this would become the norm. Most of my meals would be catered and I might have to cross my legs at times. This could tend to become very mundane, however I had taken a job to do and I'd do my best to see it to the end.

After securing the engine room and filling out the engine room log, I went above deck and found we had tied alongside the Mr. Bill. The Mr. Bill and the Chilkoot were lying alongside the Nikiski Terminal dock, one directly behind the other. Both had already been loaded with freight needed at Granite Point for the oil company's installation and both were ready to travel. I observed a large Manitowoc cable crane on the dock, which had been used to load the LCU's.

Allen met with the skippers of the two landing crafts and it was decided we would leave about half-tide on the flood the next morning around 0430 hours. They wanted to use the tide to our advantage as much as we could and, by leaving on half-tide, we could get around the East Foreland and pretty well across Cook Inlet before the tide change, if the ice wasn't too thick.

Allen contacted a couple guys at the Nikiski Terminal and told them we were shorthanded and needed to hire a deckhand. He asked them if they knew of anyone needing some work. Being this time of the year, and the icing conditions in Cook Inlet during the winter months, very few people wanted to hire out on a boat that was working in these waters. No one could be found on short notice so Allen told Tony and me we would have to make it work with the crew we had. He said we could make it work by switching out with one another whenever we needed to but did say we'd be putting in some long hours. Tony had been on boats for years and also had become acquainted with the "Bell System" when coming from Seward. He was schooled in navigation so he could relieve either Allen or me. We really had no alternative so we had to figure out the best way to get the job done with our limited crew.

Both the Mr. Bill and the Chilkoot were old military landing craft, (LCU's), and were sister ships and both measured 120 feet long by 32 feet wide, beam to beam. Living quarters and the wheelhouse were located on the stern of the vessels above the engine room compartment. This left a deck area, measuring approximately 80 feet long by 24 feet wide, for the hauling of freight and/or equipment. Both boats were twin-screw vessels, meaning they each had two shafts and two propellers, powered with twin 871 GMC diesels. A large gate was affixed to the bow of the boats and could be lowered when the boat was nosed up to the beach creating a ramp for loading or offloading the vessels supplies and/or equipment. The machines used to offload the boats could be driven aboard from the beach, via the bow ramp, thus making loading or offloading the vessels a lot easier. At the Nikiski Terminal a crane had been used to load the boats because most of the freight being loaded was not on wheels.

Granite Point was not too far from the Nikiski Terminal as a crow flies, but with the icing conditions, it could seem much farther. The Nikiski Terminal was located just south of the East foreland and Granite Point was located approximately 10 miles north of the West Foreland. The Inlet was approximately 5 miles wide between the East and the West Forelands. With the fast tides and the icing conditions, we could find it very difficult to navigate the two square nosed landing crafts though the heavy ice. This being the case we had no way of predicting an arrival time to Granite Point. We could very possibly get caught in ice flows and the tide could set us far beyond our destination. We would have to figure out what directions to take once we were underway and the number of leads, or open water areas, and would determine this by the ice flows and ice packs hindering our forward movement. We were tasked with getting both the LCU's through the ice so this meant we may have to break open areas for one LCU and then, if the other was not able to follow, we would have to return and assist that vessel. In discussing this with Allen I got the feeling he was somewhat apprehensive about what lay ahead. He said there were so many variables that we could only find out what lay ahead by getting underway and dealing with whatever we ran into.

By tying alongside the Mr. Bill we did not have to be concerned with managing the lines on the tug when the tide changed in Cook Inlet. If we had tied directly to the Nikiski Terminal dock we would need someone tending the lines to let out line as the tide went out or pick up line as the tide increased, or came in. With the LCU crew manning the lines from the dock we could catch some sleep before getting underway the next morning.

At 0400 hours Allen knocked on my stateroom door, waking me, and told me to make ready for sailing. I dressed quickly, grabbed a can of pop, and responded to the engine room. After checking the lube oil level and the water day tank I threw the lever to disengage the propeller shaft, and I started the main engine and let it warm up while running at an idle. After it came up to operating temperature I shut the engine down and re-engaged the flywheel. I buzzed the wheelhouse and told Allen all was ready in the engine room. I then stood by for directions from the bridge.

At approximately 0435 hours Allen buzzed me and asked if I had checked the water and the oil level in the main engine and I told him all was ready. I replaced the wooden plug and we then departed the Nikiski Terminal.

As best I can remember I was given 1 bell and 1 whistle, so I started the engine ahead and advanced the RPM's to 100. After only a very short time another bell was heard and I stopped the engine. The next signal was 2 bells so I started the engine in reverse position and then 3 whistles were signaled so I advanced the RPM's to 300. After a short time a single bell was signaled and I reduced the RPM's and then stopped the engine. Another single bell was heard and the engine was again started in forward and when 2 whistles were signaled I advanced the RPM's to 200. We hadn't been going forward for more than a couple minutes when the wheelhouse signaled me to stop the engine. I was immediately given 2 bells and 3 whistles so I reversed the engine and advanced to 300 RPM's. Shortly after that I was given 1 bell and I brought the throttle to idle then stopped the engine. I received another bell and I started the engine in forward gear and then 2 whistles were signaled and I advanced the RPM's to 200. The maneuvering of the boat and the forward and reversing of the engine would keep me from thinking of much of anything else. The next signal was one whistle and I reduced the RPM's from 200 to 100. Ever since I was hired in Seldovia I had been going over and over the signals in my mind hoping it would become second nature to me. I did find it to become easier as I continued to respond to the bells and the whistles.

In checking the gauges, I found all to be normal and the air pressure to be at 105 pounds. With all the starting of the engine, the compressor was continuously building pressure. It would kick off when the gauge reached 130 pounds. Air did build rapidly and, with the frequent maneuvers of the boat calling for air every time the engine was started, it was imperative the compressor kept ahead of the demand.

As we navigated through the ice flows I was often being called on to reverse the engine and advance the throttle in an effort to stop the forward motion of the tug. We had to maneuver the boat forward and in reverse often to work our way through the ice flows and assist the two LCU's. I could tell when we would nose into the ice flows, or push on them in an attempt to bust through them or break them up. At times I would try to figure out what was actually going on when we were continually maneuvering and assisting the LCU's. By feeling the bumps and grinds I could picture in my mind what was happening above deck as we fought the ice flows. The ice would make loud scraping sounds when it was going down the side of the hull and the boat would keel over to port or starboard at times when we would ride up on an ice flow in an attempt to break it up. I found it impossible trying to determine what maneuver the skipper was attempting. Regardless of what I envisioned, there was no way I would ever ignore a signal regardless of what I conjured up in my mind.

We found the ice to be heavier than it was when we were coming up the Inlet from Seldovia. We were running mostly with the tide or into it when we were traveling from Seldovia to Nikiski. It was a very different story when we were trying to go across the tide. Our first trip crossing Cook Inlet took 14½ hours of steady travel before reaching the Granite Point Terminal, all the time maneuvering back and forth. Upon reaching Granite Point Allen called me on the voice pipe and told me to get some sleep. He said he and Tony had switched off during the crossing and they were pretty well rested. He said they would stand by while the LCU's were being offloaded. Due to the icing conditions we could not anchor the tug and there was no dock, or facility to tie to, at the Granite Point location. This required two people to be awake at all times so the tug could be maneuvered around the ice that was close to the beach.

I filled out the engine room log and then, as I left the engine room, I ran into Allen. He told me he was very pleased with my work today and said he was glad he'd hired me. I thanked him and told him I figured there would be some very long days ahead. He agreed and said he would still be trying to find another crewmember to lighten the load but didn't know if he could convince anyone to hire on due to the icing conditions. I told him we'd make do either way but I did encourage him to keep looking.

It felt like the temperature had dropped since I had been in the engine room and I mentioned this to Allen. He said we were in single digit temperatures now and said this will only build the ice and make it harder for us in our crossings.

For a short time, I watched the offloading operation on the beach. Two front-end Caterpillar 966 loaders, with forks, were being used to offload the Mr. Bill. The Chilkoot was alongside the Mr. Bill on the beach, but the loaders were both offloading the Mr. Bill at this time. I also observed a D-7 Caterpillar dozer and a couple semi-trucks up on the landing above the beach. This equipment must have been moved there before the icing conditions became a problem. It was evident the D-7 Caterpillar had been used to clear the beach of ice so the LCU's could go onto the beach without taking the chance of causing any hull damage.

Tony had delivered me sandwiches and drinks in the engine room every few hours during our crossing so, not being hungry, I just washed up and went to my stateroom to get some sleep. I think I was almost asleep before my head hit the pillow. I didn't realize how tired I really was until I lay down. I think it was more mental fatigue than physical fatigue. I had been very concerned how everything would work out with it all being so new to me. I told myself as long as I kept the skipper happy I should be alright.

It took 6½ hours for the two LCU's to be offloaded and to refloat so I did get some good rest before Allen woke me and said we'd be heading back to the Nikiski Terminal within an hour or so. I got dressed and went to the galley to grab something to eat and drink before I went to the engine room and relieved Tony. He had been in the engine room since I had gone to get some sleep so he was ready to be relieved. He asked how I'd done during the first crossing and I told him Allen seemed to be happy.

He said that was all that really mattered. He said I'd done well when he had relieved Allen and was in the wheelhouse calling the signals.

Tony left the engine room and I checked the oil and water level in the #2 Lister engine and then started it, running it at an idle to warm it up before bringing it on-line. Allen had shown me how to safely switch out the generators so I waited for #2 to come up to temperature. After approximately 10 minutes I switched the power to the #2 generator and shut down the #1 engine. I checked the oil and water in the #1 Lister and found it did not need any fluids added. I then logged the time I switched out the engines in the engine room log book and noted that neither engine needed any fluids. I added our arrival time at Granite Point and the time we were departing. The engine room log was up to date and all pertinent information had been added.

It wasn't long before we got underway headed back to the Nikiski Terminal. The signals from the wheelhouse seemed to intensify and become more frequent. The bumping and grinding of the hull against the ice also seemed louder and the impacts with the ice seemed to be harder and more frequent. I buzzed the wheelhouse and Tony answered. I ask if the ice was heavier than our previous crossings, due to all the maneuvering and he said it seemed there were less and less leads and the ice had piled up more in some of the pressure ridges. He said it appeared the ice flows were growing and seemed to be more closed in and he and Allen feared it may be a lot longer trip going back to Nikiski than it had been on our trip to Granite Point.

Tony's prediction was right. With the ice pack growing it made navigating all that much harder. Due to the daylight hours being so short in the winters in Alaska, and with the Inlet making more ice, Tony was needed in the wheelhouse to operate the spotlight while Allen navigated the boat through the ice flows. The two LCU's and the tug all had huge spotlights that were constantly being used to find a path around the heavier ice flows and pressure ridges. It was much easier and safer for one man to operate the spotlight while the other operated the boat. This meant, with both Tony and Allen in the wheel house, I would not be getting relieved for any length of time, if at all, while we were underway. This was one of the many reasons we needed another crew member on board the tug.

We spent the better part of two days getting both LCU's back to the Nikiski Terminal where they could be loaded for the next trip. Tony was able to relieve me in the engine room for a couple hours on only one occasion. It wasn't a lot of rest but it certainly did help and gave me somewhat of a second wind. Everyone couldn't wait to hit the rack after we finally reached the Nikiski Terminal and were secured alongside the Chilkoot at the dock. I, however, had to top off the fuel ad water tanks before I could lie down. It took me the better part of two hours to take on the fuel and water. I was more than ready to lay down by that time.

I also had found the stool in the engine room to be very uncomfortable after only a few hours so I started thinking what I could do to make things better. While taking fuel and water aboard I checked with the crew on the Chilkoot and upon asking I was told they had some old salmon seine aboard which they gave me. I also was given some polypropylene line and I was able to put together a make shift hammock. I positioned it where I could set in it and reach the engine controls without a problem. This turned out much better than I expected. I was much more comfortable setting in the hammock than I ever was setting on that stool for so many hours and I soon realized I was not experiencing as much back pain as before when using the stool.

We continued to fight the ice and make crossings and they seemed to get longer and longer. We were now into November and the temperatures were going below zero at night and only reaching single digits during the day. Ice continued to build rapidly. The pressure ridges, which were built by floating ice overflowing stationary ice, were gaining in number and in size. The fast tides would push the floating ice over the ice that was grounded, building a large pressure ridge. When the tide came in enough to float the pressure ridges they would move out into the navigational waters and we would have to work our way around them. They were so large and thick there was no chance of breaking through them or breaking them up with the tug. On numerous occasions all three vessels would be stuck in ice flows and could not move, some times for a few hours. We would have to wait until a lead opened or the tide change broke up the ice allowing us to navigate. Allen and Tony were very good about letting me know when we were hung up. I could take advantage of that time to go to the bathroom or grab a drink or quick sandwich. At times I would lay back on the hammock and close my eyes, always listening for a bell or whistle. During these times I found the makeshift hammock to come in very handy. I could accurately doze off for a quick nap at times. Those short naps made all the difference after we'd been steadily going back and forth in the ice flows for hours. I never heard any complaints regarding slow responses when the wheelhouse would send a signal. I'm sure I would have heard about it if I'd missed any signals.

Allen, Tony and I found we did work very well together, even during the tougher trips. We developed strong bonds and mutual respect for one another during these crossings. Every time we would return to the Nikiski Terminal, Allen would check to see if he could find a deckhand but no one wanted the job. We continued with only the three of us aboard the tug but we were making it work.

The trips to and from Granite Point have become somewhat blurred in my memory in that they were all basically the same and one day wasn't that much different from the day before. Some trips would be much longer than others, due to the ice conditions, but we dealt with the same problems and hazards on each and every crossing.

During one trip in mid-December we were fighting very heavy ice flows and pressure ridges. I had been in the engine room for over 32 hours with only short bathroom breaks. We were all dead on our feet. Tony would bring me a sandwich and a can of pop when he could safely leave the bridge but that only happened during daylight hours when the spotlight wasn't needed. At one point we were navigating through heavy ice flows and Allen signaled four whistles while we were in forward motion. I advanced to full throttle and we lurched up on an ice jam. The boat lay over on the starboard side approximately 25 – 30 degrees. One bell was signaled and I reduced the throttle and shut the engine down. The tug then slid off the ice jam and righted itself. I suddenly saw smoke coming from the bilge at the back of the engine on the starboard side. I grabbed the buzzer and signaled the wheelhouse and yelled fire in the engine room. I then grabbed a fire extinguisher, lifted a floor panel and emptied the fire extinguisher into the bilge. Allen and Tony had reached the engine room by the time the extinguisher had been emptied and they also grabbed extinguishers. I hadn't seen any flames and, when I got my wits about me, I realized I didn't smell any smoke. I went to the front of the engine and checked the gauges and observed the temperature gauge for the main engine to be pegged on 220 degrees. I immediately looked up at the sight glass on the bulkhead engine water-cooling tank and didn't see any water in the glass. I yelled at Allen and Tony and stopped them from emptying more fire extinguishers. I was so beat down from the long stent in the engine room, and we had been so busy maneuvering, I had overlooked filling the day tank with water for cooling the main engine. I signaled Allen and showed him the temperature gauge. I told him the bilge water must have hit a hot pipe in the bilge when we keeled over on the ice. I was so tired and rummy from lack of sleep, the first thing I thought was smoke when the steam erupted from the bilge. I apologized and told Allen I'd failed to fill the day tank. He said he understood how these things happen with all the hours we'd been putting in. He said it was surprising more of these type incidents hadn't taken place but was very glad it was steam instead of smoke. I can't think of any scenario worse than a fire aboard a boat. Allen said another crew member would make all the difference but no one wanted to work Cook Inlet in winter time. He told me to fill the tank but said we'd give the engine time to cool off before starting it again. H was afraid of cracking a cylinder head, he said. He told me to go lay down for a couple hours and Tony would relieve me. We would continue pushing through the ice with one man in the wheel house until I got a couple hours sleep and could be back in the engine room. He said he could see I had reached a point where I had to shut my eyes for a while. I apologized again then went to my state room.

I was sleeping hard when Tony opened my state room door and woke me. They had let me sleep for three hours. I still remember it being so hard to get out of bed. I jumped up and went into the galley to get a drink and then I went to the engine room. I felt terrible about forgetting to fill the day tank, which created the problem, but I was to the point of collapsing when it all went wrong. I will say I checked the day tank after that a minimum of three times a day. I certainly didn't want any replays of that problem.

We managed to get all the freight and gear delivered to Granite Point from the Nikiski Terminal before the end of the year. We did wind up speeding Christmas aboard the tug in the ice during out last crossing when going to Granite Point.

On the 29th day of December, 1966, we left the Nikiski Terminal headed south. We had fulfilled the contract and we were escorting the Mr. Bill and the Chilkoot out of Cook Inlet. We were underway to Seward. The two LCU's were going to Homer for a much needed rest. We still had to find leads and break through some ice flows before reaching water clear of ice but we found it much easier to navigate when we were going into the tide or with it instead of having to cut across tide. We hit ice free water after passing the Anchor Point area. After we were free of the ice I felt the stress leave my body. We were maneuvering very little and I found the lack of maneuvering to become very mundane in a very short time. Tony came to the engine room and told me to go take a nap. We had been fighting the ice for a few hours before hitting clear water and I didn't argue. I was glad to get a little shuteye without the bumping and grinding of the ice down the length of the tug.

The Mr. Bill and the Chilkoot had left us and were underway to Homer. We continued underway to Seward. The two LCU's had finished the job they had contracted for even with the ice conditions being as bad as they had been. We had said our goodbyes before leaving the Nikiski Terminal and everyone was happy to have this contract behind us.

We arrived in Seward at approximately 1720 hours on December 30th and, after securing the tug, Allen took Tony and me out for a steak dinner. We had a wonderful evening with Allen and Tony sharing a lot of seafaring stories. I was young and inexperienced, compared to my two ship mates, and I didn't have any stories worth sharing at that point of my life. However, I felt I had just experienced a couple months that I could tell my kids about one day. I cannot say I was sad to see the contract end but it was an experience very few people have had. So much of what I learned on this job has been of great assistance to me later in my life as I continued to make my living working and fishing in the Alaskan waters.

I flew home to Seldovia the following day, on December 31st, so I could make ready for my wedding day.

"THE SHISHALDIN"

In 1967, after getting married, I found myself without a job. Upon checking around for work I was told the crab boat, Shishaldin, was looking for a deckhand. I contacted the skipper, Arnie Serwald, and, after questioning me about my past experience, he offered me the deckhand position. He said if I worked out I would be getting a full share, or 8% of the gross. He said we would be taking on fuel and water the next morning and, then, after taking on bait, we would get underway. I accepted the job without any hesitation and then headed home to pack my gear and let my wife know about this new employment opportunity.

The Shishaldin was an older boat, an old Army landing craft, (LCI), which had been converted to a crab fishing vessel. Its living quarters and wheelhouse were located toward the stern of the vessel. The boat measured 168 feet long and 32 feet wide. It was the largest vessel fishing king crab out of the Seldovia harbor at the time.

The boat was referred to as a bow picker. The Government originally built all LCI's to hall infantry personnel. They were vessels with a bow ramp, which could be lowered when the vessel nosed up to the beach, enabling the infantry to disembark. When they converted the Shishaldin to a crab fishing vessel, the bow ramp had been removed. A covered bow and a large bow compartment were built and replaced the old bow ramp. The anchor winch for the boat was located inside the bow compartment and a 1½ inch cable from the anchor was attached to the 1500 pound boat anchor. The Danforth style boat anchor was secured on the top deck of the bow compartment.

Two large fish holding tanks had been added amidships and salt water circulating pumps were plumbed into the tanks from the engine room. Salt water was circulated through the two tanks when crab was on board to keep them alive. The tank hatches were built up approximately three feet above the deck of the boat. Wooden planks covered both tanks and were removed to access the crab when offloading the catch at the cannery. A small 3X3 foot hatch was built into the top of each tank so the crab could be deposited into the tanks without having to remove any planking. Just aft of the bow compartment, on the starboard side of the vessel, the power block, which was used to pull the crab pots off the bottom, was attached to a metal davit constructed of heavy walled six-inch pipe. The davit could be swung to a position over the side of the vessel so the buoy lines would not chafe on the bulwarks when the pots were being brought off the ocean floor. A picking boom was attached to the back of the bow compartment and reached out above the power block and the pot rack. The picking boom was utilized to place each crab pot on the pot rack during the picking of the gear when a pot was brought off the ocean floor.

Two larger stacking booms were located just ahead of the wheelhouse. These two booms were used for stacking pots on deck, or when moving the pots off the deck to the pot rack when setting gear. The configuration of the booms enabled the crane operator to reach anywhere on the boat deck for offloading and stacking crab pots. The pots could be stacked on top, alongside and in front of one another. Up to 150 crab pots, measuring 7X7X3 feet, could be loaded aboard the vessel. The only time you would have that many pots aboard was when you were bringing them to the fishing grounds from the storage area, or following the season, when you were taking the pots back to town for storing.

The Shishaldin still had the original engines as when it was a military vessel. This consisted of eight 671 GMC diesels, four engines on each of the two propeller shafts. These engines powered the vessel. Three 471 GMC diesels were also aboard with two of them powering four kilowatt generators, for the electricity on board, and the other powering the hydraulic system. The two large circulating pumps, which circulated water through the two tanks, were located near the forward bulkhead in the engine room and were powered by electricity. On the fantail of the boat a large freezer had been added below deck, to store all the bait that was needed for the long fishing trips. A flush hatch which was located on the aft deck accessed the freezer.

I was pretty pumped after being given a job on such a large vessel. I had only worked on the smaller day fishing boats up to this point in my fishing career. It was a big deal to be able to move up to the large commercial vessels. They could hold their catch up to two to three weeks before delivering, without experiencing large dead losses. They could also fish rougher water making it more likely a deckhand could make a great deal more money. I knew there would be a lot to learn but I was determined to become a good deckhand so I could build a good reputation among the fishing fleet and continue to work on the larger vessels. Along with fishing in rougher waters, the larger boats could change areas when the season in one area closed, thus enabling them to fish more months throughout the year.

King crab fishing was comparatively a new fishery in that a market had only been developed for king crab in the late fifties and early sixties. Due to this the fishery was not regulated near as much as it became later on and the seasons, in most areas, was open year around. However, in the spring time of the year the crab would go into molt and their shells would soften and their meat would be more like jelly than crab meat. Due to this the larger vessels, and many of the smaller boats, would not fish during the molt. The skip-molts, the one's that didn't go into the molt, were still firm but they were not too plentiful and there were not enough of them to make fishing worthwhile. The molt would last for two to three months so the fisherman would work on their boats and crab gear and wait for the crab to again become firm. The crab was so fragile during the molt that the mere handling of them would kill them so, to preserve the fishery, the fisherman chose not to fish during those molting months.

The crew on the Shishaldin consisted of the skipper, Arnie, Mike, the engineer, the deck boss, Al, and a cook/deckhand combination, Ronnie. They were all older guys, in their 30s and 40s and I really did feel somewhat intimidated. Arnie had told me four of us would be on deck most of the time but at times the engineer would have some work in the engine room to do and we would be reduced to three on deck. He said it slowed the deck operation down but didn't' stop us from fishing. He told me the boat was fishing between the Barren Islands and the Kamishak Bay area. He said he hoped I could keep up the pace and wasn't prone to sea sickness. The Barren Islands are located between the Kenai Peninsula and Kodiak Island, in the Gulf of Alaska, and was known for strong winds, fast tides and rough seas. I assured Arnie that I would carry my load. I'd never experienced any motion sickness, or sea sickness, and was really hoping my luck would hold.

That evening I moved aboard the Shishaldin into a stateroom at the bottom of a ladder that lead below deck and aft of the galley. The room had bunkbeds on the port bulkhead wall, a built-in closet with drawers below the lower bunk and was heated with electricity. A thermostat was observed on the wall near the door. I was the only occupant of the room so I opened my sleeping bag and put it in the bottom bunk. I observed reading lights on the wall at the head of both the top and the bottom bunks. I unpacked my duffle bag and put my clothes away. I was very pleased with the accommodations. My fishing gear, raingear, boots and a heavy coat had been stored in the entryway leading to the living quarters off the forward deck. There was a lot of room aboard the boat and the accommodations were very comfortable.

My state room was the only stateroom below deck. The captain's stateroom was located behind the bridge in the wheelhouse with the other three staterooms being on the same deck as the galley and the head, or bathroom facility. The hatch leading to the engine room was located just aft of my stateroom.

After moving into my stateroom, I went to the bridge and found Arnie. He was relaxing and reading a book. It was nearly 1600 hours and I told him I had moved aboard and I asked if there was anything that needed done. He told me to check with the deck boss but there wasn't anything else he needed. H said I could go on home after I checked with Al and that I was to be back aboard by 0600 hours the next morning. He hoped to be fueled up, with water and bait aboard by noon and said we would leave for the fishing grounds as soon as we had everything loaded. I told him I'd check with Al and I'd be back by 0600 hours.

I left the wheelhouse and found Al in the galley. I asked if there was anything I needed to do before going home for the night and he said, other than the fuel, water and bait, we were ready to go. He told me to have a good night and he'd see me the next morning.

I was excited, finally having been hired on board a large commercial fishing boat. I still had to prove myself to everyone but I was confident I could accomplish any job they wanted done. I had fished on the smaller day boats enough to know pretty much what was expected of me. I could hand coil line, I knew the knots, I was acquainted with the way the pots were baited and I could mend gear. I'd also been taught the hazards that are always present when fishing on a crab boat.

My wife was very supportive but said she wished I could make a decent living at home where I didn't have to be gone so much. I agreed but told her it was something I've wanted to do for quite a while now and getting on the bigger boats could better both of our lives. She said she understood but still wished I didn't have to be gone so much. We had only been married a few weeks and everything was new to us but we were enjoying the education we were getting.

The next morning, I kissed my bride goodbye and went to the boat. I boarded the Shishaldin at 0535 hours and found everyone aboard making ready to pull out to the fuel dock. The main engines were running and being brought up to temperature.

At 0600 hours Arnie told us to cut the boat loose and we pulled out of the harbor and docked at the City dock. After getting secured to the dock we made ready to take fuel and water. The fuel company opened at 0800 hours and they passed down the fuel hose and the water hose. Mike pointed out where the fresh water filler pipes were located and gave me the job of seeing to it that we were topped off with fresh water. He and Ronnie were overseeing fueling up.

The water tanks were topped off just after 1000 hours and Arnie called the cannery on the radio and asked that they deliver fifty boxes of bait herring. With what we had aboard Arnie said we would have more than enough for a three-week trip, if we wound up staying out that long. The cannery delivered the bait on pallets and lowered the pallets down to the fantail of the boat with the dock crane. I opened the hatch to the freezer unit then climbed down into it. Ronnie handed the bait down to me, one box at a time, and I stacked them in the freezer. By the time the bait was all stowed I was more than ready to exit that freezer. It took a little while for me to warm up.

Mike and Al had topped the fuel off and we were ready to pull out and head for the fishing grounds. Arnie called us on the loud hailer and ask that we all come to the wheelhouse. After we all were present he said he'd gotten a weather report from a boat fishing the Barren Islands and the wind was picking up and the seas were building. The marine forecast was also calling for small craft warnings so, because it was nearing 1200 hours, and we had a good seven hour run to the fishing grounds, Arnie had decided we'd wait until 0200 hours the next morning to take off. The weather forecast was better for the next day and the wind may come down by then. We could get underway around high water enabling us to run with the tide, saving fuel. We would be getting on the grounds at around daylight and then could fish all day. Arnie felt us taking off now would put us on the grounds after dark. Because of the rough weather, it probably wouldn't be wise to leave right now. He said he had checked with the City and the fuel company to see if we could stay alongside the dock until we departed and, since they didn't expect the State ferry or any other larger vessels, neither felt it would be a problem. Arnie told me I could go home and be back around 0130 hours. He said the rest of the crew was staying aboard anyway so they could tend the lines on the dock. I thanked Arnie and I left he boat and walked home.

My wife was surprised when I walked through the door and she jokingly asked me if I'd already gotten fired. I laughed and told her I was just coming home to see who her boyfriend was. We both laughed and then I told her what Arnie had said and that she needed to have a little more faith in her husband. She said something about that being a two-way street.

At 0130 hours the next morning I boarded the boat. Arnie said we would be getting underway in a few minutes. Mike had the main engines started and were warming them up making ready for departure.

At approximately 0210 hours we untied from the City Dock and got underway. A sight southwest breeze was blowing but that was not any indication of what the weather was doing at the Barren Islands.

After securing the tie up lines I went to the wheelhouse. Arnie was navigating out of Seldovia Bay and we were going through the buoys. He told me he was glad I'd come to the wheelhouse because he was taking first watch and he wanted to familiarize me with the boats operation. I observed two 36-mile Decca radars, two depth finders, two VHF radios, a CB radio and a single side band radio. A large chart table was on the aft wall of the wheelhouse and chart drawers were built in right below the table. Two large padded chairs on pedestals were on each side of the wheelhouse and Arnie was running the boat from the starboard chair. A system for steering the vessel from either chair had been added. A jog helm lever would activate the rudder and the bridge had two sets of controls for operating the engines. A rudder control indicator was also visible on the forward wall ahead of the ships wheel. A wind velocity indicator had been installed over the window in front of the captain's seat on the starboard side of the wheelhouse and I noticed it was showing 15 mph. We were traveling approximately 10 mph into the wind so, in reality, the wind was nothing more than a 5-mph breeze.

Arnie stayed at the helm until we had cleared Seldovia Bay and headed in a southerly direction, on a course that would take us to the Barren Islands. After setting the course Arnie activated the auto-pilot and told me he wanted to show me where we would be fishing. He turned the light on over the chart table and he pointed out our location and where we were headed. He said we'd reach the gear around 0800 hours and, barring bad weather, we could get to work. Arnie told me I would be doing wheel watches as did everyone on board. He said he always spent the first watch with the new hands to familiarize them with the operations of the boat. He asked if I knew any navigation and I told him I had a little experience but hadn't really gotten far enough off the beach to really need it. He said he'd teach me some tricks if I wanted to learn. I told him I really did want to learn everything I could so he said we'd take some time for that. Arnie showed me the gauges for the engines and said it was very important that I get used to scanning the gauges often. We had eight main engines, all with separate gauges, so the panel was full of oil and temperature gauges. Each gauge was labeled with its respective engine and this simplified the interpreting of the panel.

All during the next two hours Arnie was schooling me in the operation of the boat, the deck lay out and what was expected of me. He asked me if I could hand coil line and I told him I had coiled line both off a power block and a capstan. He said I'd be switching off with Ronnie on baiting the pots once in a while but Ronnie would be handling the bait most of the time. If he was getting behind I was to pitch in and help him out. He said we had a bait grinder aboard so chopping the bait by hand wasn't going to be near as hard as whet I'd been accustomed to in the past. That was some great news. Chopping the frozen herring blocks by hand was hard work and time consuming.

Arnie did say that I'd be working the rail most of the time. This meant I would be expected to throw the hook and retrieve the buoys that marked the crab pots location. I'd then put the line into the power block and coil the line when it was bringing the crab pot to the surface. When the pot broke the surface, I would stop the power block, take the picking hook attached to the picking boom, hook it into the bridle on the crab pot and release the line from the block. Mike operated the controls of the picking boom and he'd pick the pot out of the water and place it onto the pot rack. While the other three hands sorted the crab, I would be expected to get the crab pot line and the buoys ready for either re-setting the pot or for stacking the pot on deck. If the pot was being stacked I would be tying the coil of line up, so it would stay all together, and I would put it inside the pot along with the buoys. Ronnie would handle the baiting of the pots. Each pot was baited regardless of whether it was being stacked or reset. If it was being stacked on deck, it was only a temporary thing. We would be setting it back in another area close by. The only time we didn't bait the pots was when we were moving the pots to a new fishing grounds a great distance away, or we were taking the gear to the beach for storage during the time we wouldn't be fishing.

The two hours Arnie and I spent together in the wheelhouse went by quickly and I found him to be a wealth of information. He and I hit it off and he told me if I had any questions, and he could be of any help, just ask him. He said the only dumb question is the question one does not ask. He was very easy to talk to and I did pick his brain from time to time during the two months.

Arnie told me to wake Al for the next two-hour watch and then he said I should get some sleep. He said in crab fishing you never know when you will get back to your bunk. He wanted to fill the boat as many times as he could in the next couple months before soft shell season hit us, he said. That meant we'd be fishing all the hours we could. The weather was always a factor in the Barren Islands and Kamashak Bay areas so he said we had to fish anytime the weather would let us.

I went below and knocked on Al's door. He yelled he was awake and I went to my stateroom and sacked out.

Ronnie woke me the next morning at around 0700 hours and told me breakfast was ready. I could tell by the movement of the boat we were in rougher water than when I had gone to bed. Ronnie said we'd probably be on the gear in an hour or so and we needed to get breakfast out of the way. I jumped up and dressed then went to the dining room located just ahead of the galley. Ronnie had cooked sausage, pancakes and eggs. After we finished eating I helped him clean the galley and I did the dishes. So far, the dishes had been the worst of my duties. I was the youngest of six boys back home and I got stuck doing dishes quite often. Those memories are still vivid in my mind so, even though it's not all that bad, I still don't enjoy doing the dishes.

We were nearing the first crab pot so I got my fishing gear on. Because it was still February, the weather was still cold. I dressed in layers so I could shed a sweat shirt or a light jacket if I got too warm. I put my Extra Tuffs, (boots), and rain gear on then went on deck and met with Al. He told me I would be working the rail and he asked the same questions Arnie had asked the night before. After he was satisfied with my answers he told me to get ready for a rough day.

We were quartering into the six to eight-foot sea, coming out of the west, and a little spray was breaking over the bow and the starboard rail once in a while. With the deck awash from the spray and the overflow from the holding tanks, no ice was forming even though the temperature was well below 32 degrees.

Arnie announced over the loud hailer that we were coming up on the first pot. I went to the rail by the power block and readied the throwing hook to retrieve the buoy line. The crab pots were rigged with a diver buoy, which held the tension of the line which came to the surface off the pot, and a trailer buoy, which trailed off the diver buoy approximately twenty-five feet and was always down tide from the diver buoy. When you throw the hook, you want to throw it between the two buoys so you would have enough slack in the buoy line to insure you could pull it aboard and get it into the power block. When Arnie maneuvered the boat within throwing distance of the buoys, I threw the hook and was happy with the fact that I did land between the two buoys on my first attempt. Skippers get annoyed pretty quickly if you miss the first throw because the boat was still going ahead and, if you missed, they had to reverse the boat in order to give you time to pull the hook aboard and throw it a second time. Everyone knew you didn't ever want to miss the second throw after having missed the first. You would be taken off the rail immediately. Most fishermen live by the motto that a minute lost when fishing is a minute you'll never get back. Some skippers got really upset and take the mistakes personally.

I pulled the line aboard, threw the trailer buoy behind me, put the buoy line in the power block, started the block and started coiling the buoy line. Al then moved in to run the power block. We were fishing in approximately 120 fathoms of water, (6 feet to a fathom) which meant we had 175 fathoms of line on each pot. The first 25 fathom shot of line, coming off the crab pot, is called the riser line and is a floating line, so polypropylene is used. This insures the line will float off the crab pot when it is setting on the bottom of the ocean floor while fishing. This reduced the chances of the line getting fouled with the crab pot during tide changes or slack tide, or because of any ocean movements. The rest of the line, upwards from the riser line, is a sinking line. The Shishaldin used a nylon type line, or polydacarene line, which was as strong as polypropylene but didn't float. If you use floating line reaching up to the buoys from the riser line, the line would float on slack tides and boats could get it tangled in the propellers. Polypropylene line was used to rig the diver and trailer buoys so this line would float and could be seen. This didn't really cause a problem because most mariners will avoid ruining between two buoys that are in close proximity with one another.

As I coiled the line and brought the pot to the surface I realized the power block on the Shishaldin was the fastest block I'd ever coiled behind. I had to pay close attention to what I was doing so as not to have a problem that would cause Al to have to slow or stop the power block. Al would slow the block down when a knot was brought through it. The lines were all in either 25 or 50 fathom shots, so the knots were frequently going through the block. When Al saw the pot below the ocean's surface he would slow the block down and grab the picking hook off its ring on the bulwarks. Mike, who ran all the rigging, would lower the cable to free up the hook. When the bridle of the pot would reach the block, Al would stop the power block and place the picking hook into the pot's bridle. Mike would then tighten up on the picking line and Al would reverse the power block, releasing the crab line from it. The pot would then be lifted above the pot rack and Al and Ronnie would turn it to a position where it could be set down on the rack. After it was lowered to the pot rack, Mike would lower the picking hook and Al would disconnect it from the bridle of the pot and place it back into the ring on the bulwarks. Mike would tighten the line to secure it and then we would open the door to the pot and the crab would be sorted. We all shared in the sorting of the crab unless we were stacking the gear. If we were stacking the gear, I would tie the col of line up where it would not spread out, and, after the crab were taken care of, I would throw the tied coil and the two buoys into the pot and close the door. Al or Ronnie would connect the hook, off the stacking booms, to the pot. Mike would then move the pot off the rack and stack it on the deck in an area near the front of the wheelhouse. Al would assist Mike by holding onto the pot and guiding it to the location where it would be stacked. Any crab that had yet to be sorted off the deck would be sorted and the deck, being free of crab, would be ready for the next pot to be picked.

If the pot had a lot of crab, after being brought aboard, the catch was usually dumped onto the deck by using the picking boom. After the crab was dumped on deck the picking hook would be secured in its ring on the rail by the power block. The undersize male crab, the females and any trash fish would then be sorted out and thrown back overboard. Any male king crab that measured 7 inches or more, across the widest part of the shell, was thrown onto a conveyor belt that deposited it into which ever tank we were filling at the time.

If we were resetting the pot, it would be re-baited, checked for any damage and the door would be closed and secured. I would then throw the 25-fathom shot of riser line onto the top of the pot and get ready to throw the rest of the line overboard after the pot was launched. On our first pot we had a total of 39 crabs and Arnie came over the loud hailer and said we'd be setting the pot back. As soon as he gave the signal to launch Mike would activate the hydraulic ram below the pot rack and it would push the inside part of the rack upward. The rack was hinged to the rail of the boat on the opposite side, so when the ram was activated it would raise the inside of the rack high enough to launch the pot. After the pot hit the water I would then throw the rest of the line overboard with the two buoys to follow. We'd then be coming up on the next pot and the sequence would begin all over again.

After you have pulled one pot, when crab fishing, you will find that every pot is pulled exactly the same way. This would only vary if the line was snarled or tangled or the pot was hung up on the bottom for some reason. What I was quick to realize was the larger boats worked at a much faster pace than did the smaller day boats. The pots on a larger vessel seemed to be set closer together and, with all the help on board working as a team, the gear could be gone through much faster. This enabled more gear to be gone through each day. Even in rough weather a larger vessel could still go through a lot of gear. The smaller day boats usually had a crew of two on deck and, on most of the smaller boats, the skipper doubled as one of the two on deck. He'd bring the boat alongside the buoys and then leave the wheel and come onto the deck to assist the deckhand.

As we continued to fish the wind increased, as did the seas. The wind was out of the west and, as the seas got larger, the gear became harder to handle. Each pot weighed around 800 pounds, before any crab was in them, and you had to be very careful when bringing them out of the water and onto the pot rack. The pot rack had a locking mechanism and, in the rougher weather, the mechanism had to be used to secure the pot to the rack. Mike had to be very alert on the controls of the picking boom and gauge the lurch of the boat with the sea so he did not have an 800-pound pot swinging out of control. A good operator could gauge the seas and land the pots on the pot rack at just the right time, avoiding any damage or injuries to the crew.

The catch increased as we continued to fish. We were averaging over 50 crabs per pot now and we were setting all the gear back in the water. It was getting harder and more dangerous due to the growing seas. We kept fishing as the wind increased. Arnie came over the loud hailer and told us the wind was a steady 25 mph (miles per hour) with gusts to 35 and 40. He cautioned the crew to keep our eyes open and watch out for each another. He said if the wind continued to increase we would have to secure the deck and go find shelter behind the Barren Islands.

At approximately 1930 hours, after the wind and seas continued to grow, Arnie told us to secure the deck and to tie down the power block and baton down the tank hatches. He said the wind was blowing a steady 50 mph now with gusts to 65 and 70 mph. He said we would run to East Amatuli Cove on East Amatuli Island, in the Barren Islands, and anchor up for the night. Being inside East Amatuli Cove should put us in the lee of the island where the seas could not build. I swung the power block davit inboard and tied it down. Ronnie and Al secured the hatches on the tanks. Ronnie and I stowed the excess bait in a chest freezer kept in the forward compartment and then we went inside the cabin and got shed of our rain gear and boots.

Arnie got underway heading for the Barren Islands. He said it would be a couple hours by the time we got inside and anchored up. He told Ronnie we'd wait until calmer seas before starting dinner. He said we would be catching the seas on the starboard beam when we made the turn to go in behind East Amatuli and it could get pretty rough for a short time.

I washed up then went to my stateroom to stretch out for a little while. When I felt the boat start to roll a little I knew we were making the turn to go behind the Islands so I jumped up and went up to the bridge. It was dark but you could make out the outline of an island off our starboard side. The wind velocity indicator was reading 70 – 75 mph pretty steady and then a gust up to 90 mph would be indicated. The boat would shimmy, or tremble, in the wind. Arnie said the wind was on our beam and we felt it more because of the direction it was coming from. He said the vibrations of the boat, caused by the wind, would decrease when we turned the bow into it when entering into East Amatuli Cove. The seas were decreasing quickly as we came into the lee of the Island. Arnie told me to let Ronnie know he could start dinner now. I went to Ronnie's stateroom and told him what the skipper had said. He thanked me and headed for the galley. I went back to the wheelhouse to take in the anchoring of the boat. After about 30 minutes Arnie reduced the throttles and eased into the Cove. Mike came up the staircase into the wheelhouse. He asked Arnie how much many wraps he wanted to let out when anchoring. Arnie said he wanted three full wraps out tonight due to the heavy winds and needing more scope than usual on the anchor. He told Mike we'd be standing watches tonight with the main engines running. Arnie said he felt the anchor could drag if the wind picked up anymore. We were going to keep the engines running and put them slow ahead in gear if needed to keep that from happening. Mike commented that he was glad these big storms didn't happen too often even though the Barren Islands sure seemed to have more than their share. Arnie agreed and said it was a rough place to fish but it usually paid off if a guy stuck it out and stayed with the grind.

Arnie told Mike to get ready to set the anchor and he turned on the deck lights. He told Mike to be careful walking up the deck to the bow compartment. Mike assured him he would be fine and he went below to get ready. In a couple minutes Mike was observed leaning into the strong wind when working his way to the bow. Arnie, using the loud hailer, asked Mike if he had the anchor ready to go and Mike yelled back that all was ready. Arnie reversed the engines then told Mike to drop the anchor. We were in 50 feet of water when we anchored the boat and it was only an hour before low tide. When the three wraps were out Mike asked Arnie if he could dog in the winch. Arnie threw the engines in neutral and told Mike to dog the winch. We waited until the boat stopped and settled in and then Arnie took a radar bearing. If the boat did drag anchor we could tell by the radar bearings that he took. Arnie called to Mike on the loud hailer and told him to come on inside and told him it looked like the anchor was holding.

Arnie kept watch for another 20 minutes before being satisfied that we weren't dragging anchor. He told me the person on watch will have to be alert tonight. If we started dragging anchor we could get into trouble if no one noticed it soon enough to make the needed corrections. He said I would stand the first two-hour watch and he showed me what I should be watching for. He told me if we did start to drag anchor that I was to wake him immediately. The Shishaldin was so big, he said, it was like a big kite and caught a lot of wind. Due to its size it sometimes would drag anchor where a smaller vessel wouldn't have any problem. Ronnie yelled up to the wheelhouse that dinner was on the table and we went below to eat. Arnie fixed him a plate and headed back to the bridge.

After dinner I went to the wheelhouse and joined Arnie. He showed me the controls for the main engines as well as for the spotlight. He said when I was on watch I was to keep an eye on the oil and water gauges and if anything was climbing into the red, to let him know. He showed me how the spotlight reached out and lit up the beach on East Amatuli Island. I don't think I'd ever seen a brighter light. It seemed to almost turn night into day.

Arnie shared that we had pulled a total of 68 pots today and caught around 3500 crab. He said with the weather being snotty all day he felt this was a good day of fishing. He also told me I seemed to be working out fine and he asked how I felt about working the rail after my first day. I shared that it was a much faster pace than on the smaller vessels and the gear was much heavier than I was used to but I had been able to keep up with the power block and that had been a major concern of mine. Arnie said I was doing fine on the rail and he'd keep me there as long as things were working out. I felt I'd been accepted as a crewmember now and I was getting much more comfortable with the position.

It was 2230 hours when Arnie told me he was going to lay down and I had the watch. He told me to wake Al in two hours to take over. He was very insistent that I never hesitate to wake him if I feel something is wrong. He said he'd rather be awakened for little or no reason than to let something go wrong to a point that it would be hard to correct. I told him I wouldn't hesitate to call if a problem did arise. He told me to keep an eye on the wind velocity indicator and, if the wind did reach a steady 90 mph I was to let him know. The wind was blowing 70 mph pretty steadily and, when a gust would hit, the indicator would read upwards of 90 mph. I had never experienced these kinds of winds and it was very concerning to me.

Arnie went to bed and I took up a position by the spot light. I turned it on and scanned the water and the beach. The salt water had white caps everywhere but no large swells due to us being inside behind the Island. The wind would pick up the water and throw it, creating a smoke like appearance on the water's surface. The spray was continually hitting the boat and covering the windows. Some ice crystals were forming but no serious ice was building at this point. I kept checking the radar every few minutes to make sure we were not dragging the anchor. All during my watch the wind howled and the boat would shimmy, or tremble, when a strong gust would hit us. The two hours I was on watch seemed to last forever. I was so concerned about dragging the anchor, or something else going wrong, that I stayed on my feet the entire time. I repeatedly checked the oil and temperature gauges, as well as the radar, and I nearly burned a hole in the beach with the spotlight. Thankfully nothing did happen during my watch and, when my watch was over, I woke Al so he could take over.

The wind velocity indicator was now holding a pretty steady 75 mph, with stronger gusts, but it had not reached the steady 90 mph that Arnie told me to watch for. The water still appeared to be smoking and the boat still trembled when the stronger gusts would hit. I observed one gust to reach just over 100 mph but then it quickly settled back down to a steady 70 to 75 mph. This had been quite a first day aboard the Shishaldin. I was already questioning myself as to what I was doing out here. I have to admit, it was a pretty concerning in the life of this 21-year-old kid.

Amazingly I slept pretty hard through the night. I awoke at 0650 hours and I got up and dressed. I went to the bridge to find Mike on watch. The wind velocity indicator was now hitting a steady 90 to 95 mph. Gusts would hit and the indicator would peg out on 120 mph. It would hold there for a short time and then come back down to 90 or 95 mph. 120 mph was as much as the indicator would read. The high winds were stressing the boat and the anchor line.

It was still dark and the darkness made it even more eerie when the gusts would hit. I asked Mike if he'd ever seen this kind of winds before and he said he had but they were rare. He said he'd listened to the marine forecast earlier and a full storm warning was in effect from Lower Cook Inlet, through the Barren islands, all around Kodiak Island, in Shelikoff Straight and reached as far west as Cherikoff Island. He said it was supposed to diminish in the afternoon and be down to 35 to 50 mph tomorrow. Mike said we'd not be going anywhere today and possibly not tomorrow. After a blow like this it takes a day or two for the seas to subside he said. He had kicked the main engines ahead an hour earlier after the winds started pegging on 120 mph, he told me.

Arnie came out of his state room and asked Mike for an update. Mike told him the same information he'd shared with me and Arnie told him he wanted to let out another wrap of anchor line to make sure we didn't start dragging anchor. He told Mike to stay low when working his way forward to the bow compartment. Mike left the bridge to get his coat on and go forward. As Mike worked his way to the bow he stayed low as possible, letting the built up railing shield him from the wind. It was still blowing 90 mph. When Mike reached the bow compartment he signaled Arnie that he was ready. Arnie picked up the RPM's on the engines to move forward to ease the tension on the anchor line. Mike had already started the engine that powered the anchor winch and he picked up on the anchor line enough to enable him to release the dog and unlock the winch drum. At that point Arnie brought the main engines to an idle and took them out of gear. The wind set the boat back and the cable started reeling off the anchor winch. When it was nearing the end of the fourth wrap, Mike signaled Arnie that he was going to again dog in the wince. Arnie put the engines in slow ahead, bringing the boat to a stop. He then told Mike to set the dog. Mike set the dog and the boat settled back against the cable. Arnie told Mike all seemed well and he could shut he engine down and come on inside. We watched as Mike worked his way back to the cabin from the bow compartment.

Around midafternoon the wind started to decrease in velocity. At around 1800 hours the wind was down to 40 mph and the gusts were getting less and less. When they did hit they would only reach upwards of 60 mph. Everyone was either reading a book or playing solitaire. Al had tried to teach me cribbage and I was catching on but was overlooking a lot of points when I would count. He assured me it would get easier as I continued to play.

The next morning the wind was still blowing 30 to 35 mph but Arnie said we'd wait one more day to let the seas subside. We would get an early start the next morning he said.

When you're anchored up on a boat, waiting out the weather, you find time to go by very slowly. You do a lot of reading or, as in Al and my case, you play a lot of cribbage. I took a nap in the afternoon and awoke just in time for dinner. We ate steak that night and had a piece of white cake that Ronnie had baked. We were all stuffed by the time the meal was over.

The wind had come down and was only blowing 20 to 25 mph now and there were no hard gusts. The main engines had been shut down and no one had to be on watch during the day.

Arnie told the crew at dinner that we would be fishing long hours and would be turning over all the gear we could. He said we had less than two months to make the season a success. He cautioned us that the seas would be rough at times and we needed to stay on our best game to avoid getting anyone hurt. He said he hoped we didn't have to move a lot of gear and the best-case scenario would be if we could just pick and set back.

During the night we each stood a two-hour shift. I was on watch from ten to midnight. The wind was still hitting 15 to 20 mph but that didn't affect us at all. As I scanned the water and the beach of East Amatuli Cove, I observed some Kittiwakes on the beach and some Black Ducks and Golden Eye swimming near the shore. During the last couple days, we hadn't seen any wildlife. The wildlife, and all the fishing boats, had hunkered down throughout the blow. There was no way a bird could have ever flown in that wind.

While on watch I thought back over my life and I realized I had experienced quite a bit for a young man off a southern Illinois farm. I had moved to Alaska at a very young age and had worked in a king crab cannery, had fished king crab on the smaller day boats out of Seldovia, I had spent two months as an engineer on a tug boat working in the ice in Cook Inlet, I had gotten married and now I was on the largest king crab boat fishing out of Seldovia. I also thought about the last couple days when I was questioning what I was doing out here. I felt a lot better now that the wind had subsided and we had ridden out the storm. I felt I would not be as impacted by the next storm and I'd gained a lot of Respect for eh Shishaldin's ability to withstand the assault the weather imposed on it.

I had only fished one day on the Shishaldin but I had a good idea now of what was expected and everyone on board seemed to accept me as an equal. My being the youngest man aboard was somewhat concerning to me in that the seasoned fisherman didn't often accept the new guy right away. That didn't seem to hold true on this boat and I felt very accepted by the crew. I vowed to myself to work as hard as I could for the next couple months and to learn all I could from these seasoned fishermen. In doing so I felt I could build a reputation as a good hard-working crew member and one who worked well with others. This could prove to be very beneficial when I applied for work on another large commercial fishing vessel.

We got underway at 0500 hours the next morning and ate breakfast while in route to the fishing grounds. At 0715 hours we reached our first string of gear. The wind was blowing around 20 mph and the seas were 8 to 10 feet, still out of the west. It was cold but the bow compartment did shelter us somewhat when we were running between pots.

After picking a dozen pots Arnie came on the loud hailer and told us we had a 40-minute run to the next string. We had been averaging over 75 crabs per pot so we were able to set all the gear back and not have to stack any gear and move it. If this kind of fishing kept up, and if the weather let us continue to fish, we could fill both fish holds in another

4 to 5 days. Fishing with this kind of an average would insure a pretty decent pay day for the crew.

The crew went inside the cabin to grab something to drink. The wind had decreased somewhat and was only blowing 10 to 15 mph now. The seas hadn't come down too much but the swells did seem to be smaller. At least we weren't dealing with any breakers or heavy seas now.

The rest of the day was decent fishing with us holding an average of around 75 crabs per pot and the weather kept coming down making it much easier, and faster, to work the gear.

Flocks of Myrrhs were seen off and on all day, flying near the surface of the water. The Tufted Puffins were also plentiful as were the kittiwakes and other sea birds. The ocean was alive again following the storm. Sea lions were seen quite often swimming around the boat. I was told the Barren Islands was a rookery for the sea lions and that the animals went ashore to bear their young. The spring of the year brings thousands of them to the area for calving, I was told. They are huge animals but are very graceful in the water. When nearing the boat, they would swim around the bow for miles, diving and then surfacing again on the opposite side of the bow. It appeared to be a game with them. They would swim much like a porpoise, jumping up out of the water every time they surfaced. It was beautiful to watch. The sea lions did create some problems for the crab fisherman from time to time. The buoys, which marked the crab pots, would become toys for the sea lions. They would knock them around and, at times, would bite them causing them to deflate. The buoys would then sink and the crab pot would be lost. Some crab fisherman, in later years, came up with a solid Styrofoam buoy with a hole through the middle of the buoy to run a line through. A plastic insert was installed through the middle of the buoy to prevent any chaffing. The foam buoys would be positioned behind the trailer buoy, rigged to a ten to twelve-foot line. This would enable the fishermen to retrieve their gear if the plastic inflated buoys were damaged by the sea lions, and sank. The cost of the pots mandated someone come up with some kind of sea lion proof buoy. The Styrofoam buoys were labeled "Sea Lion Buoys" and were used by the majority of the larger crab boats fishing the waters frequented by sea lions.

Arnie signaled we were coming up on the next string of gear and we all returned the deck. We started picking pots and found the pots were not producing near as well as the previous string so we started decking the gear to move to another area. Up to this point we hadn't decked any gear so this would be new to me. I pulled enough line off the coil to tie it up and then, after the pot was cleared of crab and rebaited, I threw the coil and the two buoys inside and closed and secured the door. Al hooked up the stacking hook to the bridle of the pot and Mike picked the pot off the rack and, with Al holding to and guiding the pot, stacked it on the port side at the front of the cabin. The pot was lowered to the deck with one side leaning against the boat's railing. The edge of the fish holding tank supported the crab pot. The stacking hook was secured to its position near the crab rack and we were pulling the next pot. After the pot was taken off the rack for stacking, Arnie would be coming up on the next pot to be pulled and Ronnie and I would attend to pot until Al was freed up. Al would then take over running the power block from Ronnie who would then go attend to his bait.

We wound up stacking the entire string of gear, which consisted of 32 crab pots. After we finished the string, Arnie told us we would have around an hour run to get to where he wanted to set the gear we'd stacked. Ronnie said he had to get some bait ahead and would be in after a while. I asked if I could be of any help and he said I could assist him in getting some bait from the freezer compartment on the aft deck. He and I transferred a dozen boxes of bait forward from the freezer and Ronnie ground up a couple boxes. That put him ahead on the bait so we wouldn't have to wait on him when pulling the pots. The skippers didn't like the operation slowed down for any reason and most felt bait should never be the reason we weren't fishing.

Arnie told us we were getting close to the area where he wanted to set the gear so we all put on our fishing gear and headed back out on deck.

Mike and Al hooked up the first pot and moved it to the crab rack. Ronnie and I opened the door and I pulled out the line and the buoys. Ronnie closed and secured the door on the pot. I untied the coil of line, threw the riser line on top of the pot and waited for the signal from the bridge. We set all 32 pots in one string. Each pot was set exactly the same as the one before and, before long we had a rhythm down and everything worked like clockwork. Arnie told us we had a 30-minute run to the next string. We all again went inside and I went up to the bridge. Arnie said it appeared the crew was working well together and that I was working out just fine. I, of course, felt very good about the compliment and I thanked him, telling him the crew was really easy to work with. He said they were a group of great guys.

It was nearing 1800 hours and Arnie said we'd probably pick gear a couple more hours before quitting for the night. He said the fishery had changed a lot with the introduction of the bright crab lights all the larger vessels were using now. They consisted of 3-4 huge Halogen type lights they had mounted to the forward most mast. They were positioned to shine to the front and both sides of the vessel. The lights were so bright you could see the crab pot buoys from up to 200 – 300 yards away in calm waters.

A number of large vessels, both out of Homer and out of Kodiak, fished the Barren Island/Kamishak Bay areas and they were easily seen with the big crab lights they were using. On this day I had counted 7 boats within 5 miles of us.

We were nearing the next string of gear and Arnie asked if I'd let the crew know we were getting close. I went below and alerted the crew then got into my fishing gear.

We picked pots for another 3 hours before Arnie told us to secure the deck. We had been getting better numbers and no one wanted to quit fishing. The last string had been showing 75 – 110 crab in the pots. I had never seen that many crabs in one pot. A couple of the pots had over 100 crabs in them and looked as if there was no room for another crab to enter. The most I'd remembered seeing in one pot, on the smaller boats, was around 35 or 40 crabs. That was good fishing in Kachemak Bay back in the late 1960's. I couldn't believe we were getting the numbers we were on this last string. It sure seemed to keep the crews spirits up. Everyone was in a great mood.

For the next 5 days we were able to fish and the numbers were still holding with more than a 70-crab average in the gear. We'd stacked some gear now and then but, by the time five days had past, we'd moved the gear into a general area and the run between strings was minimal. We were able to set back and not stack gear, which only increased the number of crabs we were catching. When we didn't have to stack and move gear, we could pull considerably more pots. On the morning of the 6th day Arnie told us at breakfast we were nearly topped off in both holding tanks. He said we'd fish until around noon, in hopes we'd top off both tanks, and then we'd head to town to deliver.

It was close to 1100 hours when Al yelled to Arnie and told him we were full and couldn't put any more crab on board. Arnie told us to secure the deck and we'd head for Seldovia.

After the deck was secured I went inside and washed up. I grabbed a can of pop from the galley and headed up the stairwell to the bridge. Arnie was still on the helm and he told me it would have been a perfect trip but for the storm for the first couple days. He said he rarely seen fishing this steady. He'd seen high numbers of crab but said it was usually found in just one or two of the strings. Good fishing throughout all the gear was rare indeed. He told me not to get my hopes up thinking this would happen on every trip. I told him I'd never seen anything like this before. I added that the weather also fit into that same category. I'd never been in a full storm before, even on the beach, let alone on a boat. He said thank God it wasn't something that happened too often but said we were fortunate to have a cove with good anchorage. He'd seen storms when they didn't have the protection we had and they would have to jog into the sea until it lay down. He said those were some miserable times.

We reached Seldovia at 1820 hours and we tied up to the cannery dock. We would lay there for the night and would start to offload the catch the next morning. After we were tied up and secure, Arnie told Mike he could shut down the main engines. He told us we could go ashore but to be back aboard by 0800 hours. The cannery had told him we were scheduled to start offloading at 0900 hours, he said.

I climbed the ladder to the cannery dock and then walked home. My wife was surprised to see me but seemed pleased none the less. We talked and talked. I told her all about my first trip on a large commercial vessel and I left out very little. She was shocked, as was I, that the wind can blow that hard and a boat can survive it. I told her about the large numbers of crabs we'd caught in the gear and how well the crew worked together, each man having his duties made the deck flow smoothly. I also told her if the fishing kept up like it was on this trip, the money I would make would far exceed the wages I was making on the smaller boats. I shared that it was long hours and strenuous work but I also was enjoying what I was learning. The worst part of the job was my having to be away from home so much. We both agreed but we were thankful for the opportunity this was giving us. Out future looked much brighter now than it had a month ago when I was looking for work.

I boarded the Shishaldin at 0745 hours the next morning and found Al, Mike and Ronnie already removing the planks off the two fish holds. I joined them and within a few minutes the tanks were open and ready for offloading.

The Shishaldin was rigged different from any of the larger boats that I had ever seen. The two holding tanks had been fitted with a false bottom covering the floors. Long rods were attached in all four corners of the false floors and reached high enough where they could be hooked into the stacking booms hook. This enabled the crab to be lifted by picking up on the picking boom winches. The holding tanks were not pumped down and the crab was never completely out of the water prior to being offloaded. When being offloaded they were thrown onto a conveyor belt which deposited them into one of the canneries off-loading bags. The bags were placed in front of the forward tank at the end of the conveyor belt. When the Shishaldin was converted to a crab boat, the owners felt keeping the crab in circulating salt water at all times, even while being offloaded, would greatly reduce their dead loss. They felt by pumping the tanks dry when offloading, as most all the boats do, many more crabs are killed. The offloading crew stands on the crab in knee deep water and throws them onto the conveyor belt. When they need to be lifted up the engineer would raise the false bottom in the tank, forcing the crab upward and keeping the offloading crew from going over the top of their hip boots.

We had the conveyor in place and everything ready when four cannery workers came aboard to offload us. I asked Al if I should also jump in the tank and help offload the crab and he said the cannery workers took care of all the offloading. Al said I would be busy enough just handling the bags they were filling. The dock crane operator lowered the bags down to the end of the conveyor belt and Ronnie and I were expected to keep a bag under the conveyor belt at all times. When a bag was filled with crab Ronnie or I would hook the bag to the dock crane, the operator would lift it out of the way and we would slide another bag under the end of the conveyor belt. The bags filled up quickly with four men feeding the conveyor belt and Ronnie and I were kept pretty busy.

Offloading the boat was completed at 2100 hours. We'd taken a break for both lunch and dinner. Following the offloading Mike pumped the tanks down and Ronnie and I climbed down into them and cleaned both tanks. Barnacles, crab legs and other pieces that had broken off, had to be removed and the slime that covered the bottom of the tanks, had to be scrubbed off.

At around 2240 hours the tanks were cleaned, the planks had been replaced and the deck was secured. Arnie came on deck and told us the total delivery was 160,000 pounds. The cannery was paying $.10 cents per pound so, after doing the math, I was ecstatic with my first trips earnings. If I received a full share, I'd earned better than $1200.00 myh first trip on the boat.

Arnie told us we could take off and be back by 0800 hours the next morning. He said we'd be taking on 20 boxes of bait and then we would get underway to the fishing grounds, weather permitting. He asked Mike if we were alright on fuel and Mike said we could make a couple more trips, if they were like the last one, before needing any fuel. Arnie said he'd see us in the morning and he left the deck.

I told the crew goodbye and I climbed the ladder to the cannery dock and walked home. My wife was still up when I got home and she said she was wondering if we took off. I told her what Arnie had said and we talked for a little while before going to bed. She was really pleased when I told her about our delivery. I said, I felt like I was carrying my weight on deck and I got along well with the crew, so I felt I would be getting the full share of 8%. Her eyes really lit up when I told her, if I was paid a full share, I had made better than $1200.00 om my first trip. Fishing had been amazingly good and, this wasn't always the case, so we had no idea what the next trip would bring. The weather could keep us from fishing or the crab could move off the gear and we'd have to locate them again. When crab fishing, there are no guarantees.

At 0745 hours the next morning I boarded the boat. The engines were running and everyone was in the galley drinking coffee. The cannery hadn't delivered the bait yet. When they did arrive with the bait Ronnie and I would stow it in the aft freezer.

Arnie told us we had a decent forecast so he wanted to shove off as soon as the bait was aboard. At 0805 hours the cannery crew delivered the 20 boxes of bait. Ronnie and I stowed it away then let the skipper know we were ready on deck. We untied the boat at his direction and got underway to the fishing grounds.

For the next 6½ weeks we filled the Shishaldin tanks three more times. The weather was pretty rough most days but was not so rough we couldn't fish. We all were getting tired of the grind day after day but that is the life of a crab fisherman. The numbers were less than the firs trip, and we did have to shuffle gear quite often to stay on the crab. Arnie had been fishing king crab since it became a fishery and he had a knack of finding the crab when they moved off the gear. He was a hard worker and knew the king crab fishery as well, if not better, than most.

On the last load the crab only averaged 7½ pounds, which I was told indicated the soft shell season, or the molt, had started. Our last delivery totaled 92,000 pounds of crab. We had not had a great deal of dead loss up to this point but, on the last load, we lost more crab than on all the other trips combined, another indication of the molt. We cleaned up both tanks and then pulled over to the fuel dock to top off on fuel and water.

The Shishaldin was heading south to Seattle and I was getting off. Arnie was in the wheel house when I went to the bridge. He said he'd been more than satisfied with my work and that I would be getting a full share. He said if he needed a deckhand in the future I could look for a call. I, of course, was flattered but, at the same time, I felt I'd earned my stripes. I'd worked hard the entire time I was aboard the boat. I had done everything that was asked of me and I felt I'd succeeded in building a good reputation that hopefully would spread among the larger crab fleet.

Arnie gave me my final check and we said our goodbyes. I went below and said bye to Mike, Al and Ronnie and told them I'd really enjoyed working them and thanked them for all they had taught me. They each said they had enjoyed working with me, as well, and hoped to work with me again in the future. I retrieved my gear from my stateroom, grabbed my rain gear and boots and climbed the ladder to the City Dock. I waved to the crew as I got into the rig my wife was waiting in.

In a short 8½ weeks that I fished aboard the Shishaldin, I made $9,600.00. This was a very good payday for a 21-year-old kid in the late 1960's. But, even more importantly, I learned a great deal and I met four top hands I could call friend.

The word did get around and, because of my time on the Shishaldin, I was approached by Joe Kurtz and asked if I'd go to work for him aboard the 91-foot crab-fishing vessel, Amatuli. I spent nearly four years fishing Alaskan waters on the Amatole's from Kachemak Bay, Lower Cook Inlet, the Barren Islands, Port Lock Banks, all around Kodiak Island and, out as far as the Bering Sea. I learned a lot, met a lot of great people and I made a lot of money.

My parents' teachings at a very young age, paid off in huge benefits. The value of hard work and being respectful to others, helped me to become an experienced crab fisherman. I was now pretty well known in the crab fishing industry and I felt I could most probably get a job on any crab boat that needed an experienced hand. My life was going great and, little did I know, I had many more exciting adventures and experiences which lay ahead.

"CRIME DOESN'T PAY"

As a teenager on May 1st, 1964 I arrived at the remote town of Seldovia, Alaska traveling from my home in Missouri. My plan was to spend the summer with an older brother who was living and working in a cannery there. That was many years and many memories ago. I wound up staying in Seldovia and marrying a local Athabascan girl who was, and still is, the prettiest girl in town. Together we raised a daughter who now lives in Washington State with our grandson. But this story is not about that part of my life. This writing is about a series of unexpected events that took place in 1968, which could have cost my brother-in-law and me our lives. The memories I have during this episode of my life are now very dear to me.

I've had many exciting adventures in my life, some which could have been life threatening. My brother-in-law, Harry Yuth, became a very important person in my life during one such occasion. He passed away in 1997 after a long battle with cancer, which makes my memories even more special. Harry was a gentle man with a quiet strength. He was a native-born Alaskan who was very knowledgeable when hunting and fishing in Alaska's harsh terrain and climate. For the greater part of his life he had commercially fished for crab, salmon, and halibut in Alaskan waters. With his being well schooled in battling the elements of this harsh land, I felt very fortunate to have been in his company during one such adventure. The events we encountered leave little doubt we both survived our ordeal through our friendship and trust in one another and by the grace of God.

Harry and I were not criminals but we were about to knowingly break one of Alaska's hunting laws. We were gearing up to go on a moose hunt even though it was well past moose-hunting season. We had both been working during the moose-hunting season and were not able to hunt for our winter meat. We justified the illegal hunt in our minds by convincing ourselves we needed the meat and we only planned to take one moose. This would be meat enough to feed both our families and, with the price of beef, we felt we needed to get our meat by hunting for it.

It was February in Seldovia and winter had set in. The temperature was nearing the +10 degree mark and the skies were clear. Harry and I felt it the perfect day to begin our trip. We were traveling to Sadie Cove for the hunt.

We carried our hunting gear down to the boat harbor and loaded the skiff. There was a lot of gear but we had room in the skiff and knew we needed all the gear we were taking to be on the safe side. We were going hunting in the winter in Alaska and you need to be prepared. The weather is unpredictable and you have to be ready for almost anything. Our transportation was a small, 14-foot, wooden work skiff Harry had borrowed from his boss. It was a heavily built work skiff with a square bow and wide beam. The bow was covered over with plywood to make a weatherproof storage area, otherwise known as a whaleback. A 40-horsepower long shaft Johnson outboard powered the skiff, and we brought along a 25-horsepower Johnson for a spare, which we stored in the bottom of the skiff. We had three outboard tanks full of gas, as well as three full five-gallon cans aboard. We put the six cans of 2-cycle outboard motor oil in a plastic bag and tied the top of the bag. A box of tools was loaded for any mechanical problems we might have and we had packed enough food for a week and a half. Harry brought a sleeping bag, rated to be good to –40 degrees below zero, and I brought a mummy bag with another heavy-duty bag. We also brought two tarpaulins, an 8' X 10' and a 20' X 20'. Each of us had a shotgun and a rifle along. We planned to go duck hunting on the trip as well as hunt for moose. I'd brought my 30-40 Craig rifle and Harry had his Remington 30-0-06. Our shotguns were both 12 gauge, Remington model 700's. We told our wives to expect us back in three-to-four days. They were told of our destination and we felt we had planned everything out and covered all the bases. We got underway and the outboard was running well, we were dressed for the weather and we had a favorable forecast. We headed out on our hunt in good spirits looking forward to a, hopefully, successful hunt.

We enjoyed the scenery as we traveled out of Seldovia Bay and headed north past Barabara Point. We went behind Hesketh Island and through Eldridge Passage on our way to Sadie Cove. Sadie Cove is located approximately 10 miles north from Seldovia on the east side of Kachemak Bay. It reaches easterly nearly five miles between mountains that seem to go nearly straight upward from the beach on both sides of the bay. We arrived at the mouth of Sadie Cove at around 11:00 a.m. on that brisk Monday morning. A slight southwest wind on our stern helped to push us along. As we started into the Cove the southwest wind was picking up and we could feel a drop in the temperature. The sky was clear. It was a good sign that we wouldn't be getting snow for a day or so. As we traveled we watched the winter ducks; butterballs, golden eyes, and black ducks, as they took to wing ahead of us. Two seals were seen swimming near the south shore and upon seeing us they dove, disappearing from sight only to come up again further to the east in the Cove. A pair of eagles kept watch from aloft with wings spread wide floating on the air currents. Numerous seagulls sounded off as they fed on baitfish toward the middle of the bay. The Cove was full of life and it was exciting to watch all the activity taking place. Snow was blowing off the mountaintops and one could tell there was considerably more wind aloft than at sea level. As we continued into Sadie Cove we continued enjoying all the animal activity around us.

After a few minutes we rounded a point and were able to see the head of the bay of Sadie Cove. What we saw shocked both of us! Ice had formed and reached out nearly a mile from the head of the bay, a fact that would certainly change our initial plans. We found the ice too thick to take the skiff through and we had to beach it nearly a half mile from where we planned to make camp.

The tide was still coming in when we beached the skiff just to the west of the ice flow. The beach was covered with loose rocks but the heavily built work skiff should be fine when the tide did go out. We didn't think twice about leaving the skiff secured on the beach. We beached the skiff and readied our packs with cooking utensils, enough food for a couple days, our sleeping bags and one of the tarps. We decided we would hike into the camp and come back the next day for the rest of the food and gear. We planned to check the area for moose in the afternoon, after setting up camp. We put our packs on, threw our rifles over our shoulders, and started out for the camp site. The remainder of the food, the shotguns and the other gear we stowed under the bow of the skiff so it would be out of the weather in the event it did snow.

We were anxious for the hunt and having to beach short of camp was considered only a small inconvenience. As we hiked in we found the beach was covered with two or three inches of snow, above the tide line, and it was very easy walking. We made good time and it was nearing 1:30 p.m. when we reached the place we were going to camp. The area was perfect for a camp with four trees spaced just right for hanging the tarp overhead. We could have a fire in the middle and our sleeping bags would be out of the weather if Old Mother Nature decided to throw a little snow our way. We had decided not to bring a tent along using a tarpaulin for a shelter. We had made camp like this in the past and it had worked very well. A tent would have been too big and would have taken up too much room. A small stream ran down the mountain just a short walk to the east from camp, and we needed only to break through the ice for our water supply. We were located on a small knob that jutted out from the foot of the mountain just west of the head of the bay. It would be a perfect location for a base camp and it provided a beautiful view of the bay to the west. We were twenty to twenty-five feet above sea level with good access to the beach on both sides of camp.

In the winter in Alaska the daylight hours are short. We had approximately six hours of daylight this time of the year so we had to set up camp quickly if we were going to get any hunting in before dark. We set up a quick, temporary camp then took up our rifles and headed east toward the head of the bay. The valley continued easterly between the mountains and widened out somewhat as we continued on.

We were hoping to get a lay of the land and possibly see if any moose had been in the area on this first short hunt. As we walked into the valley we found some old moose sign but nothing that appeared fresh. It looked as if a few moose were wintering in the area and we felt good about what lay ahead. After walking for approximately half a mile we decided to split up so we could cover more ground and get a better feel for what lay ahead. I kept with the original trail while Harry walked to the south. He planned to go to the foot of the mountain and then turn east. We would meet back at this location a half hour or so before dark, which was only an hour or so away.

We had not been apart for long when I came upon a large tree that had fallen across the trail. I headed into the timbered area to the north to go around the tree and found myself having to cross a small ditch. I worked my way down the bank and jumped to the other side. The tall grass obscured what lay on the ground and I landed on a broken branch. The branch ripped open my right boot on the inside by the ankle and, at the same time, I lost my balance and fell, dropping my 30-40 Craig rifle. I pulled my boot off and found I had skinned my shin and it was bleeding a little. It was not a serious wound but it was painful. I put the torn boot back on and picked up my rifle, surprised to find the stock broken in half in the area just back of the action. Disgusted, I picked up the two pieces of my rifle and, with the light fading, started back toward the trail to meet with Harry.

I found Harry already there and waiting for me when I arrived. I told him about my fall, about the boot being ripped, and about the rifle stock being broken in half. He said, "Murphy's Law is sure alive and well, huh?" He then said he had seen some moose sign but it, too, was old and he was not sure any of the moose had stayed around for the winter. We had to pick up the pace now to reach camp before darkness fell.

We walked into camp at dusk and got busy building a fire. We then set up the rest of the camp. While Harry opened a can of beans and put on the coffee I gathered firewood for the camp. There was no shortage of wood around the camp and I didn't have to travel far to find enough fire wood to last for a couple days. Harry announced dinner was served and we feasted like kings on beans and hot dogs. After dinner I washed what dishes we had used and then we sat back and enjoyed the fire. The southwest wind had picked up and could be heard in the trees above camp and, even though we were in a protected area, we felt the wind when it whirled down from off the mountain and into our camp. The fire would blow around a little but the wind tended to fan the flames and make it burn brighter and hotter. We visited and Harry told me of the time he'd spent in the Army as a paratrooper and about the many jumps he'd made. He talked about the guys he'd met and of his time in Okinawa, Japan. It was evident that he had enjoyed himself immensely while serving his country and he was eager to share these times with me. Harry's stories were very interesting and time passed quickly. After talking for a couple hours we each spread our sleeping bags on separate sides of the fire and settled in for the night. We visited from our sleeping bags, planning our next day. We decided to take another walk into the valley to hunt for moose. We'd go at first light. With the tide being high it made it nearly impossible to walk the beach back to the skiff. We would make our morning hunt a short one and come back early so we could go to the skiff to get the rest of the gear when the tide was ebbing. This would make walking the beach much easier. If we were lucky enough to get a moose we wouldn't go to the skiff until the next day. We still had food enough for a couple days so this wasn't really a problem. If we did get a moose we certainly wouldn't be worried about groceries. Later in the night the wind picked up and we could hear it howling through the trees. The temperature dropped considerably and we snuggled deeper in our sleeping bags in an attempt to keep the noise and the cold from invading our little world.

Harry peeked out of his sleeping bag, at one point, and saw the Aurora Borealis, the Northern Lights, doing their dance in the Northern sky. He woke me and we both watched for a time and then got out of our warm bags, put on our coats, and walked to the edge of the trees where we could better see this fantastic show of nature without any obstructions. The lights danced across the sky in a multitude of different colors; pink, orange, deep red and light blue. They sky would brighten in one area and become waves in another, dancing and darting as if in competition, each showing an array of different colors. As one area would fade another area would brighten in intensity. A beautiful curtain would form in the sky and then lights would streak across the sky from a different direction. It was one of the most spectacular sights I'd ever witnessed. So many lights were in play that we found it difficult to take it all in. We watched the show for the better part of an hour and then, when the lights became less, we returned to the warmth of our sleeping bags. With my mummy bag inside of the larger bag I warmed up right away. It wasn't long before sleep came.

It seemed only a short time before Harry called me saying it was time we got up. The fire pit still had warm embers in it and, by placing the dry wood in the embers we were able to get another fire going very quickly. We were cold and the fire felt good. It was hard to leave the warmth of the sleeping bags and I was glad I'd taken the time to gather extra wood the night before. In a short time the fire was raging and we had to back away from it to keep from getting too warm. Harry required his morning coffee and he put a pot of water on to boil. Not being a coffee drinker I'd brought a few packages of hot chocolate along. Harry cooked breakfast, which consisted of bacon and fried potatoes with onions. We sat enjoying our hot drinks and again realized how good food tastes when it's cooked out of doors over an open fire. We felt great after the warm food and drinks hit bottom and we were both anxious to go hunting. Daylight was breaking as we finished washing the breakfast dishes.

The wind was not blowing as hard as it had during the night and it looked as if the skies were still clear. We wanted to find that early morning moose. The problem was we now had only one rifle to take on the hunt and I had this large hole in my right boot. My ankle was tender but not so tender as to stop me from going on the hunt. We each lit a cigarette, a habit we both shared at that time, and then we got underway. We now would stay together due to our only having one rifle. We checked the tide book and found we could hunt until noon and then must return to go get the rest of the gear from the skiff.

As we walked we saw very little moose sign and what we did see was old. The moose could be farther back in the valley so we continued on the old trail that led to the east. When we came to the tree across the trail where I'd torn my boot and dropped my rifle, we were careful to find an easier and safer way around it. We hunted for a couple hours, and still not finding any fresh moose sign, we decided to head back to camp and grab a bite to eat before we went to the skiff for the rest of our gear. We had almost given up on the idea of getting a moose out of this valley. We sat down, smoked a cigarette, and hashed out what we would do the following day. We decided to give it one more day. We would go farther into the valley and see if the moose had wintered farther back in.

Right now, it was time to head back to camp. My right foot was wet from trudging through the snow and I needed to put on a dry pair of socks. I was wishing I had brought a second pair of boots on the hunt but when planning the trip we hadn't considered having that kind of a problem. It was just past noon when we reached camp. The wind was still blowing a little but was down from when we'd left. Harry opened a can of Spam and fried it up, along with the last of the onions we had with us. We ate a couple sandwiches and I drank the last of the hot chocolate I'd brought from the skiff. Harry made another pot of coffee and drank it. We were nearly out of food so it was important that we go to the skiff, if only to replenish our food supply.

As we started to walk on the beach we found it hard going with the ice now reaching to the top of the beach. The high tide had moved the ice up the beach covering it which made walking somewhat difficult. We had to pick our way through it, which made it very slow and tedious. We noticed the wind had blown the floating ice toward the head of the bay now making it possible for us to bring the skiff right to the beach near the camp without endangering it. Harry noticed, what appeared to be, a red gas can in the edge of the ice flow approximately two hundred yards offshore. He and I both agreed the item looked like a partially sunken red outboard gas tank like the ones we had stored in the skiff. We felt a little twinge in our stomachs, but we agreed it could have come from anywhere and was probably not one of our tanks. The skiff was not visible due to the points of land that jutted out from the toe of the mountain. We were anxious to see the skiff after rounding each point of land but again and again we were disappointed. It is hard to imagine how many points of land are actually jutting out until you walk the beach. We didn't talk much after spotting the floating tank but we picked up our pace a little, anxious now to prove to ourselves the tank didn't come from our skiff. Finally, as we rounded one of the points of land, we spotted the skiff. It appeared in good shape, being high up on the beach and sitting upright. Harry and I looked at one another and smiled, sighing with relief. It took only a few more minutes to reach the skiff. Upon reaching it we were shocked and couldn't believe what we were seeing.

The skiff had set down on a sharp rock and a hole was punctured completely through the plywood bottom. Anything in the skiff that hadn't floated off was now soaked with salt water. The oars were gone, as were the gas tanks and the gas cans. The only exception was the gas tank that was being used when we arrived. It was still there due to the gas line being connected between it and the outboard motor, anchoring it. Closer inspection of the 40-hp Johnson outboard, on the transom of the skiff, showed it had also been swamped. Any food left behind had either floated out from under the bow or had been ruined by the salt water. The two shotguns were wet and lay in a combination of ice and water in the bottom of the skiff. The 25-hp Johnson outboard also was lying in the water and ice. The skiff must have set down on the rock when it had gone dry on the first tide after we beached it and then swamped on the next incoming tide during the night. It had been awash on two more tides before we had arrived. Approximately 50 feet past the skiff, and at the high water mark, we saw the oil we'd brought which we'd placed in the plastic bag. I retrieved it and brought it back to the skiff.

After the shock had somewhat subsided we began unloading the skiff so we could attempt to repair the damage. We found a couple cans of pork 'n beans that had survived the flood but that was all the food left in the skiff. The rest of the food had been stored in a plastic cooler and it had floated off. The two cartons of cigarettes we'd left behind were also gone and this was a major loss at this time of my life. What we found when we turned the skiff over was shocking. This heavily built work skiff had a bottom that was only ¼ inch thick. Someone had slapped the ¼ inch plywood on as a temporary fix and hadn't finished rebuilding the boat. Had they finished their job and put the right bottom on the skiff, Harry and I wouldn't be facing the hardships which lay ahead. Had the boat's bottom been the same thickness as the sides, the rock most probably would not have penetrated it. Regardless, we knew we had to fix it. It was now a matter of survival. Now we were only interested in repairing the damage and figuring out how we would get back home to Seldovia. Our hunt for moose had come to an abrupt halt. We didn't discuss the seriousness of the problem but we both knew this could very well become a life or death matter.

The whaleback on the skiff came in handy when looking for plywood material to use for a patch. Harry took a patch off the bow using a hammer and his knife. He pulled a few nails out of the plywood that held the whaleback in place. The skiff was only 14 feet long but it was heavily built and both Harry and I had to summon all our strength to roll the boat over so we could put the patch on the bottom. After we finally got the boat rolled over, we proceeded to patch the hole. After the patch was in place and nailed down, we felt we should caulk it to keep it from leaking. We gathered some moss from the bank and worked it in under the patch with a hammer and screwdriver. Having finished, we looked at our masterpiece and Harry said something about our being rough carpenters, with the emphasis on rough.

Our good feelings were short lived because when we turned the skiff back over and launched it we found it leaked nearly as much as it had prior to our patch job. We again summoned all our strength and turned the skiff over a second time, hopefully for the last time. We removed our caulking and then nailed the patch back in place. The moss caulking had pushed the patch away from the bottom of the boat making it impossible for it to seal. We launched the skiff again and it still leaked a little but not nearly as much as it had with the moss caulking. We could easily keep up with the incoming water with the hand bailer so we felt the patch job was a success, temporarily anyway. We loaded the gear, including both motors, and then, with two round-nose shovels we had earlier stowed under the bow, we started rowing out to retrieve the gas can from the edge of the ice. With daylight fading we had no time to linger and we rowed as fast as we could. Little was said as we edged our way into the ice and retrieved the outboard gas tank. It still had some gasoline in it but we were afraid the seal had leaked and salt water had gotten in. We discussed the water problem and decided we would try to separate the water and the gas but we would have to clean up the outboards first as we would have no use for the gas if we couldn't get an outboard running. In fact, we had a lot of work ahead of us. We headed toward the beach below camp, using the shovels to propel us along. Neither of us talked much as we pondered what lay ahead. When we beached the skiff below the camp we discussed what our next move would be. Harry felt we should carry the outboards to camp where we could go through them and see if we could get one of them running. We had to try and separate the gas and water from the two gas tanks. The shotguns had to be gone through and cleaned up, as did the rest of the remaining gear. With that decided, we began unloading the skiff and packing everything up the bank to camp.

For dinner that night we ate the rest of the pork 'n beans and Harry had his coffee. I had devoured all the hot chocolate so I settled for drinking water from the stream. Night had again come to our Sadie Cove campsite and we, again, kept the fire stoked with wood to warm, as well as light, the camp. Harry mentioned how dark it gets when you are setting by a fire trying to peer out away from camp. He said Sasquatch could probably see into camp a lot better than we could see out. We discussed the likelihood of Sasquatch being real and both decided we hoped not, given the area we were camped in.

Along with the darkness came the bitter cold but along with the cold also came those beautiful northern lights. We, again, stood in awe of the lights dancing in the skies. The show was not as outstanding as the previous night and didn't have near the colors but they were beautiful, just the same. We watched for quite a while before the cold became too much. Harry said it would be great if the northern lights would come out when it was just a little warmer. We both intentionally skirted discussions of the seriousness of our situation and tried to keep one another's spirits high.

The wind had died down and it was calm now, with only a slight breeze out of the southwest, but the cold cut to the bone. We knew it was dipping below zero, possibly into the double digits, but we had no way of measuring just how cold it really was. We stood and visited by the fire for a while warming the front side of our bodies then turning around to warm our backsides. This continued until we both finally gave in and crawled into our sleeping bags for the night. We planned what we would do the next day from the warmth of the sleeping bags. Harry, being a good mechanic, and the only mechanic on this trip, would see if he could get one of the outboards running while I would see if I could separate the water and ice from the gas in the two outboard tanks. We could then head out after one outboard was running. I had worked on the shotguns but they needed a lot more care. The stocks and actions were still in need of attention but all of this could wait until later. Right now we were both tired from a day full of unwelcome surprises. We didn't visit much that night, both thinking our own thoughts and each not wanting to voice our concerns of what lay ahead.

Daylight was just arriving when I peered out of my sleeping bags to see Harry looking at me. Harry told me to pick a number from one to ten and if I got it right he'd get up and get the fire going. We were so warm in the bags we were hoping the other would jump up and start the fire. We chuckled at Harry's suggestion and then we both quickly exited the bags and stoked the fire. Since all of our food was gone, Harry suggested I should start drinking coffee. I told him I didn't want to be sick as well as hungry. He still had a little coffee left, along with the box of sugar cubes he'd thrown into his backpack the first day we left the skiff. I settled for a couple sugar cubes and a drink of water. Harry kidded me that he really did make good camp coffee and even I would like it. This little bit of humor made us feel better but I still didn't take him up on the offer. We both knew we had to keep our spirits up and lean on one another if we were going to make it out of the mess we'd gotten into.

I gathered more wood for the campfire while Harry worked on the 40-hp Johnson. After I'd gathered quite a bit of wood and had the fire burning pretty high, I set the outboard tanks as close to the fire as I dared, in an attempt to melt the ice that had formed inside. Any small particles of ice would be a big problem in the carburetor of the outboard. I attempted to pour the gas from one to the other using a makeshift funnel. I stretched a cloth across the tank filler spout to screen out the ice, but it didn't work as well as planned. Ice had adhered to the bottom of both tanks and they had to be warmed up to a temperature that would melt the ice without igniting the gas. I kept the fire burning high into the afternoon hours and kept pouring what little water off as it melted. At one point Harry asked that I help him carry the outboard to the skiff. He planned to hang the outboard on the transom where it would be in the water for cooling purposes and he'd try to get it running. The gas cans by now had thawed as much as they were going to and most of the gas had been poured into one of the cans. After carrying the motor down to the skiff Harry said he still had to do some work on the carburetor before he was ready to start it. I returned to the camp to continue cleaning the water soaked items. In a short time I heard Harry cranking on the outboard and heard it fire, trying to start. I was working on my shotgun at the time and, with the stock still wet, I propped it up by the tree nearest the fire in hopes the heat would dry it, then I went down to help Harry crank on the outboard. The outboard kept trying to start but would only kick over, start and then die. We cranked on it for a long time but couldn't get it to stay running. Harry said it was most likely ice particles in the carburetor and he would have to tear it down again. Harry seemed to be taking it all in stride but I was starting to get a little concerned. I'm sure he was concerned as well but voicing our concerns wouldn't help the situation at all. We lifted the motor off the transom and packed it back to the camp. When we reached the camp I found my shotgun stock was on fire. It was burned so badly that the spring and metal works were visible and the stock would have to be replaced. I was hoping the heat hadn't warped the action. Disgusted and upset I asked Harry, "What next?" He could see my disgust I guess, because he said, "It could be worse; we could be out of sugar cubes."

As strange as it seems, that statement eased the tension and, somehow, I knew we'd be all right. I again found Harry to be an extraordinary person, a man who had known a lot of diversity in his life and a man who knew how to deal with most any circumstance. He seemed to have a sixth sense about people and knew just the right things to do and say at just the right times. He was so comfortable with himself and his abilities that all of this appeared to only be a small inconvenience to him. I'm sure he knew the seriousness of our predicament but he didn't show it and this had a real calming effect on me. I was again glad that I was with Harry

Yuth. If I had planned to have a trip like this, with all its problems, I'm sure I wouldn't go if Harry wasn't along for the ride.

The afternoon passed without incident but we both were suffering from hunger pangs. We would eat a sugar cube and it seemed to help for a time. We were also down to only a couple cigarettes and, being highly addicted, this was a big concern of mine. Harry was a social smoker and could take them or leave them alone but I had been smoking a couple packs a day and was really starting to worry. That night the hours dragged by slowly and Harry kept working on the outboard with the light of the fire. With nothing for dinner but sugar cubes and, with Harry drinking the last of his coffee, we knew we had to do something the next day to bring in some food. We decided I would go hunting and see if I couldn't get a rabbit or a duck while Harry continued trying to get an outboard to run. With our plan in place we settled in for the night. It was so cold I kept waking up and I'd throw more wood on the fire to keep it going. I had placed the wood close to my sleeping bag before turning in so I could feed the fire without having to leave the warmth of the sleeping bag. It worked well and the embers were still glowing red the next morning.

As I was waking from a sound sleep I felt something tickling my nose. Closer inspection revealed I had kicked the end out of my mummy bag and the feathers were everywhere. Harry saw this and couldn't keep from laughing out loud. He said, "All we need now is a little hot tar." When I inspected the bag I found a big hole in the foot of it and feathers loose inside both sleeping bags. I gathered them up, as best I could, and stuffed them back into the hole in the mummy bag and then tied it closed with a piece of twine. It would work but the bag ended up a little shorter and a whole lot less comfortable than it was before my repair attempt. The sleeping bag was pretty important with the temperature dropping to below zero every night.

While I was working on the sleeping bag, Harry built up the fire. Keeping with the humor, Harry asked how I liked my sugar cubes, over easy, fried, or poached. I told him to just serve mine straight up and we both chuckled, again trying to relieve the stress of the moment.

Being daylight Harry again started working on the outboards. He'd decided to work on both outboards in hopes he could get one of them running. He would work on an outboard for a time and we would then carry it to the skiff and hang it on the transom of the skiff so it was in the water. This was done repeatedly throughout the day with both engines but we were never fortunate enough to get one started. Harry thought it was due to the ice particles in the gas tanks. He'd been cleaning and cleaning the carburetors on the motors and they still would only kick over as if they were trying to run but never would start and stay running.

While he continued to work on the outboards, I took Harry's shotgun and started walking westerly from camp. I was looking for any rabbit sign in the snow and, at the same time, staying on the bank near the beach where I might find a duck swimming along. As I walked along I thought about our situation. I knew we could be in real trouble if we didn't get out of this bay. No one ever traveled into Sadie Cove in the wintertime so we couldn't expect any help if we stayed here at the head of the bay. We came here to hunt a moose out of season knowing we wouldn't be interrupted. The cold weather was a major problem. It was so cold a person had to be careful to keep warm but not get overheated to the point of sweating. The weather was changing with the southwest wind blowing less and a few clouds gathering in the east. If an easterly did come in it would bring warmer weather. As I walked along I said a little prayer, hoping that the good Lord would take pity on us, even if we were on an illegal hunt and were knowingly breaking the law. It wasn't like we'd shot a moose but, I had to admit given the chance, we certainly would have.

The good Lord must have been listening because I'd hardly finished my little prayer when I saw two black ducks land near the beach below me. I stood dead in my tracks for a while until the ducks moved in toward the beach under the cut bank and was feeding close to the beach and out of my line of sight. If I couldn't see them they couldn't see me and I started edging my way down closer to the beach. When I again saw them, I tried to keep a tree between the ducks and me where I still couldn't be seen. This worked until I had only a few feet to go. The ducks saw me then and started swimming quickly away from the shore. It was apparent they were going to fly off so I stepped out from my cover and shot one still on the water. The other duck was just starting to fly when I pumped in another shell and shot him. Now both ducks were floating dead out in the water and I had no way to retrieve them. As I sat trying to figure a way to retrieve the ducks I noticed a slight breeze was still blowing out of the west and it was moving the ducks, ever so slowly, toward the beach. I decided I would just have to wait until they floated in where I could reach them. I lit the last half of my last cigarette and settled back to wait. As I waited I noticed two eagles circling high over the bay. They kept circling, getting lower and closer to our floating dinner. I started wondering how an eagle would taste on a spit over the fire. To avoid this temptation, I moved down to the beach where I could be seen and the eagles decided to keep their distance. It took quite a while for the two ducks to drift into the beach but patience did prevail and I walked back to camp proud to have gotten something for our dinner.

When I reached camp I found Harry carrying an outboard back up from the skiff again. He was discouraged. He told me we were not going to get the motors running unless we were able to get some good, clean gasoline. The ice particles kept plugging the carburetor, keeping the motors from running and, without clean gasoline we didn't have a chance of making them run.

While cleaning the ducks, in an area out away from camp, we discussed plans for the next day. We knew we had to get to the mouth of the bay where we could signal anyone going by on a boat. Harry knew about a gravel pit, on the south side at the mouth of the bay. He remembered an old bunkhouse being there where we could stay until we could get help. We decided we would row out of the Bay using the shovels as oars. With the plan in place we finished cleaning the ducks and walked back to camp.

Harry informed me I was about to learn a lesson in cooking ducks over an open fire. First we cut two forked sticks and put them through the ducks, length ways. Our first attempt didn't work to well. The sticks were not heavy enough and the wood kept flaming up and, after a time, the weight of the duck broke the burned stick and my duck fell into the fire. After fishing the duck out, we cut two heavier forked sticks, hoping to avoid a second mishap. Harry called me the "Galloping Gourmet" while laughing at his own wit. He said something about the lengths a starving man will go to for something to eat. Cooking the ducks seemed to take forever and we went over our plans while we rotated them over the fire.

Darkness arrived and the breeze switched around and was now coming lightly from the east. We decided, if the Easterly wind remained, we'd build a small sail to help us when traveling out of the bay. We had the small tarp and we would cut a couple willow trees to make the mast and the cross arm. We would nail the mast to a rib in the bottom of the skiff, and to the whale back, and would tie the cross arm, with a line, to the mast. We could put a line from the top of the mast to the bow and to the stern to ensure it stayed in place. The small tarp could be tied onto the cross arm and onto the mast. To steer the boat, we'd turn the cross arm by pulling on the ropes that would be tied to the ends of the cross arm. The shovels would act as oars and we would work our way to the mouth of the bay. We were excited about the move even if it was only part way to Seldovia.

With plans made we began eating our dinner. The ducks were dry and the taste left a lot to be desired, but they did fill the need and we felt better than we had for two days. I told Harry about the eagles wanting to eat our ducks and about my fleeting thoughts and he told me next time to take the bigger bird. Both of us laughed at that, wondering at the same time, how they might taste. The warm food in our stomachs, regardless of how it tasted, and our plans to move to the rock pit, made us feel much better about what lay ahead. Following our feast we gathered up the camp and made ready to leave the next morning. We cut the willow trees that would make the mast and cross arm for the sail, and tied them together. We could fit the tarp to them in daylight before we got underway.

It was important to get started around first light so we would have all day to reach the rock pit. We had a good five miles to travel and we didn't know what obstacles lay ahead. With everything packed and ready we put a couple of logs on the fire and got into our sleeping bags. We could tell the temperature was getting warmer, above zero anyway. It was hard to get to sleep with the anticipation of our next day's travels. We knew we were not out of trouble but just having a plan and a destination was very uplifting. At least we weren't just sitting there and taking it. We were fighting back, even if it was just to the head of Sadie Cove and not all the way home. At least boats did pass the mouth of Sadie Cove and from the gravel pit we could possibly signal someone.

The next morning, we were up before daylight and had a hurried breakfast of two sugar cubes each. We were just carrying the last of the gear to the skiff when daylight came. In a few minutes the mast was up and the sail was tied in place. We were looking forward to seeing if our makeshift sail would work. The wind was blowing lightly from the east.

We loaded the rest of the gear aboard the skiff and pushed off. As if on cue, the wind stopped blowing completely as soon as we pushed off the beach. Murphy's Law was still in effect. We looked at one another, shook our heads and picked up the round-nose shovels and started rowing toward the west. The patch on our skiff had worked loose a little, and we found ourselves having to bail more often than before. It seemed we would row for ten minutes and bail for five. The wind was still calm and it looked as if we were going to have to row the skiff all the way with no help at all from Mother Nature.

After about an hour of rowing, Harry decided to pull the skiff along with the bowline as he walked near the beach. He had his hip boots on and, while I kept the boat bailed, he trudged through the water with the boat in tow. With my torn boot I couldn't help him tow the skiff along. He pulled the boat along for the better part of an hour and then we again took up the shovels and rowed toward the mouth of Sadie Cove. The temperature had warmed up and the clouds had gotten heavier and it looked like snow was coming.

It wasn't long before the snow started falling and within a couple of hours better than an inch covered the whaleback and the boat. Visibility was restricted and we could not see over a few hundred feet ahead of us. We couldn't tell how far we had come but guessed we were better than half way. We were tired of rowing but the sail had failed us and we knew there was no quitting until we reached the gravel pit. After a time the snow subsided and we again were able to see out of the bay. This picked up our spirits a little and we rowed a little faster. Row and bail became the pattern, row and bail, row and bail. We tried to keep each other entertained by discussing many different subjects. We talked about other hunts, about experiences we'd had in our different jobs and about our families. We discussed anything that came to mind. Harry again talked about his time in the Army. He told me about the times they had the war games in the Army and how they had to camp out in the wooded areas in Japan where the snakes became more worry than the enemy they were competing against. We continued to visit as we rowed and bailed, rowed and bailed. It was around 2:30 p.m. when we finally rounded a point and could actually see the gravel pit which was only a few hundred yards ahead of us. We were both so anxious to reach the beach, the talking stopped and the rowing picked up in intensity.

When we were within 30 feet of the beach Harry jumped onto the bow, getting ready to jump ashore. The snow that had fallen made the whaleback slick and Harry's feet went out from under him and he went overboard and disappeared under water. When he surfaced I grabbed him and pulled him aboard the skiff. The forward momentum of the skiff brought us into the beach. Harry was sputtering and spitting out water and we realized instantly how serious the situation was. I estimated the temperature at around +10 to +15 degrees and I knew Harry could freeze to death in a very short time. I told him to get ashore and to keep moving. We had to unload the skiff before it sunk and I threw the gear to Harry as fast as I could. He carried it up the beach and out of the tide line. This took around five-to-ten minutes. As soon as the boat was unloaded we headed up the hill to the abandoned bunkhouse. Harry nearly ran up the hill in an attempt to keep warm, but it took a little longer for me to get there.

When I was nearly half way up the hill I spotted an old wooden Blazo fuel box and noticed a chain saw blade sticking out of it. Closer inspection revealed a McCullough chain saw had been stored inside the box. Was this the work of a greater power? I threw the saw over my shoulder and continued up the hill to the bunkhouse. When I reached the bunkhouse I noticed an old discarded barrel stove outside by the building. I went on inside and found Harry jumping around, rubbing his legs with his hands, and trying to warm up. An oil stove, with a stove stack still on it, sat in the middle of the room. I hurried back outside and grabbed the barrel stove and brought it in and placed it under the window. The window was made up of eight small windowpanes. I knocked one of them out and placed a section of pipe, taken from the oil stove, onto the wood stove. A pipe elbow, also taken off the oil stove, was placed on top of the other pipe section and was pointed out through the hole in the window to let smoke escape. I then picked up the chain saw and pulled out the choke and, saying a little prayer, pulled the rope crank. On the second pull my prayer was answered and the chain saw started. A number of bunks had been made out of 2X4's and most of the bunk frames were shortly cut up and became firewood. Harry was busy getting a fire started while I cut up the bunk frames. By the time I'd finished with the bunks he had a good fire burning. The room was partitioned on one side but the other side was open, leaving quite a large area to heat. In a corner of the room I found a large section of plastic. We used the plastic to cover the opening between the partition and the outer wall of the bunkhouse, hoping it would help to keep the heat from escaping. It seemed to help and I filled the stove with more wood. In only a short time the fire was burning so hot the top of the stove started glowing red. Harry had taken off his wet clothing and was slowly warming up. His shaking had subsided and he was talking again, telling me he could never remember being so cold. From the time we'd left the skiff until the fire was blazing in the barrel stove, very few words passed between us. We knew what had to be done and we set about doing it. Finding the useable chain saw and the discarded barrel stove seemed to be more than just a coincidence.

After we had thawed out and Harry's clothes were dry again, we walked back to the skiff to get our sleeping bags and the 40-horsepower outboard. Harry was determined to make one of them run. What we hadn't noticed when we had arrived was a small tract loader had been left at the rock pit. The loader had a gas engine and I told Harry I'd see if I could borrow some clean gas while he was working on the outboard. When I inspected the loader I found a line on the bottom of the gas tank that could be loosened, letting the gasoline drain out. I took one of the outboard cans and carefully loosened the line. It worked perfectly and in a few minutes we had nearly three quarters of a tank of good, clean gas. I mixed oil with the gas and then carried the can up the hill to the bunkhouse.

Night was coming quickly now and, with it, fatigue. We had put in a long, hard, energy-draining day. We were very hungry as well, and the sugar cubes were nearly gone. They didn't seem to do much for us anymore and we hoped we would have some real food, very soon. We located a few old cigarette butts that had been discarded by those before us and we tried to smoke them but we only managed to get a coughing fit. I'd never tasted anything so gross. We put more wood in the stove and crawled into our sleeping bags. The heat felt good and Harry said, after being so cold, he was happy to be here, inside a building, and was glad to have the heat. We talked briefly about the day's events and our plans for the next day. We both agreed that swimming would not be on the agenda. I told him it wouldn't be nearly as cold if we would do our swimming during the legal hunting season. Again, humor helped to lift our spirits.

We decided we would work on the outboard the next day and try to get one going with the new gas. If the 40-horsepower motor would not start, we'd go to the skiff and bring the 25-horsepower outboard to the bunkhouse. If we could get one going we would head for Seldovia as soon as we could load the skiff. While Harry worked on the outboards I would go to the flat and build a signal fire to alert others to our plight. We would only use the fire if we couldn't get one of the outboards to run. With our plan in place we bid each other good night and settled in to get some sleep.

When I awoke the next morning the room was already warm and Harry was putting more wood in the stove. I found it much easier to get up in warm surroundings and I told Harry I expected this to happen for the remainder of the trip. He chuckled and said he was really hoping we would be in our own beds at home tonight.

Harry was going to tear the outboard carburetor down again and I couldn't do anything to assist him so I walked down to gather some wood for a signal fire. I also figured the skiff could probably use some attention. If it had swamped during the night I would bail it out and get it ready to go. I had faith that Harry would get the outboard running and we could head home but I needed to stay busy so I would gather the wood for the fire right away. When I reached the skiff it was high and dry on the beach but it had a lot of water in it. I bailed the water out and then dismantled the make shift sail we'd built. I took down the pole and cross arm and folded the tarp. I then walked over to the beach facing Hesketh and Yukon Islands and started gathering wood for the fire. After completing this I walked back up the hill to the bunkhouse to see how Harry was doing. I'd been gone for a couple hours by this time and it was already afternoon. When I stepped inside I found Harry still working on the outboard. He had it hanging on one of the remaining 2X4 bunk frames, and was hooking up the gas tank. He told me he was going to try to start the engine dry, just to see if it was going to run. He had taken the carburetor off two times today and hoped he'd now gotten it fixed. He said, when it started, he would shut it off before it damaged the water pump. He was holding out a lot of hope with the new gas he said. After priming it with a couple pumps on the outboard gas hose bulb, Harry pulled the cord and the engine fired but didn't start. The second and third tries ended with the same result. On the fourth pull the engine started and continued to run. Harry shut it down quickly to keep from damaging the water pump and then he jumped up and down with joy. Words couldn't begin to explain our feelings when the outboard kept running. We gave each other a high five and without another word we gathered up the motor and other gear and headed down the hill to the skiff.

When we reached the skiff the tide was coming in and the stern was just starting to float. We quickly got the engine in place and then got the boat into the water and loaded the remainder of the gear. With a couple pumps on the gas bulb, and a couple cranks on the cord, the motor started, even though it was running rough. After an adjustment of the carburetor the motor smoothed out. I looked at my watch and was surprised to find it was already after four in the afternoon. I untied the skiff and shoved it off the beach. When I jumped aboard the bow I was careful not to slip on the ice as Harry had. I sat down on the port side and Harry dropped the outboard into forward gear. It immediately died. Our hearts sank, thinking we still might not be out of the woods. Harry pulled on the cord once and again and nothing happened. I grabbed the gas line bulb and pumped on it. This time when he pulled on the cord the engine again started running. He again dropped the motor into gear and this time the skiff started moving. We smiled at one another and, as if on cue, the motor started dying out. I grabbed the gas bulb and started squeezing it. The motor picked up rpm's and we were finally underway. As we traveled the motor would start to die and I would pump the gas bulb. It would pick up again and we would go a short time before having to repeat the process. This became the routine. For the next three quarters of an hour we traveled southerly, Harry steering, me pumping on the gas bulb. We noticed the wildlife, the ducks, the seals and the eagles, but they didn't hold our interest as they had in the past. We were interested only in traveling the 10 miles from the rock pit to Seldovia where we could dock the skiff, go home to get something to eat and then sack out in our own beds.

After reaching the mouth of the Seldovia Bay it seemed to take forever to reach the boat harbor. When we entered the breakwater opening of the harbor, the outboard motor died. I pumped the bulb and Harry cranked on the motor but it didn't do any good. We were out of gasoline. We grudgingly took up the shovels and rowed the skiff to the float and alongside the tugboat, Lempira IV. We hurriedly unloaded everything onto the tug including the motor off the transom. We knew the skiff would swamp and all the gear would again get wet if we didn't unload it. As soon as everything was off loaded we headed up the boat float to the harbor parking lot. It was around 5:00 p.m. and six days had passed since we had left this harbor. It seemed as if it were two weeks or more.

Our wives had gone to the store together and were returning when they spotted us approaching the harbor parking lot. We told them we hadn't eaten for days and were starving. They commented on our body odor and our unkempt looks. We commented on their beauty. Our mother-in-law, Tania, lived only a block from the harbor and the girls decided they would take us there and let her feed us. When we reached her home, Tania also commented about the smells that were present and about our unkempt appearance. While she cooked we told them of our hunt. Our wives said they were concerned when we didn't return when we were scheduled but were afraid to send anyone to look for us. They had discussed sending an airplane to look for us but, if we had killed a moose and were taking longer than expected to pack it out, we would be in lot of trouble. We had to agree and came to the conclusion we should possibly do our hunting during hunting season.

Tania cooked some bacon, eggs and toast for us and, after eating only a small amount, we felt as if we had eaten a T-bone steak. We couldn't eat nearly as much as we thought we could. Harry also got his cup of coffee which I'm sure was an addiction for him. We were both more than content now. Coming into the warm house and having full stomachs seemed to sap what little energy we had left. We were drained and anxious to sleep in our own beds. We thanked Tania for the food and agreed to meet the next day to deal with the hunting gear. We then parted and went to our respective homes, where, following a nice hot shower, I anxiously crawled into bed where I would have the best sleep I'd had in days.

With the hunt now being over I am left with memories that will be with me for the rest of my life. I believe everything that happens has a purpose and, even though I don't really know what the purpose of this hunt was, I do know that I became better acquainted with my brother-in-law, and learned many very important things from him. I learned to be patient, even in times when the future doesn't hold much hope, and I learned to rely on one's own abilities. Probably the best lesson I learned from Harry was what you can do when you insert a little diligence, patience, and a little thought. These things I learned have helped me throughout my career. You may find it hard to believe but at the time of this writing I am the Chief of Police for the City of Seldovia and have held this position for over 29 years. I often think back about all Harry and I went through and all the lessons learned but I believe one of the most important lessons I learned through all of this was that **CRIME DOESN'T PAY!**

HIGH TIDE MARINE

My experiences in and around Cook Inlet are numerous. For a few years I ran boats on a lot of different contracts for three different companies. Most of the work was done for the oil companies with oil platforms and on-shore installations in and around Cook Inlet. The first time I actually ran a boat in Cook Inlet was in the spring of 1971. I took the position as a boat operator for High Tide Marine, who operated out of a yard on the waterfront in Anchorage.

I was at my home in Seldovia when I received a call from a man named Jack, who was the owner of High Tide Marine in Anchorage. He told me he was looking for a boat handler and heard I was a good hand with a lot of experience on the water. He owned a landing craft, an LCM, and had a contract with an oil company that had oil platforms located in Cook Inlet. He'd taken a contract to deliver freight from Anchorage to the platforms. Jack said most of the freight would be on pallets, and any freight not on pallets would be configured to be picked off the landing craft by a crane.

It was the spring of the year, and the King Crab fishing season had just ended. I had been working the crab season for Joe Kurtz on the fishing vessel, Amatuli, a Seldovia based crab boat. Since the season was over, the boat had gone to Seattle for some shipyard work. I could have gone to Seattle and worked in the shipyard, but after discussing it with my wife, Ann, I had decided to stay home and look for work around Seldovia.

Jack told me the job running the landing craft would be a seasonal one, and he would hopefully have a contract with the oil company for the next couple years. He said as skipper I would be expected to deliver supplies to the platforms, which meant I would be working the tides. He said there would be no set working hours or certain days. I would work the tides, and the freight orders would dictate my schedule. I would be expected to maintain the boat, including all repairs, fueling and upkeep. Jack would provide a deckhand, who could double as an engineer. He said all expenses would be borne by High Tide Marine. I told him I would need some time to discuss this with Ann, but would let him know right away. He said he needed someone rather quickly, and had a load of freight that needed to go out on Monday of next week. We discussed wages, and I told him I'd get back to him the next day with an answer. I asked about living arrangements, and he said I could stay aboard the boat. It was equipped with a galley, bunks and a head, or bathroom, he said. The office, located in the yard, had a shower facility, and I could use that anytime I was in town. He said he really needed to hear from me right away and was hopeful I would take the job. I thanked him and told him I'd talk to him soon.

While talking it over with Ann, I found she was not at all happy about the idea. She said we had discussed my staying in Seldovia, instead of going to Seattle on the Amatuli, so I could find a job locally and not have to be away from home. She asked if she and our daughter, Donica, would be expected to move to Anchorage. I told her the job was only for the summer months, and then I planned to go back on the Amatuli for the winter king crab season. It didn't make a lot of sense for us to move everything to Anchorage, just for the summer. I also told her that Jack had said I could live aboard the boat, and that would cut expenses considerably. It appeared I would be spending most of my time out on Cook Inlet and wouldn't be in Anchorage much anyway. After more discussion, we finally decided I should take the job. There was not a lot going on around Seldovia, so work could be hard to find. We started packing the gear I would need to take with me.

The next morning I called Jack and told him I was interested in the position as skipper of the LCM, and I would be in town on the weekend to move aboard. He told me to call him when I reached Anchorage, and he'd give me a key to the gate and show me aboard the boat. He said he was happy to hear I was taking the job. He said he had a deckhand named Tommy, who would also double as an engineer, however, Tommy would not be living aboard the boat. Tommy was married with two children and had a place in Anchorage.

I was on the first flight out of Seldovia on Saturday morning. It was a short fifteen-minute flight over Kachemak Bay to Homer, where I kept a pickup truck. I threw my gear into the truck and headed for Anchorage. I arrived in Anchorage just after 1600 hours, stopped at a gas station, and called Jack. There were no cell phones back in the '70's, so communication was not as easy as it is today.

Jack gave me directions to the High Tide Marine yard on Dock Street, and told me he'd meet me there. I could feel the excitement start, and I was eager to begin this new job. I had worked in Cook Inlet as an engineer on a tugboat in the winter, fighting the ice, but I'd never been the master of a boat, where I had to make all the critical decisions. The fast tides, the tide rips and the weather were all hazards that would be a challenge. Even though I felt a little anxious, I believed I could do the job.

I arrived at the High Tide Marine yard before Jack. When I observed a big Lincoln town car arrive, I got the impression I was hiring on with a guy who must be doing well for himself. Anyone wealthy enough to drive this expensive automobile must be a very good businessman. Jack was dressed to the tee in slacks, a blazer and a nice shirt. He was around 5' 8" tall, and was all smiles when he exited the vehicle. He walked up to me and held out his hand and introduced himself. When we shook hands, I noted he had a good firm grip and a confidence about him, which I admired right away. He told me he had talked to an old skipper of mine, a guy named Allen, who had hired me on as engineer on an old military tug. I told Jack I knew him well, and that he was a good guy and a great skipper. Jack said Allen had nothing but praise for me, and that I'd reportedly done a great job for him. It was good to hear that Allen was happy with my work, but it meant even more to me that he had mentioned me to Jack, when he found Jack needed a skipper.

Jack unlocked the gate and told me to pull my pickup into the yard and down by the LCM. I pulled in and he followed me in his town car. I saw a two-story building in the middle of the property I assumed was the office for High Tide Marine. I later found the bottom level housed a small office and a shop, while the upper level housed the business offices. I observed a landing craft tied to a float that led from the edge of the yard. The tide was out and the two floats and tug were setting high and dry on the mud. A walkway led to the float from High Tide Marine's yard. I pulled down by the walkway, so I could move my gear aboard the boat. Jack and I walked down the walkway onto the float; then boarded the vessel. I noticed "High Tide 1" printed on the starboard bow of the boat. Jack said he'd named it after his company.

We went aboard the High Tide 1, and Jack explained the layout. Down each side of the deck from the bow was a walkway, approximately 2' wide. Two fuel tanks were located on opposite sides of the boat below the walkways, and two fresh water tanks were located ahead of the fuel tanks. The boat was 56' long with a gate on the square shaped bow. The gate had been lowered onto the ground making a ramp, so the boat could be loaded with freight. An open cargo hold, with high sides, reached from the bow to the back of the cargo hold, where a metal door which opened to the engine room compartment was observed. The deck was approximately 35' long and 12' wide. A two-story metal house was located just aft of the open cargo hold. A fantail deck, approximately 18' long, housed a rudder compartment, or lazarette, with a flush, waterproof access hatch. A ladder on the port side of the back of the cabin led to the roof of the wheelhouse, where the antennas were located for the radars and the radios. The running lights, the large vapor deck lights, a 10-man canister life raft and the ship's spotlight were also mounted on the roof of the cabin.

At the foot of the ladder leading to the roof of the wheelhouse was a 2" gas powered water pump and the exhaust hose. They were secured to the ladder for easy access. The pump was kept aboard for any emergencies the boat may run into or for assisting other vessels in distress. A five-gallon plastic gas can was also secured beside the pump. The entry door to the cabin was on the aft wall near the starboard side. The galley had a stove, one bunk, a refrigerator with a small freezer, a small table with two chairs, and a ladder leading down to the engine room on the port side. Another ladder on the starboard side led up to the wheelhouse.

The wheelhouse had a single bunk on the aft wall and a chart table, which was hinged to the ceiling, so it could be lowered onto the bunk for plotting courses and other navigational purposes. Two Decca radars, a 12 mile and a 24 mile, were located one on each side of the ships wheel. A large compass was mounted just ahead of the steering station, and a ship's log book was lying on the counter beside the compass. Two VHF radios, a depth finder and a CB radio were mounted just over the top of the windows ahead of the steering station. Below the bunk a navigational chart drawer, housing navigational charts and the necessary tools needed for plotting courses, was found. Below the chart drawer were two more drawers where one could stow personal items and clothing.

Two 671 GMC diesel engines powered the LCM. A small two-cylinder Wisconsin engine, located ahead of the main engines, powered a generator supplying the 120-volt AC electrical system aboard the boat. The boat also had a 12-volt system for all the lighting aboard. Large 120-volt vapor lights were mounted to the top of the wheelhouse. When turned on they lit up the fantail of the boat as well as the cargo hold. The light plant had to be started when these lights were needed. The bow ramp, or gate as it was referred to, was also powered with 120 volts, and the generator had to be utilized when raising or lowering the gate. 12 volts powered all other lighting on board.

Following the tour Jack asked if there was anything I needed, or if I had any questions. I told him I thought everything I needed was aboard, and I would probably have more questions after I got better acquainted with the operation. He said we'd need to go shopping for groceries Sunday morning. A crew was scheduled to load the boat Sunday afternoon in preparation for our first trip on Monday morning. The tide would be high at 0830 hours Monday morning, and the boat would be floating around 0630 hours. He said the next day we'd go over the charts, and he'd point out the oil platforms I would be delivering freight to. He gave me a key to the gate, shook my hand and again welcomed me, saying he looked forward to working with me. I told him I'd do everything I could to satisfy his contracts with the oil company. He left, and I went to my pickup to get my gear and move it aboard.

That evening I drove up town and had a steak dinner with all the trimmings. I thought I'd better treat myself now, because I had a feeling I wouldn't often have the chance to pamper myself with a good meal. Call it a premonition, but I had a feeling I would be earning every penny I was paid, and having gourmet meals would be way down on the priority list.

Before heading back to the boat, I called Ann and told her everything that was going on and our plan to leave for the Bruce platform on Monday morning. She told me to be careful and to call when I had a chance. She said everything was fine at home and for me not to worry about her and our daughter.

I drove back to the yard, unlocked the gate, and drove down near the High Tide 1 and parked. It was close to 2000 hours when I went aboard the boat for the night. I went down into the engine room to better acquaint myself with the layout of the boat. Two electric bilge pumps and one belt driven bilge pump were found, as was a lube oil tank that housed the lube oil for the engines. I found the boat was set up with a 12-volt system throughout so running lights, reading lights and such could be used without needing the generator. The electronics in the wheelhouse were all 12 volts, which included the two radars, the VHF radios and the depth finder. The only time we'd actually be using the generator was to light up the decks of the boat, when raising or lowering the front bow ramp, or to run a battery charger or other motors powered by 120 volts. I observed an engine room log book setting on a shelf in the engine room and found its last entry was the fall of the previous year.

After I checked everything out, I found the boat had been maintained well and, even though it was an older vessel, it seemed to be in good shape. I stowed my gear and stretched out on the bunk in the wheelhouse with a book. I don't know how long I read before I fell asleep. The drive up the highway and the stress of beginning a new job all seemed to play a role in my being so tired. I was eager to go to work but at the same time nervous due to the amount of responsibility I was taking on. I was confident I could do the job, but anything new always seems to be somewhat daunting, when you are just starting out. This was the first time I had ever been the captain of a boat, and Cook Inlet was full of hazards. I would have to stay alert and be on my best game all the time to prevent any major problems. It was a good feeling, knowing I was being entrusted with this responsibility. They had enough faith to trust that I would be able to do the job and make any critical decisions. Still, at the same time, I was somewhat overwhelmed by it all.

I was up at 0730 hours on Sunday morning, and at 0900 hours Jack came to the boat. He told me a crew would be coming down within a couple hours to load the boat with freight, which we would be delivering to the Granite Point platform, 'Bruce'. He said the freight would all be on pallets and would be wrapped in plastic to insure it would not get wet. A tarp would also be used to cover the load to further insure it stayed dry. The oil company had a crew who would be loading the boat with a forklift. When we reached the platform a couple roustabouts would be sent down on the man basket to rig the pallets for offloading. Jack said my job was to get the freight to the platform and to hold the boat in position under the crane, while it was being offloaded. The oil company would see to all the loading and the offloading. He instructed me to tell my deckhand to stick to his deckhand and engineer duties and not to get involved in assisting the oil company in loading or offloading. Jack told me all the oil platforms all stood by on channel 16 on the VHF radio but, since that is a Coast Guard distress channel, I should call them on VHF 16 then switch over to channel 10 to talk.

He said, after I was unloaded, there was no sense to start back to Anchorage when the tide was ebbing, or going out. He said all we would be doing is burning fuel and not really making any headway. He said the oil companies had long cables shackled to the platform legs, so I could hang off them when waiting for a tide change. If we started back to Anchorage a little before low water, we could make it back just prior to, or right at high tide. This would enable us to get high enough on the beach, where they could load another load of freight without too much difficulty. This way we would be getting the boat loaded, while it was high and dry on the mud. He said the timing should work out so we would be ready to go on our next trip around high water or just before. If everything worked as he hoped it would, we would be making a round trip every day and a half or so, but we had to be traveling with the tide for the most part. He felt, even with weather holds or any other problems, the oil companies should be more than satisfied getting their freight within that kind of a time frame.

Jack said a fuel truck was scheduled to come to the yard at 1500 hours today to top the boat off with fuel. He then pulled out a navigational chart and pointed out the Bruce platform, stating that is where we would be going. He also pointed out the location of the platform Anna and the platform Granite Point. We'd be delivering to all three platforms throughout the summer, all of which were located off Granite Point, he said. Hilcorp managed the platforms. Jack said this was the first year he'd been involved with Hilcorp, and he really wanted to make a good impression. If Hilcorp liked what we were doing for them, it could mean contracts for many years to come. A lot was hanging on how this job went. He said he had a lot of confidence in me and was sure everything would work out fine. I told Jack I'd give it my best shot, but I did feel the pressure this placed on me.

While Jack and I were visiting, the deckhand, Tommy, arrived. He came aboard and Jack introduced us. We shook hands and Tommy said he looked forward to working with me. He was around 30 years of age and stood nearly 6' tall with a lean build. He seemed very pleasant and quick to smile. My first impression was that he was a very likeable guy. I had a feeling we would work well together.

Tommy asked about the plan, and Jack related what he'd shared with me regarding the loading of the boat, the fueling and the departure time. He told Tommy that I could stick around for the loading of the freight, and he and Tommy would go to the grocery store and get the needed supplies. Jack said they wouldn't be gone too long and would return prior to the fuel truck's arrival. If everything went as planned, we should be ready to shove off around high tide in the morning. High tide was at 0830 hours, so I said maybe we'd shove off around 0630 or 0700 hours after the boat was floating. Jack said it appeared everything was covered, and he and Tommy left to get the groceries. Before leaving Jack handed down a water hose from the yard and told me to top off the fresh water tanks.

Jack and Tommy arrived back at the yard at 1410 hours, and I went ashore to help carry the supplies aboard the boat. I told Jack the loading crew hadn't shown up, and he said he'd check on them. Tommy and I finished stowing the groceries just in time to see the fuel truck enter the yard. We went out to meet the driver, and the fuel hose was passed to us. We topped off both fuel tanks, and the driver pulled the hose back aboard the truck. Jack came out of the office and met the driver to sign for the fuel. He told us he had contacted the loading crew and they would be down around 1730 hours. They were behind schedule after running into a problem wrapping and waterproofing the pallets. They told Jack, after they got it figured out, that everything went a lot better and should alleviate any major problems in the future. They now knew what was needed, Jack said. He remarked, "I guess we're all in a learning curve." Jack then told us to stick around and see to the loading of the freight aboard the boat. He left around 1450 hours and said he'd see us in the morning before we shoved off.

Tommy told me he had gotten acquainted with the High Tide 1 after being told he would be working on board this summer. He said he knew how to start the main engines, the generator, and how to work the bow ramp. He said he didn't know anything about sailing but was anxious to learn. I told him I thought we'd do fine together.

At 1745 hours three men arrived from the oil company with two 40' flatbed trailerloads of freight, all on pallets. The fork lift, belonging to High Tide Marine, had been made available for their use. Tommy and I went out to meet them, and they started loading the boat. The pallets were stacked two wide and two high, and when the boat was loaded the load reached the full length of the cargo hold. A large special-order tarpaulin was then pulled over the top of the load from the bow to the engine room bulkhead. It was tied down and one of the men told us to tell the roustabout crew to roll the tarpaulin up and store it near the back of the cargo hold by the hatch leading to the engine room. They said the tarpaulin could not be taken aboard the drill rig and that it was a special order built for the High Tide 1's cargo hold. We assured him we would bring it back with us. They thanked us and told us they would see us when we got back. We said our goodbyes and they left the yard. After they left Tommy started the generator, and we closed the bow gate. Two turnbuckles were used to secure the gate with one on either side. The light plant was shut off, and the boat was ready to head down Cook Inlet.

While the crew was loading the boat, Tommy and I got better acquainted. He told me that he had never been out on the ocean before, but he was eager to try it and would appreciate anything I could teach him about deck handing. He said he had been around equipment and didn't really think the engineering part of the job would be that difficult. However, he was somewhat nervous about knowing what to do on deck. I told him we'd work things out. Most of it was common sense, and he struck me as one who used his head before jumping into something. I told him I didn't want him out on deck without a life jacket on. Cook Inlet with its fast tides was a dangerous place, and you had to be very careful. The vest type life jackets were comfortable and the company had a number of them aboard the boat.

I showed Tommy a couple tricks about securing a boat to a cleat, so it wouldn't tighten up to the point where you couldn't get it loose. He thanked me saying it made good sense. I told him I thought he'd do fine, if he took a moment to think before acting. He seemed to be very attentive and thanked me for the advice. I told him to never hesitate to ask questions, and that the only dumb question was the one that wasn't asked. He told me I might be sorry I said that. He had a great sense of humor.

Tommy said he had been married nine years and had two children, a girl 4 years old and a son 6 years of age. His wife was born and raised in Anchorage. He'd moved to Alaska with his parents when he was a freshman in high school, and graduated from West High School. He now lived in a trailer park out near Muldoon. He'd been working for High Tide Marine in the yard for 4 months doing a lot of different things and he said he really liked Jack. He also said a guy named Gene, who usually worked during the week, was the foreman for the yard operations and I'd be meeting him soon. He commented that High Tide Marine had treated him well and was a reputable company. Tommy asked me some questions about my home and family and about my experience on the water. When I mentioned I'd been king crab fishing, he told me he would love to be a fisherman. I informed him it wasn't all that it was cracked up to be, and was a whole lot of hard work. He said he didn't mind working hard if he was making a good pay day. Tommy was easy to talk to, and I was looking forward to getting better acquainted with him. I had a good feeling about this job.

Tommy asked if there was anything else we needed to do to be ready for the trip down the Inlet. I told him I thought everything was pretty much taken care of. He said he'd be heading home then and would be back by 0600 hours the next morning. I told him again I looked forward to working with him. He told me goodnight and left the boat.

After Tommy went home, I left the yard and went up town to eat dinner. I went to a pizza parlor and had a pizza and a couple beers. I arrived back at the boat at around 2200 hours. I read for a short time then went to bed.

I got up at 0530 hours and made ready for our first trip down Cook Inlet to the Bruce platform. The tide was just reaching the hull of the boat. We'd float in a half hour or so. At 0600 hours Tommy arrived at the boat. He said good morning and asked me if I wanted him to make some coffee. I told him I didn't care for coffee, but if he was a coffee drinker to go ahead. He put water on to boil and brewed some up.

Jack pulled into the yard around 0620 hours and came down to the boat. He came aboard and asked if we were ready for the trip. I told him I thought so and didn't think we'd overlooked anything. He again told me to contact the Bruce platform when we were a half hour or so out, and they would be ready to unload us when we arrived. He reiterated that we should call on VHF 16 and then switch over to channel 10. If they wanted another frequency, they would tell me which one. I told him monitoring VHF 16 is very common among all the mariners I've been around. Jack said when we were coming back we should be able to reach the yard on VHF 16m when we were nearing Fire Island. Fire Island was only about 8 miles from the High Tide Marine yard. The High Tide 1 only made 8 – 10 knots, depending on how fast the tide was running, so that would put us an hour or so out of Anchorage when we called.

The boat was floating and we were getting a good jump on the tide. I told Tommy to warm the engines up and then to check the bilges and the forward deck to make sure we weren't taking on any water. The pallets put a pretty good load on the boat. I'm not much for surprises, so we wanted it checked prior to taking off. Tommy started the main engines and, in a few minutes, he joined Jack and me in the wheelhouse. He said the bilge looked good and the forward deck was dry. Jack told us to have a good trip and reminded me not to even think about starting back until we could catch the flood. I told him not to worry, and he went below and exited the boat. I told Tommy to cut us loose, and Jack threw off the lines when Tommy released them from off the cleats. I then told Tommy to stow the lines in case we hit some rough weather. We didn't want the lines washing overboard and fouling the propellers. I backed out of the slip and swung the boat hard starboard. We worked out into the tide, which was still coming in, and headed down Cook Inlet. It was just coming daylight as we got underway. I wrote our departure time down in the log book and noted we were underway to the Bruce platform in the Granite Point area.

Tommy came up into the wheelhouse and said the lines were secured and he wandered what else he should do. I told him for the first couple hours to check the engine room every fifteen minutes or so to insure we didn't have any leaks in the stuffing boxes on either propeller shaft. I too was new aboard the boat and we'd have to get acquainted with the vessel together. I told him I'd teach him about navigation, how to run a course, how to read the radars and the depth finder. I'd also teach him radio language. He again said he was looking forward to learning all he could.

The weather was calm with a light breeze out of the west but not enough to cause any problems. We were just past Fire Island when the tide changed and started going out. We would be running with the tide all the way to the Bruce platform, if things continued to go well. I showed Tommy how to read the compass and what to watch for on the depth finder. I also turned on the 12-mile radar and let it warm up, so I could teach him how to adjust and read the radar. Tommy showed a genuine interest when I was showing him the radar and explaining different things about working on a boat.

We were making decent time on our way to the Bruce platform. When we were about 10 miles from them, I called on the VHF radio on channel 16. They answered and asked me to switch to channel 10. I switched over and told them we would be arriving within an hour or so. They said they would be ready to offload us when we got there. I signed off and we continued on our way. I kept one VHF radio on channel 16 and the other monitoring channel 10, so both frequencies were covered if they tried to contact us on either one.

As we traveled down Cook Inlet I showed Tommy the tide rips and what to watch for and what to avoid. The rips could be full of logs and debris and a boat could get in a lot of trouble trying to go through them. Even if it took you out of your way, it's best to avoid the bigger tide rips.

We arrived at the Bruce platform at 1420 hours. The tide was still ebbing but had slowed down considerably. The tide book showed the tide to be low at 1443 hours. We would be offloading through slack tide, but it would be changing and starting to flood before we got all the freight offloaded. I figured it'd take at least two hours to offload the pallets. I told Tommy it would be difficult for me to see where the crane was dropping the line due to the platform being so high up and my view being obscured by the roof of the wheelhouse. He'd have to be on deck and signal if I drifted too far off. Once we started offloading, I could position the boat by referencing the distance from the legs of the platform. Tommy seemed to understand, and said he'd do whatever needed done.

I called the platform on the radio, and they said they would be sending two men down on a man basket with a set of pallet slings in about 10 minutes. I told Tommy to go out on deck, ahead of the wheelhouse where I could see him, and to get me into position when the man basket was being lowered. It was only a few minutes, and the man basket was lowered onto the deck with the two roustabouts. Tommy signaled me, as I got the boat into position to take them aboard on top of the tarp covering the pallets. The crane operator took the man basket back up to the platform. The men got busy and rolled the tarpaulin back to the engine room bulkhead, uncovering all the pallets.

I kept the boat close to the same position. Within a few minutes the pallet slings were lowered down and the first pallet was lifted off the boat. During the offloading operations I told Tommy to stay on deck and keep me in position. The tide was starting to flood by the time the last pallets were lifted from the boat. Positioning the boat was fairly easy with the conditions being what they were. The west wind had subsided, and not even a breeze was blowing as we offloaded. I was thinking this would certainly not be the case every trip. It had taken two hours and ten minutes to offload all the pallets. The man basket was lowered down following the offloading of the last pallet, and the two roustabouts waved to me when they were lifted off the deck.

Tommy came up to the wheelhouse and inquired as to what he was to do now. He understood we were going to tie off to the platform leg, but really didn't know how to go about it, he said. The tide had changed and was about an hour into the flood. I told Tommy I had decided we would head back to Anchorage. Barring any problems, we should be able to still get into the yard at High Tide Marine, even though we'd probably be bucking tide for an hour or so before reaching Anchorage. I told him the tide didn't run too fast until a couple hours after tide change. If we got underway right away, I didn't think we'd have a problem. At 1645 hours we were underway back to Anchorage.

Tommy offered to fix some dinner, if I wanted him to. We only had a sandwich for lunch, so I told him I was overdue. He said they'd bought some steaks, so he'd fix a couple steaks, a salad and put some potatoes on to boil. He almost had me salivating before he went below to cook.

As we headed back to Anchorage a southerly wind started to come up with the tide. Since it was with the tide the little swell it created was on our stern, so it didn't create any problems for us. The engines were running well, and we were making good time. All the gauges were in the green, and it was a beautiful day to be on the water. Tommy readied a plate for me and handed it up through the hatch. He then joined me with his dinner, and we visited as we chugged along. The tide book listed 2114 hours as being high tide, and I was sure we'd be able to get into the yard when we arrived. We were just approaching Fire Island at slack water, which meant we were about an hour out of town. I was glad I'd decided to head back. For 1½ hours we were bucking tide, but at 2255 hours we tied up to the float at the High Tide Marine yard. We were able to get into the yard without a problem, but we would have to move the boat ahead on the next high tide for loading purposes.

After we secured the boat Tommy shut the main engines down and checked everything over. He reported that all looked well, and asked if he could head home. He said he had brought the engine room log book up to date. I told him that was great and to go ahead home, but to come down around 1100 hours in the morning so we could move the boat further into the yard. He said he'd be here, and he left for the night. Jack didn't expect us back this soon, but I decided to get with him in the morning. It wouldn't benefit anyone if I were to wake him this late at night, just to let him know we were back. I was tired and went to bed falling asleep right away.

At 0830 hours Jack came aboard the boat and said he was surprised to see the boat back already. I told him about the first run, and the fact we made good time getting to the Bruce platform. They had offloaded us in good time, so I decided to come back even though it was better than an hour after low water. Jack said it was a good call, and he'd contact the loading crew and have another load brought down this afternoon. We could take off just before high water tonight. That would put us out of Anchorage around 2230 hours. Jack left the boat to go contact the oil company for another load. So far everything was working ahead of what had been planned. I just hoped our luck would hold, and we could fulfill the contract to everyone's satisfaction.

I went up to the office, took a shower, and called my wife to let her know about our first trip down the Inlet and back. She said she was wondering how it was going and was happy to hear everything was alright. She said everything was quiet around home, and she hadn't heard of any jobs that I could have taken that would have kept me home. Taking this job was probably a good idea, she said. We both would prefer being together, but we still had to have an income. I told her I'd bring her to town when I got a few days off in a row. She said she would be looking forward to that. We signed off, and I went back to the boat.

Tommy arrived at the boat just after 1100 hours, and he started the engines to warm them up. We moved ahead into the yard. Tommy started the light plant, lowered the bow ramp, and then shut the generator down.

We were ready for the loading crew. I told Tommy to stick the fuel tanks to see how much fuel we'd burned. He checked and reported each tank was just shy of ¾ full. I figured we would fuel every two trips, if we didn't run any longer than we had on this first trip. Jack called me on the VHF radio and told me the loading crew would be down around 1600 hours to load the boat. The boat would again be high and dry while being loaded. This seemed to work well, so we would probably be timing all loading to take place under those conditions.

Gene, the yard foreman, came aboard and Tommy introduced him to me. Gene stood around 5' 8" tall and was somewhat heavy set. He was quick with a smile, and I found him to be very outgoing and friendly. He shook my hand, and said if I ever needed any assistance just to let him know. He told me he was the yard foreman, and had been working for Jack ever since Jack had gotten the yard. He had been out picking up some things for the yard this morning, and he'd just gotten back. He asked me about Seldovia, having talked with Jack and finding out that was my home. He said he'd visited Seldovia one time a couple years back and really liked the place. I told him I'd moved there in 1964 and had been there ever since. We talked about crab fishing and about many different things. He said he was originally from Indiana, and I told him I was born in Illinois. Gene said he was Jack's first cousin and had been in Alaska for two years. He had moved to Alaska, after Jack had called him and asked him to come to work for him. Gene was very pleasant and easy to talk to, and I liked him right away. He then mentioned he had some work to do and again told me to let him know if I needed anything then he left the boat.

Just before 1600 hours the crew arrived with two flatbed trucks full of wrapped pallets, just as they had for the previous load. They got busy right away and loaded the boat with the pallets. I went down on deck to meet them, and they said this was working out well for them. If we kept up this schedule, we'd have all the freight hauled within a month. I told them the first trip had gone very well, but I was sure every load wouldn't be so easy. They agreed and wished me good luck in the future. They finished covering the pallets with the tarpaulin and then left the yard. Tommy started the generator and closed the bow ramp. We put the turnbuckles on, and the boat was again ready to travel.

At 2240 hours we left Anchorage and headed down the Inlet with the High Tide 1. Tommy was concerned about traveling at night. He asked if we used the spotlight when traveling, to see where we were going. I told him we would not be running with the spotlight on. The radar and compass would keep us on course. We hoped we didn't get into a tide rip that caused any problems. As we approached Fire Island we picked up a 10 – 15 knot wind out of the east. Being in the lee of Fire Island, the seas were only a foot or so, and the wind being offshore kept them from building. I was somewhat concerned about what we would run into when we broke out behind the Island and entered more open water. As I feared, the wind continued to come up and was blowing 20 to 25 knots once we passed Fire Island. We were then taking a two to four-foot chop on the port beam of the boat. It was uncomfortable, but this was not anything the boat could not handle. It would take another hour or so before we would be past the mouth of Turnagin Arm and past Point Possession. I was hopeful the seas would be less due to the wind then coming from offshore. Tommy seemed very nervous about what was taking place and, even though he didn't say it, I could tell he was greatly concerned. I tried to ease his worry by telling him this was normal in Cook Inlet. We had gotten a little spoiled on our first trip. I reiterated there was nothing to worry about.

As we worked our way down Cook Inlet, the wind seemed to stay about the same. The seas did subside somewhat, but it was still sloppy and uncomfortable traveling in the trough. We still had a three=foot to four-foot sea hitting us on the port beam. When we were a couple hours from reaching the Bruce platform, I called them on the radio to get an idea of what the seas were doing at their location. I wanted to find out if it would be too rough to unload. The platform reported six-foot to eight-foot seas, and didn't think we'd want to try offloading until it calmed down. Not wanting to hang off a leg of the platform and ride out the weather, I decided to go to the Arness Terminal just north of the East Foreland, and tie up. They have a couple of liberty ships they use as dry docks, and I needed to check and see if we can stay there until the wind goes down. I told Tommy of my plans, and that we might be at the Arness Terminal for a couple days. We never really knew how long these storms would last. I called the Arness Terminal on the VHF radio and asked permission to lie alongside the dock until the weather broke. They wanted to know what company I was with, their mailing address and phone number. After giving them the information, they told me to feel free to tie up and to let them know when we were planning to leave. I thanked them and told them I'd be in touch.

I again called the Bruce platform and told them of my plans. I asked them to call me on the VHF, when they felt it was calm enough to offload the boat. It was imperative they kept me aware of the sea conditions at the platform, because I would be in calm waters at the Arness Terminal and wouldn't have any way of knowing how rough it was at their location.

After making all the arrangements I tried to contact the High Tide Marine office by radio. Unfortunately, I was too far away, and it was too late at night for anyone to be there. I called the Nikiski Marine operator, who takes calls from mariners and patches the radio call through the telephone lines, and gave them Jack's home telephone number. This was another form of communication that was widely used by mariners. After Jack answered and the Nikiski Marine operator informed him this was a ship to shore call from the High Tide 1. Jack acknowledged and I told him about the weather and our plans to tie up at the Arness Terminal. He asked me to call him every day with a progress report. He told me to be careful and thanked me for calling and keeping him in the loop.

At 0645 hours we were secured at the Arness Terminal, and both Tommy and I decided we needed to get a couple hours sleep. Tommy checked the engine room and shut down the main engines. He reported he'd checked the bilge and the cargo deck, and all looked good. He said he had filled out the engine room log. We decided to eat some breakfast before lying down. Tommy said he would make a couple omelets and fry up some bacon. I was finding out Tommy was a decent cook, as well as becoming a good deckhand.

The wind blew for the next couple days, and we didn't move from our moorage at the Arness Terminal. I checked in daily with the Bruce platform and then reported our status to Jack. Even though we were eager to get the boat unloaded and head back to Anchorage, we were controlled by the weather. Tommy and I played cards, chess and some checkers to keep from dying of boredom. We were getting better acquainted, and Tommy was continually asking questions regarding fishing, boats and navigation. I started teaching him some navigation using a local Cook Inlet chart. He was very interested and caught on quickly. Within a couple hours I had him plotting a course, checking distances, and giving me true versus magnetic headings.

After being tied up for two days and nights at the Arness Terminal, the wind started to subside. I received a call from the Bruce platform around 0850 hours telling me that it looked like we would be able to off load the boat in a few hours, if the wind kept subsiding. Tommy and I got breakfast out of the way, and then Tommy started the main engines to warm them up. At 1015 hours I called the Arness Terminal office and told them we were leaving. They thanked me for the information, and told me to feel free to come back anytime I had to lay in for weather. I thanked them and signed off. I then called the High Tide Marine office via marine operator and told Jack of our plan. He thanked me and said for me to keep in touch and to be careful.

Shortly after noon we reached the Bruce platform. The seas had come down considerably and we only had a wind of 5 to 10 mph. There was a small chop, but I felt I could hold the boat without any problem during the offloading. The tide was coming in. It was around mid-tide now, so it was running at its fastest. This could be an asset, because I could stem the tide without having to maneuver too much. The wind was still on the port beam, but it was not enough to create a major problem. I sent Tommy out on deck again to give me directions of where the man basked was going to be landing. Shortly after we reached the platform and were in position to offload, the crane operator sent a man basket down with two roustabouts. I was able to hold the boat in position with Tommy's help in directing me, and the boat was free of freight in 2½ hours. The tarpaulin was again stowed by the engine room hatch, and the two roustabouts left the boat on the man basket. The tide had slowed considerably and it would be high water in another half hour or so. Due to the tide we would have to tie off to the platform leg and wait to leave for Anchorage. Both Tommy and I wanted to get back to town, but we'd be bucking tide if we left now. Even if we did buck tide and make it back to town, we'd still have to wait for high water before we could get into the High Tide Marine yard. I decided to hang off until just before tide change.

I moved down tide of the platform to show Tommy the cable we were going to tie off to. I showed him the shackle that was hanging on the eye of the cable. I wanted him to put the tie up line eye through the shackle, without removing the pin, and then to hook the eye over our cleat on the boat. I'd then let the boat drift back, and he could feed out line until I signaled for him to secure it. I instructed him to take three or four figure eight wraps around the cleat, as I'd shown him in town, and then to secure it with a half hitch. This way, when we were ready to cut loose, he would only have to loosen the line. Throw the loop end into the water, and then pull the line through the shackle to be free. He wouldn't have to mess with the cable or shackle at all this way. If the weather did come up to the point we had to cut loose, I explained I wouldn't have to maneuver the boat close to the platform leg which is hazardous. Tommy said he understood and left the wheelhouse to get ready to tie up to the leg of the platform. I pulled up close to the leg, and he put the eye of our tie up line through the shackle and then through the eye over the cleat on the starboard bow of the boat. He then fed out line, as I backed away from the leg. When we were far enough back I stopped the reverse motion of the boat and tapped the horn for him to secure the line. He did exactly what we had talked about and everything went smoothly. Tommy was becoming a very good hand aboard the boat.

While we were waiting on the tide I filled out my log book and got it up to date. Tommy checked the engine room and the lazarette to make sure we hadn't developed any leaks. He reported the lazarette compartment was dry and checked the rudder stuffing boxes. Everything appeared to be working fine, and he had made sure the flush access hatch was sealed when he exited the compartment. We both got a book and lay in our bunks reading, while we waited on the tide change.

At 2015 hours I told Tommy to get ready to cut the boat loose. He headed for the engine room to start the engines. We cast off around 2030 hours and were underway to Anchorage. There was only a breeze now, but it was still out of the east. We were just ahead of the tide change when we left the platform, so we should have enough water to get into the yard without having to wait when we arrived in Anchorage. We reached Anchorage at 0105 hours without incident and were able to get into the slip without any problems. After securing the boat and shutting down the engines, Tommy left to go home for the night. He said he'd be back by noon the next day.

As the summer continued we kept making round-trips to the platforms near Granite Point with load after load of freight. We delivered freight to the platform Anna and the platform Granite Point as well as the platform Bruce. On a few occasions we had to go to the Arness Terminal due to bad weather, but when the weather was cooperating we were moving freight.

Tommy and I became great friends. It seemed he couldn't get enough information, always asking questions and putting my sailing knowledge to the test. I taught him how to run a twin screw, or dual propeller boat, and things to watch for that would give him indications when bad weather or high winds may be coming. He was like a sponge and remembered everything I told him. It was easy to see he had a real passion for working on the water. I had no doubt he would be running a boat one day in his future.

It was mid-August and we were only a couple trips from finishing the contract for Hilcorp. We had a load of pallets aboard for the platform Anna. As we were getting close to the platform I received a call from the platform Granite Point. They wanted to know what our schedule was. I told them we were a couple hours out from the platform Anna with a load and planned to return to Anchorage after we were offloaded. They said they had blown an engine and were having one sent down to the Nikiski Terminal, and wondered if we could run over and pick it up for them. I gave them the phone number to the High Tide Marine office and told them to give them a call. Whatever they figured out I'd be happy to do. I also asked that they have High Tide Marine call me via the marine operator after a decision was made. With that said, the Granite Point platform acknowledged and signed off. Tommy and I continued to the platform Anna with our load of freight. The wind was light and variable, so the unloading would take place as soon as we reached the platform.

When we arrived at the platform Anna they were ready to offload us. We pulled up under the crane, and in an hour and forty-five minutes we had all the freight off the boat, and the roustabouts were on their way back aboard the rig. I still hadn't received a call from High Tide Marine or the platform Granite Point, so I called the platform on the radio. They said they had talked with Gene but Jack was not available. They said Gene didn't have a problem with our picking up the engine. I told them I'd be calling the yard, but didn't really see any problem and would be heading to Nikiski Terminal right away. I gave them an estimated time of 1930 hours for arrival at the Nikiski Terminal, and asked if they would be sure and have a crane operator available to load us. They confirmed they would see to it. I told them if any plans changed I would get back to them on the radio. We signed off and continued toward Nikiski.

I called High Tide Marine via the marine operator and talked with Gene. He told me to go ahead to Nikiski and pick up the engine and deliver it. He said we had a couple more trips, and we'd be finished with the contract. He didn't feel we would be crowding any schedules if we delivered the engine before coming back to Anchorage. I told him we would be delayed through a tide and a half because of the detour, but he didn't see a problem with that.

We pulled into the Nikiski Terminal at 1945 hours, and a crew was waiting on the dock to load the engine aboard the boat. The engine was already on a pallet and was wrapped in plastic. After they set it aboard, Tommy unhooked the pallet slings, and we left and headed back for the platform Granite Point.

We arrived at the platform Granite Point just before 0100 hours. I told Tommy to start the generator, so we could light up the cargo hold for offloading the engine. I called the platform on the radio and told them we were a few minutes out, and they said they would be ready. I told them to send the pallet slings down and we would hook them up. I didn't see any reason to have a roustabout ride the man basket down just for one lift. Tommy started the generator, and I threw the deck lights on illuminating the deck. I pulled up under the crane, and they lowered the pallet slings. Tommy hooked them up, and they lifted the engine from the boat.

The tide was flooding, and it was better than half tide, so I decided we'd hang off the platform leg through the rest of the flood and most of the ebb, leaving around an hour before low water. If we were to leave directly after offloading the engine, we'd have to wait on the Anchorage end to get into the High Tide Marine yard anyway. We would also be bucking tide more than half way, and that meant we'd be burning a lot more fuel. We would hang off the platform leg and get some rest. I told Tommy what I'd decided, and he went out to the bow to tie the boat up. At slack water we had to move off the north leg of the platform and tie to one of the south legs, so the ebb tide wouldn't push us under the platform. We had only a breeze blowing, and changing legs went without any problems.

We returned to Anchorage as scheduled. The last two loads of freight were delivered without any problems. After being offloaded on our last trip, the tide was wrong. We would have to hang off for about eight hours before heading back in. Because this was the last trip, the waiting to head back to Anchorage was considerably more difficult. We had been making plans to go out to dinner with our families, after we were done for the season. I was planning to bring my wife and daughter to town, so we could do some shopping before heading back home, so this would work perfectly. I was getting anxious, so I called my wife via the marine radio and told her of the plans. She was a little timid being on a radio telephone, but said she'd make plane reservations as soon as I could give her a solid date. I told her I'd call her from Anchorage after we got back in. We said our goodbyes, and I signed off with the marine operator.

We impatiently waited the eight hours before cutting loose and heading for Anchorage. I told Tommy that those eight hours were the longest we had spent this summer, and he readily agreed with me. We arrived in Anchorage shortly after noon and checked with Gene in the foreman's office. He said the oil company was very happy with the job we had done, and it would probably open some doors for them in the future. I asked Gene what I needed to do, in reference to the boat, prior to heading back to Seldovia. He said he'd get with Jack, but thought everything would be taken care of by the yard hands from this point. I went back aboard the boat and started packing my gear.

Tommy came to the boat and said Gene and Jack were in Gene's office and wanted to see me. I walked back to the office with Tommy. Jack shook my hand when I went inside, and told me we'd done a great job. He couldn't thank us enough. I told him all had gone pretty well, but I couldn't have done it without a top hand like Tommy on board. Jack inquired as to my plans, and I told him I had a winter king crab fishing job starting in late September. I told him I was flying my wife and four-year-old daughter to town for some shopping before we headed back home, and that it'd be nice if we could all get together for a dinner while we were in town. Jack said we'd do that. He said he'd bring his girlfriend and we could bring our families. Jack told me I could stay aboard the boat until my family came to town, if I wanted to. I thanked him, and said I'd take him up on that. He told me my check would be ready in a couple hours. I shook hands all around and then went to call my wife and have her make reservations for her and my daughter to come to town. She was excited and looked forward to hitting the stores she said. I told her I thought she would be more eager to see me than to go shopping. She said yeah, that too. I told her I'd call her later in the evening to check on her arrival time. I kidded her by telling her I may or may not pick her up at the airport. She said she knew I'd pick her up, because she'd have my daughter with her. We had a chuckle, and I told her I'd call her later.

Ann and Donica arrived in Anchorage at 1330 hours on Saturday afternoon, and I met them at the gate. We picked up their luggage and headed downtown to the Sheraton Inn. I called Jack to tell him they had arrived and where we'd be staying. He told me he had made reservations at Stuckagain Heights for 1900 hours, and he gave me directions on how to get to the restaurant. He said it was a good drive up the hillside, so I might want to start out a little early. I told him we'd see him around 1900 hours.

After we checked into the room, we went to the Sears Mall where my wife and daughter did the girl thing. My daughter, who was only four years old, already liked shopping. I was thinking I'd need two jobs, just to keep up with her, once she became a teenager. While she and her mother enjoyed the mall, I sat out in the hallway people watching, one of my favorite pastimes.

We arrived at the Stuckagain Heights Restaurant just before 1900 hours. It was located high up on the side of a mountain. The view of Anchorage and Cook Inlet was breathtaking. Jack had pulled out all the stops and had gotten a banquet table next to huge windows with an unobstructed view. Tommy and his family were already there, as was Jack and his girlfriend, when we arrived. Tommy introduced us to his wife,

Tammy, his daughter, Carla, and son, Kenny. Jack introduced Marie, his girlfriend, and I introduced my wife, Ann and daughter, Donica. We had hardly gotten through the introductions, when Gene arrived with his wife, Joanne. With everyone present and the introductions out of the way, we found our seats and started, what was to be, a most memorable evening.

Drinks were ordered, and Jack ordered appetizers. As we enjoyed our beverage, Jack told us he and Marie had been together for five years. Both had been married previously, and Jack had two daughters from his first marriage. He said they lived in Indiana, where he was born and raised. He told Tommy and me that he couldn't have had a better crew on the High Tide 1. He really appreciated the job we'd done for the company. He then passed down two envelopes, one for Tommy, and one for me. He told us to wait to open the envelopes until later, but did leave the impression we would be happy with the contents. He also said the oil company had been very satisfied with our work and hinted to him about future contracts.

Gene told us he and Joanne had been married three years. He was a first cousin to Jack. He laughed and said his being related had nothing to do with his being hired by High Tide Marine. He swore it was just an insurance policy, because he just knew the company would have gone under without him. The evening was one to remember. We all got better acquainted, and I invited everyone to visit Seldovia sometime. They all agreed that they would do that one day.

Most everyone had steak, and we were all so full we could hardly walk when we left the restaurant. In the parking lot we said our goodbyes, and Jack said he would be calling me when he needed a good skipper. I told him I'd be glad to work for him again, if I was not employed.

After we reached the hotel room, I opened the envelope Jack had given me. It contained a short letter thanking me for a good job and a check for $1500.00. Needless to say, I was very happy to see the bonus, and I thought back to something my father had told me as a youngster. He'd said if you have a job and you give a man eight hours work for eight hours pay, you will profit the company you're working for, and you will benefit yourself in ways you can't even imagine. I felt good about the job we'd done, and it even felt better to know the company also felt the way they did about my work. I told my wife that I would definitely consider working for them again, if they called.

We stayed in Anchorage for two more days, did our shopping, and took in a couple kiddy shows. We headed down the road early on Thursday morning, so we could catch the ferry to Seldovia from Homer on Thursday evening. It would be good to get home.

High Tide Marine sold out that winter to Active Diver's Inc., a firm who owned two barges, one tug and a diving boat. I would become very much involved with them. They also contracted with the oil companies in Cook Inlet on a much larger scale. But as they say, that is another story.

ACTIVE DIVER'S INC.

It was the first Sunday in March 1974 when my phone rang, and I answered it from my home in Seldovia, Alaska. On the other end was Gene, an old foreman of mine from High Tide Marine in Anchorage. I had operated a boat, an LCM, hauling freight to the oil platforms in Cook Inlet a couple years back, and that's when I met Gene. He asked how I was doing, and if I was working. I told him I had been running equipment for a logging company out of Seldovia, ever since the job ended with High Tide Marine. I asked what he had going on. He told me High Tide Marine had sold out to a firm called Active Diver's Inc., who also worked closely with the oil companies. They were a much larger company than High Tide Marine and had considerably more equipment. They had commercial salvage operations, and they bid diving contracts for the oil companies or with anyone needing commercial divers. Gene said he had been hired when Active Divers had taken over the yard and was still pretty much doing the same job. Active Divers owned a small tug boat, a diving boat, two barges, plus three cable cranes and yard equipment, such as loaders and forklifts. He was calling because they were looking for a crew for the season and needed a skipper for the boat, as well as laborers to work in the yard. At present they were only looking at operating seasonally, up until the ice hit Cook Inlet. Gene told me they had a much larger yard now. They had driven sheet piling all around the old High Tide Marine yard making an "L" shaped docking facility. Both of Active Diver's Inc. barges were tied to the dock right now, one on the face of the dock and the other in, what they referred to as, the slip, he said. The two boats were on dry dock in the new yard that had been built when they backfilled behind the sheet piling. Gene said both boats had been lifted out of the water with a 4500 Manitowoc cable crane that was kept aboard the larger barge. He said I wouldn't recognize the yard, since all the changes had been made.

He told me they had some contracts with the oil companies that would keep the diving boat busy most of the summer. If I went to work for them, and wanted to stay on for a while during the early winter, they would have some boat and barge maintenance and some yard work that would last into the late fall. He told me two men named Ted and Roger owned Active Diver's Inc. Roger had a background in commercial diving operations, while Ted had owned and operated a company that worked closely with the oil companies. Ted had kept busy as a liaison to the oil companies in Cook Inlet, by setting up contractors to do whatever work needed to be done by the oil companies. Both Ted and Roger were businessmen, who had been affiliated with the oil companies for a number of years and were very well known in, and around, the oil patch. Ted, being well acquainted with the needs of the oil companies, built a diving boat that he named the Active Diver. The boat had been used in Cook Inlet for a couple years before they had purchased High Tide Marine. When they told Gene they would need a skipper for the boat, he said he told them about me and the job I had done for High Tide Marine. They asked him to see if I'd be interested in working for them. Gene said they paid well, and I would probably be working in two different pay scales. When I was out of town on a boat I would be getting a day wage and when I was working in town, in the yard, I'd be paid by the hour. I asked when they would need me to be there, if I decided to take the job. He said they would be starting up operations around the last week of April, but they needed to line up a crew now. I told him I'd been working for the logging outfit ever since I'd left High Tide Marine a year and a half ago. I would want to give them at least two weeks' notice if I decided to take the job. He said he didn't see a problem with that. I told him my wife, Ann, and I would have to sit down and discuss the offer. She was used to having me at home every night, and I didn't know how she would feel about me being gone again. Gene said he figured I couldn't give him an answer today, but did say this could really work into a good position possibly lasting for a number of years. I told him I'd be getting back to him with an answer soon. If I did take the job, I'd have to take a little time to get things taken care of here at home, before I could come up. He said that was not a problem, since it was still early, but he really did need an answer by the end of the week. I told him I'd get back to him after Ann and I had time to look at all my options. Gene said he understood and would be looking forward to hearing from me. He said he really hoped I would come to work for them.

Ann and I sat down and talked about the offer from Active Divers. She said even though logging didn't pay all that well, I was home every night. The logging company, Southcentral Timber Inc., usually shut down for a couple months during the worst part of the winter. While they were shut down this past winter, Joe Kurtz, the owner/operator of the king crab boat, Amatuli, had called and asked if I'd fly out to Dutch Harbor and rotate the crew for six weeks. He said he wanted to give each of them a break, and since I was not working right now, and was able to do all the different jobs aboard, it would work out great if I could do it. I had flown out to Dutch Harbor, and Ann mentioned that when I was gone for those six weeks, she and my daughter, Donica, really missed me. She was hoping I could stay home. I told her we had a few days to think about it, but it could be quite an opportunity for us to get ahead financially. She said she didn't want to spend another summer by herself, without my being home, but as she always did, she said we'd do whatever I decided. I told her this was going to be something we both agreed on, or it wasn't going to happen at all.

I went back to work in the woods on Monday morning, and all day long, while I operated a Caterpillar building spur roads, I was thinking about the offer from Active Divers. I loved the work in the woods, and I loved running heavy equipment. However, it didn't pay all that well, and I really wanted to start making a decent wage. We were living paycheck to paycheck and weren't able to put anything away for a rainy day.

When I got home, Ann and I again talked about our future. I told her we would not be able to ever get ahead with me working for Southcentral Timber. If I didn't work in the woods, I would have to go back on the crab boats and would still spend a lot of time away from home. Even though I didn't think she'd ever be in favor of it, I asked her if she would consider moving the family to Anchorage. It was 1974, and Donica was going to be 6 years old in December. We were not any better off financially than we were when she was born. Much to my surprise, Ann didn't immediately say no, and I could see I'd started the wheels turning. She was thinking about what moving would entail. I told her to think about it for a couple days, because we didn't have to give Gene an answer until the end of the week. It was a big decision. I did tell her that even if we did move to Anchorage, I would be gone quite a bit, because I would be on jobs in Cook Inlet. She said at least we'd be making a decent wage, and when I was in town, we would be together. Maybe I wouldn't be gone as long as I was when out on the crab boat fishing trips,

Ann had been born and raised in Seldovia, and Seldovia had always been Donica's home, as well. Moving to the big city from a small community was quite a leap of faith, and I would be asking a lot of both of them. It wasn't something where a decision should be made without some serious consideration. The more I thought about the job, moving to Anchorage, and the chance to make a better living for my family, the more I favored the idea. I was going to stick to my original statement though, and the decision would be a family decision, not just a decision I would make. I knew if I told Ann we were moving to Anchorage, she would not argue and would go along with whatever I wanted, regardless of how she really felt. But we were a team, and this was going to be something that would greatly impact our family. It had to be something we both agreed on.

When I got home from work on Wednesday evening, Ann asked me what I truly felt about moving to Anchorage. I told her I felt it might be a good opportunity, but I really didn't like the thought of living in a large city. She said maybe we could try it for a while and see how it went. She said if it wasn't working out, we could always move back home. She said I could probably get my logging job back, or I may have to go fishing again.

She told me she had been putting a lot of thought into it, and she really felt the move might be the best thing for our family. At that moment I again realized why I had married this lady. She always put a lot of thought into everything important and weighed the pros and cons before reaching a decision. Ann always put the family first. She said we could try it for a season. I told her I'd call Gene, and she should start packing boxes. I also mentioned that I'd ask if he knew of any rentals that might be available for us. I think we both felt like a heavy weight had been lifted off us, after finally having reached a difficult, but definite decision.

Gene had given me his home phone number and after dinner I called him and told him of our decision. I also insisted I be able to give the logging company two weeks' notice, and then I asked about housing in Anchorage. Gene said no problem with the time frame of two weeks, and asked what I was looking for, and what I would want to pay a month. We discussed the prices for Anchorage rentals, and I decided we should probably think about a mobile home to start with. Gene said he'd check around and get back to me with some prices and locations. He told me he was glad to hear I was taking the job, and that he looked forward to working with me again. I told him I was also excited and was hoping to hear from him soon regarding a place to live.

I went to work the next morning and told my side rod that I would be leaving in two weeks. I told him about the job offer, and that I'd be moving my family to Anchorage. He thanked me for giving him two weeks' notice, and said if he had an opening when, and if, I ever needed to go to work, that a job would be waiting. I thanked him and jumped on my Caterpillar and started pioneering another spur road.

A week had gone by, when I received a call from Gene. He had checked into some rentals in a couple different trailer parks and had phone numbers for four different landlords. I thanked him, and told him we hoped to be moved to Anchorage within three weeks. He said that would work out about right for the start of the season in Cook Inlet.

We spent the next couple weeks packing and making arrangements for our move. I was able to locate a trailer we could pull behind my pickup, which would enable us to move all our belongings in one trip. On April 21st we boarded the State ferry, *Tustumena,* and left Seldovia with all our belongings and a lot of anticipation for what lay ahead. I had talked to two different landlords, who owned mobile homes in Anchorage. We would be checking both of them out to see which would suit us the best. We were excited but still somewhat apprehensive. We were more or less taking a leap of faith, and it was somewhat concerning.

We reached Anchorage without incident and got a hotel room for a couple days, until we could check out the rentals Gene had told us about. Within the next two days, we looked at four different mobile homes in four different parts of town. We settled on a two bedroom mobile home in Mountain View, two blocks from where my daughter would be going to school. We took a couple days getting moved in and organized. Then I called Gene and told him we were settled, and I was ready to go to work. He told me to come in the next morning at 0800 hours.

I arrived at Active Diver's yard at 0745 hours and found Gene was already there. He welcomed me into his office and handed me an application form, he said I needed to fill out. It was a couple pages long, and he told me to go into the break room, just adjacent to his office, where I would find a table to use.

When I'd driven into the yard at Active Diver's, I wasn't sure I was in the right place at first. The sheet piling they had driven made a much larger yard out of what used to be a small area, when High Tide Marine owned it. I realized I was in the right place when I saw the tugboat, Fair wind, and the dive boat, the Active Diver, both in cradles in the yard. A large barge was tied inside on the north side of the dock with a smaller barge moored on the face of the dock. An American 60 ton cable crane was mounted on a pedestal on the deck of the smaller barge. A large Manitowoc crane on tracks was sitting on the deck of the bigger barge, and the boom appeared to be 120 – 130 feet long. It had to be a 150 ton rig, if not more. A blue Manitowoc crane, on tracks, was sitting in the yard next to the tugboat, Fair wind. It had approximately 60 foot of boom and appeared to be a 45 ton rig. A D-7 Caterpillar tractor and a 955 Caterpillar loader were parked behind the office building. Two forklifts were parked in front of the building. After seeing the boats, barges and equipment, I felt good about making the decision to move to Anchorage. This company appeared to be a going concern.

As I filled out the application, four men arrived at Gene's office. They were the yard crew of Active Divers and had already been working. Gene introduced them as the yard hands. There was Bill, David, Laurence and James. He told them I had moved to Anchorage from Seldovia and would be the equipment operator and boat handler. Gene told all of us that it appeared we had a lot of work coming up, and we would be very busy. I shook hands with the crew, and told them I looked forward to working with them. All four seemed pleasant and were curious about Seldovia and my past work experience. We didn't have time to visit, as Gene told me to go ahead and fill out the paperwork, while he gave the other foursome directives regarding the work they were to do.

After a time, I finished filling out the employment application and took it into Gene's office. He called upstairs on the phone and asked for Ted. I heard him say I'd finished the application, if he wanted to see me now. Ted, one of the owners, came to Gene's office from the main office upstairs. Gene introduced us, and Ted shook my hand and told me he'd heard a lot about me and was glad to meet me. He said he wanted to give me a personal tour of the Active Diver. He shared that he had built the boat, and it was his pride and joy. He said he had worked around dive boats quite a lot down in the Gulf of Mexico with the oil companies. So, when he came to Alaska, he wanted to build a boat that would handle the Cook Inlet waters and would be specifically built for hard hat and Kirby gear type diving. He and Roger, his co-owner, were talking about starting a diving company, and High Tide Marine had a yard leased that would be perfect for what they had planned. Jack, High Tide Marine's owner, was ready to slow down, and they were able to cut a deal for the waterfront property. He and Roger had been in business for a couple years and had acquired a lot of equipment. Ted said the diving boat, Active Diver, was his idea. Upon hearing this, I was experiencing a little pressure first hand.

Ted and I walked out into the yard and boarded the Active Diver. He took me all through the vessel and showed me everything about it. The Active Diver was built specifically for diving operations in and around Cook Inlet. Ted said he and Roger combined their past knowledge of boats and diving operations and came up with the boat design. It measured 62 feet long with a 14 foot beam. The boat was a twin screw vessel powered with Volvo Penta, 6 cylinder diesel engines. Two water proof flush hatches, located on the aft deck, could be opened to gain access to the engines. The hatches were hinged on the outer side so lifting the inner part of the hatch could open them. They were also reinforced so they could be utilized as additional deck space, when they were in a closed position. A bulkhead separated the engine room compartment from the amidships compartment. The amidships compartment was accessed through a hatch located just aft of the wheelhouse. For additional headroom in the amidships compartment, the deck had been raised 2½ feet, but because it was flat, it could also be used for additional deck space. A diver's decompression chamber was mounted in the amidships compartment below deck. Inside the wheelhouse there was a small stove, a table for two, a bunk on the port side and the steering station with the electronics mounted above the front windows. The electronics included two VHF radios, 24 mile radar, a CB radio, a depth finder, a loran C and a compass. Another bunk was located in the forepeak of the vessel, just ahead and below the steering station. A second steering station, a compass, a VHF radio and a depth finder were located on the open flying bridge on top of the wheelhouse, along with a 12 volt spot light. Four flood lights were mounted to the front and back of the wheelhouse, so the stern deck and the area ahead of the boat could be lit up at night. Also on top of the wheelhouse, a 12 man canister life raft was mounted. The antennas for the radios and the radar were mounted on a mast that was fastened to the rear of the cabin and extended above the wheelhouse approximately 15 feet. A crossbar on the mast housed the radio antennas, while a platform off the front of the mast held the radar antenna. The running lights were also mounted on the right, left and rear of the cabin. A single white mast light was mounted on top of the mast.

It was easy to see that Ted was very proud of the boat. The fact that he had built the boat and was entrusting it to me made me feel proud, but at the same time, somewhat apprehensive. I had never before operated a diving boat, but I couldn't see where it would be that much different from running any other twin screw vessel. I told Ted I had a lot to learn about the diving world, but felt confident that I could handle the boat without endangering anyone. He told me the divers and the dive tenders were all good men to work with and were all professionals. He said none of them would have a problem answering any questions I might have about the diving operations. My job was to keep the boat close enough to provide life support for the diver, without endangering him. Ted showed me the propellers, which had guards to reduce any chance a hose, line or cable could get entangled in them. He said I should never have the boat in a position where there was a chance of entangling the air hose, any lines, or a cable. But, he said the tide did create unexpected hazards at times, and they wanted to address all concerns. He assured me the guards around the props did not take away from the maneuverability of the vessel.

When Ted had finished showing me the boat, he told me I had come highly recommended. He had no doubt I would do a good job. He said they planned to launch the boat within the next day or so, because we had a contract to walk an oil pipeline in Cook Inlet. He said the tide runs so hard in the Inlet, that it changes the configuration of the bottom in areas where the silt is heavy. The tidal action will undermine an oil pipeline at times, leaving a huge void under it. If that happens, there is a chance the pipeline could sag so much that it could split a weld, or even break a pipe. He said the oil pipeline we were going to check hadn't been walked for a few years, and the oil company wanted to make sure there was no imminent danger of it getting damaged.

Ted explained that anytime a dive was made, two divers were dressed down in diving gear. One would be diving, while the other was on standby, in the event the man in the water needed assistance. Two tenders for each diver would also be aboard. The head tender would be directing the dive and communicating with the diver via radio/intercom, while the other tender would be tending the air hose and line, feeding it out, and taking it in as the diver moved along the bottom. The diver's life support was all aboard the boat. There would be two dive compressors aboard and hose enough to support both divers in the water, even on deep dives. Each diver wore a bottle of compressed air, they referred to as a bailout bottle, which when utilized, would give him five minutes to reach the surface, in the event their air was cut off from the boat for any reason. Ted said at times, even though very rare, both divers may be in the water, and all four tenders would be busy with the dive. The dive suits were called dry suits, and they used hard hat and Kirby diving gear. The suits were completely waterproof, and the diver wore long johns, sweaters and other clothes inside the suits to stay warm in the cold water. The diver's helmet was a round brass helmet with port holes, for viewing purposes, and vent valves with connections for the air hose and communication equipment. The hard hat locked onto the dive suit with a threaded surface that insured no water could enter the suit. The Kirby mask had soft headgear, which also had a threaded connection, to insure no leakage. Unlike the hard hat, it was affixed with a rubber cap and a built in face shield for viewing, much like a scuba diver would use. Ted told me I'd be learning a lot about diving and the gear they used, including the decompression of the divers. When the diver stayed down for any length of time, nitrogen bubbles would build up in the joints and organs, when surfacing, the bubbles can get lodged in the joints and organs of the diver causing immense pain and can be life threatening. The diver would then need to decompress, letting the nitrogen bubbles leave the body. He said all of this is good knowledge, and in a couple dives I should be well versed on how a dive was done correctly. However, he shared that all of this was just information, and my job was to operate the boat and keep everyone safe. I told him I understood and was really looking forward to our first trip. He said as soon as they figured everything out regarding the scheduling, he'd get with me and bring me up to speed.

Ted went back upstairs, and I went to see Gene about what he wanted me to do. He told me I could change the oil in the main engines on the Active Diver. He took me into the shop and showed me where the oil filters and lube oil for the boat was kept. He told me he wanted me to get acquainted with the boat. They planned to launch it within a day or two, and he wanted me to know the boat inside out, when I left the dock on our first trip.

Cook Inlet stretches approximately 180 miles from the Gulf of Alaska to Anchorage in south-central Alaska. The Inlet then branches into the Knik Arm, to the northwest, and Turnagain Arm, to the east. Cook Inlet and its tributaries are very dangerous bodies of water with extreme tides that reach upwards from -4.0 to 35 feet in approximately six hours. Due to the narrowing of Cook Inlet, off the Gulf of Alaska, the amount of water filling the Inlet creates a tide that runs like a river. On the extreme tides, speeds can reach upwards of 12-15 mph. When the tide flows into Turnagain Arm, just south of Anchorage, a wall of water 2–6 foot high is often created on the extreme high tides. This wall of water is known as a bore tide and occurs due to the large amount of water flowing into the Turnagain Arm from Cook Inlet. The shallowing up and the narrowing of Turnagain Arm from Cook Inlet creates this phenomenon. The boar tide only occurs on extreme tides, when the tide is coming in, or flooding, into Turnagain Arm. No bore tide is created when the tide is going out, or ebbing, because the fast water is flowing into the wider and deeper Cook Inlet. Whether flooding or ebbing, the tide runs the fastest at mid-tide, or half way into the flood or the ebb. Turnagain Arm is said to have the third fastest tide in the world, which only enhances the dangers when diving.

As Gene suggested, I changed the oil and the filters on the boat and then checked everything else. In the engine room I located the battery bank and the two 2" electric bilge pumps with auto-switches. There was a fresh water system on board, and I found its pump and the pressure tank mounted on the starboard bulkhead. I checked the oil in the reductions, and I greased the stern bearings and checked the stuffing boxes. I also checked the rudder stocks and the two flanges. All seemed to be fine but would need to be checked after the boat was floating. I then went to the wheelhouse, where I ran all the electronics on board and made sure the boat was in good shape and ready for sailing. I found the nautical charts and the charting tools I'd need for Cook Inlet. I checked below deck in the forepeak, and I found four survival suits and eight life jackets that were stored under the bunk. I decided I would take the bunk in the forepeak and let the deckhand have the bunk in the wheelhouse. In my tour of the boat I found four fire extinguishers that were up to date, so they didn't need to be replaced or refilled. The 12 man canister raft was also up to date and didn't need inspected, so I was pleased to find everything ready for sailing. I did see some areas on the hull, above the waterline, that could use some fresh paint.

I went to Gene's office and told him I'd found everything to be in really good shape on the boat, and that it was ready for launching. I did tell him about the areas that needed some paint, and he told me we had another day or so before they would be putting the boat in the water. If I wanted to, I could prep the areas and get them ready for painting and he'd get me some paint and whatever I needed to do the job. I told him I'd need a grinder and some primer along with the paint. He said he had an expediter who would pick up whatever I needed. He told me where the grinder and extension cords were, and I went to work. I was impressed with Gene's response to my suggestion about the needed paint, but I did take note that I'd have to be careful what I asked for. I could very easily make too many suggestions.

My first day on the job went well, and I was feeling good about our move. I just hoped it would work out for my family. I headed home to see how their day had gone. Ann said she'd spent the day unpacking and getting the trailer set up. She had dinner nearly ready, and I spent some time with my daughter, while she was finishing up. I really enjoyed the times we spent together, and Donica seemed to enjoy them, as well. I told the girls we were going to launch the boat in the next couple days, and then I would be going out on a dive and would be gone for a few days. Ann asked me how long I'd be gone. I told her I had no idea at this point, but would have a better idea before we left. I did share that I'd never done this type of work before, and really didn't know what I was getting into. I didn't know anything about diving, but I did feel comfortable with my boat handling abilities. Ann said she had no doubt I'd do fine. I told her I wished I had her confidence. She finished putting dinner on the table, and we enjoyed it together.

The next morning when I arrived at work, Gene handed me some paint brushes, a roller and a couple cans of paint. I had prepped the boat the day before, so I got busy painting the areas I had ready with the primer. It was fast drying, and I could start putting on the finish coat immediately after finishing with the primer. By the time I finished with the painting it was lunch time. After lunch Gene said they were bringing a fuel truck in to fuel the Active Diver. He said it was a lot easier to fuel it in the yard, than it was when it was tied alongside the barge. I ask him about the added weight being a problem, and he said the 4500 Manitowoc crane on the barge had no problem picking the Active Diver fueled or empty.

The fuel truck showed up at 1510 hours, and I topped off the two fuel tanks aboard the boat. Gene said the pile bucks would be there first thing in the morning to ready the boat with the diving equipment. He said it would take most of the day to get the boat set up, and he wanted me to work with the dive tenders in an effort to learn all I could about the diving operations. He also told me he wanted me to run the forklift for loading the equipment on board the boat, since the tenders were not equipment operators.

The next morning four dive tenders arrived at the yard to rig out the Active Diver. Gene introduced me to them, and told them I'd be working with them in getting the boat ready. We started by loading the equipment aboard the vessel, which included two dive compressors and two pallets loaded with the diver's hoses, which also housed communication wire and cable. The air hose, communication wires and a 3/8 inch cable were all married together with electrical tape wrapped around them every two feet. The cable was needed to carry the load that would be applied when the tender was hauling in the diver, or when the tide was running hard. The communication wire had fittings attached to the ends for hooking up the hard hat and Kirby gear to the dive radio. The air hose was for the diver's air supply. The dive hose was made up in 50 feet sections and could be attached to one another to add or reduce their length, depending on the depth of the dive. There was 300 feet of hose on each of the two pallets that were brought aboard, totaling 600 feet of dive hose. The air hose had to be hooked up to the compressors on board the boat, and the communications cable had to be plugged into the radio box, which was kept on the flying bridge. The decompression chamber also had to be hooked up to an air compressor. The dive suits, helmets, hard hat and Kirby gear had to be brought aboard and protected at all times to insure no damages could occur to the water tight seals. Both dry suits and helmets had guards placed over the threaded areas so nothing could damage them. Numerous fittings and tools were brought aboard, so repairs could be made when we were on location.

Everything was loaded and hooked up before quitting time and Gene told me I should plan on taking off on the boat on Friday morning. He said we'd pick up some groceries and supplies the next morning, and I should pack what personal items I would need for at least a week out on the water. He said Ted wanted the boat launched tomorrow afternoon and was anxious to get us out on the job checking the pipeline. The divers and the tenders would be flying out by helicopter to the oil rig, and we'd be picking them up off the rig when it was getting close to dive time. Throughout the job the divers and their tenders would be staying aboard the oil rig and then come aboard the boat when it was nearing time for the next dive. My deckhand and I would tie the boat off the oil platform leg between tides. Gene said all the oil platforms had cables hanging off the rig's legs for boats to tie off to, so we wouldn't have to anchor. I thanked Gene for the update and then headed home to inform the family what was going on.

When I got home I found Ann had made friends with the Smiths, who lived next door to us in the trailer park. Ann had told Mrs. Smith, Jud, we'd drop by after dinner, so we could meet her husband, and they could meet me. Ann told me they had a daughter and three sons, and Donica would be going to the same school as their younger kids. This was a real blessing, because Ann would have someone close by, who she could reach out to, when I was out of town. We had dinner, and around 1930 hours all three of us walked next door, and I was introduced to Al and Judy, or Judd as she was known to her friends, and their children, Gary, Anita, Rod and Aaron. Anita was around four years older than Donica, but they hit it off immediately. Al was in sales, and Judd was a stay at home mom, as was Ann. On weekends when I was in town, we started hanging out together, having picnics, camp outs, and attending church. As time went by, our friendship grew into something very special for all of us.

After I arrived at the yard on Thursday morning, Gene and I went to the grocery store and bought groceries to last us a couple weeks on the boat. We were limited on freezer and refrigerator space, so a lot of what we bought was canned foods. It was evident they wanted us to eat well, and Gene told me to pick out any kind of groceries I wanted. We bought everything we'd need and then some.

When we returned to the yard we found the dive tenders already aboard the Active Diver testing all the dive equipment. They were meticulous in their work, and it was easy to see they were professionals who knew what they were doing. It was imperative that the equipment is in excellent condition, and that everything be double checked before a diver went into the water. The divers and the dive tenders were all members of the pile drivers' union and were paid very well. Diving is a hazardous business with many challenges, and Cook Inlet, with its fast tides and muddy/silty water, only enhanced the existing dangers.

Gene told me James, one of the yard hands I'd met on the first day, would be my deckhand on the Active Diver. Gene said he had been on a boat one summer in Southeastern where he'd fished salmon, but he was not an experienced deckhand. He did say he was a good worker who took directions well, and Gene felt he'd be a good man on the boat.

At 1500 hours the 4500 Manitowoc crane was swung into position to pick the Active Diver and set it in the water alongside the SS-12 barge. The crane was rigged with spreader bars and large nylon straps. The straps would be placed under the boat's keel in the bow and stern for lifting it. The tide was coming in, and there would be enough water to float the Active Diver by 1530 hours. The dive tenders finished their work and exited the boat. All was ready, and the yard crew rigged the boat for the pick by getting the nylon straps into position. Two long tag lines were tied to the bow cleat and the stern cleat aboard the boat. This allowed the men on the ground to turn the boat into position when lowering it into the water alongside the barge. Gene had given orders to get the boat ready to pick, but not to pick it until he told us to. He said he wanted Ted present for the pick. At 1540 hours Ted arrived at the yard, and the pick was made. The crane operator had no problem picking the boat, and it was lowered into the water alongside the SS-12 barge without any problems. The tag lines were used to secure the boat to the barge, once it was set in the water and was floating. One side of the nylon straps was released, and the crane operator lifted the rigging high over the boat, and then swung it aboard the barge.

I went aboard the Active Diver to make sure no stuffing boxes were leaking or any problems existed. I exchanged the tag lines with tie up lines to insure the boat was secure. Finding no problems below deck I went to the wheelhouse. Ted came aboard and told me he wanted to go over the chart with me, to show me where we would be going, and what he wanted us to do. I pulled out the Cook Inlet chart and he pointed out the oil platform, Anna. This was the platform that would house the divers and their tenders. The pipeline we were going to check was just east of the platform, and it ran to the south across Cook Inlet, ending at the East Foreland facility. He said the first dive would probably be the most difficult of the dives, because we had to locate the pipeline. We would be marking the pipeline with a buoy where we ended each dive, which would mark our starting point on the next dive. We would leapfrog the buoy as we walked the line, marking where we ended each dive. If we did find a problem, we'd be marking that location with buoys as well. Ted told me the boat crew didn't have to worry about this, because the dive tenders would be taking care of those details. He reiterated that my job was to stay close enough to the diver to provide life support and to keep everyone safe. He did say that I was in charge of the boat, and if I felt the need, I could call the dive off for any safety concerns. He also was adamant that, regardless of who might argue with me, I had the final say, and I should demand the diver be brought up, if I felt he was in danger. The dive tenders didn't know the first thing about running a boat, he said. He also shared that at times the tide could be running in two different directions, one direction on the surface and the opposite direction on the bottom. When this occurred the air hose could get a belly in it and could create a hazard by getting near the propellers. Ted said he'd been on a number of these dives and things could go bad quickly. I needed to keep my mind on operating the boat and let the tenders take care of the diver in the water. He warned me that to lose track of the diver's bubbles was a recipe for disaster. I needed to know where the diver was at all times, and if I did lose track of the bubbles, I was to let the head tender know immediately, so he could point them out to me.

The tides in Cook Inlet were hazardous, and we could only dive on slack water, when the water is running slowly, or not moving at all. Each tide was different, but on the large tides we would not have that much time on the bottom, before the tide would change and pick up speed again. Ted said for this reason, we should be on location a little early on each tide and stay down as long as it was safe. He told me to keep in contact with the dive tenders, when they were aboard the oil rig, via VHF radio, and make sure we didn't miss any dives due to them not being ready. He also said the weather could be a factor, and I would have the responsibility of calling off a dive, if I thought it was too rough, or there was a hazard of any kind. I told Ted I'd never run a boat with a diver down, but I had run twin screw boats enough to know what to expect every time I maneuvered the vessel. I assured him the diver's wellbeing was my greatest concern. He told me he felt comfortable sending me out to run the boat, but if I had any questions I should not hesitate to ask the tenders or a diver. I told him when I got on location I may have a number of questions, but at this point I couldn't think of anything to ask. Ted wished me the best of luck and told me that I should plan on departing Anchorage around 0430 hours the next morning. We had a 30.9 foot tide at 0629 hours, and by leaving a couple hours before high water, we could possibly arrive at the oil platform in time to pick up the crew and get a dive in at the low water slack, which was at 1312 hours. Low water was a -0.7 foot tide. If we did arrive late on that tide, at least we'd be ready for the next high water slack, he said. He shook my hand, wished me well, told me good luck, and then left the boat.

I went to Gene's office and told him I thought everything was ready to go on the boat. The dive tenders had left the yard shortly after the boat was launched and told me they had everything ready. Gene told me to go ahead and go home and be at the yard at 0400 hours to warm up the boat, before we left at 0430 hours. He said he'd tell James the time we were leaving and have him come down at the same time. He said he'd also be down to see us off. I left the yard and headed home. I wanted to get as much sleep as I could, before we left the next morning. I didn't know at this point if I could leave James alone at the wheel, so I didn't plan to sleep too much the next couple days. I wanted to feel comfortable that James could do the job, before I put too much responsibility on him.

At 0350 hours, Friday morning, I arrived at the Active Diver's yard. I unlocked the gate and parked inside the yard. In a few minutes both Gene and James showed up. I had the engines running, warming them up and making ready for departure, when they arrived. The boat was floating, but I wanted a little more water under it, before I got underway. Taking off this soon, before tide change, would give us a real jump start, and would hopefully insure we arrived in time to make a dive on the low water slack tide.

After James boarded and everything was checked out, we had sufficient water under us, so we could leave the slip without digging a propeller into the muddy bottom. I wanted to be sure we had enough water under the boat, because we didn't need any problems that would delay our departure. Gene told us to stay in touch on the VHF and to be careful. I assured him we'd be careful and would be in touch. I told James to cut us loose from the barge, and secure the tie up lines so we wouldn't have a problem if the weather did come up, and the boat became awash with water. When leaving, I ran the boat from the open bridge and backed out of the slip. I then turned into the tide and headed down Cook Inlet. We were bucking tide, and it was running 6 or 7 mph at this point, but it would slow down considerably as we traveled south. With the tide elevation changing over 31 feet in approximately 6½ hours, the speed of the water leaving Cook Inlet had to be moving pretty fast. Ted had mentioned that we wouldn't have a lot of time on the bottom. The tide turns quickly, and sometimes it seems to just swing around and never actually stops moving when changing directions. This is also a time when the air hose can get a big belly in it and has to be watched very closely. Ted said abort any dive when any hazard to the diver exists, and I had already made up my mind that I would not endanger a diver for any reason. No job is worth taking a chance of injuring, or killing anyone.

We had a good trip down the Inlet and arrived at platform Anna at 1150 hours. The ebb tide was slowing down considerably, and, if the divers and tenders were ready, we could probably make the low water dive. I had contacted the platform on the VHF when we were around 45 minutes out, and they told me they would tell the dive crew so they could be ready. I pulled up alongside the oil rig under the crane. In a few minutes the man basket with six people aboard was lowered to the boat. James assisted by holding onto the man basket when it was lowered aboard, while I kept the boat in position. The two divers were already dressed out in diving suits and only had to put on their helmets, weight belts, ankle weights and gloves to be ready to go. All the other diving equipment was already aboard, and the dive tenders had everything hooked up and ready to make a dive.

Ted had shown me the general area on the chart, where we should jump on the first dive to locate the pipeline. I headed to that location, while the tenders got the first diver ready to go into the water. They introduced me to Scooter and Jim, the two #1 divers for Active Divers. I had already met the dive tenders. They all worked together like a well-oiled machine. It was easy to see that everyone knew their job, and not a lot of directions were needed. I told James to just stand-by, and they would call on him, if they needed his assistance.

When I arrived in the general area where we would be diving, I stopped the boat and waited for directions from Scooter's lead tender, Dave. Jerry, Scooter's assistant tender, lowered the dive ladder over the side, and the tide's speed was checked. After the tide had slowed to a point they felt was safe, Scooter, with both tender's help, put on his gloves, his weight belt, ankle weights and the brass hard hat. The brass helmet was locked in place, and the air hose with the communication wires and the cable was fastened to an eye bolt built into the dive suit. The eye bolt insured any pulling on the hose would be absorbed by the dive suit, and not the diver's helmet, or any of the communication wires or air fittings on the air hose. Jim, the stand-by diver, was ready to dive if Scooter needed assistance or got into trouble. Jim's tenders, Al and Hank, had started one of the air compressors and were standing by, if any additional help was needed. As I watched the operation, I could tell these men were all seasoned professionals, no nonsense hands, who were well aware of the hazards that existed when diving in Cook Inlet.

Dave took a position on the bridge beside me at the helm, and I told him I was up tide from the area where I was told the pipeline was located. The diver would be moving with the tide when attempting to locate it. Dave thanked me and asked if I was ready to send the diver down. I told him I was, if he felt the tide was slow enough. This was the first time I had ever run a boat with a diver in the water. I was very alert and conscious of everything that was going on. Dave communicated over the radio dive box with Scooter, telling him he could descend at any time, and to go with the tide when he got on the bottom. Dave told me to be sure to keep the boat up tide with the props away from the diver. I nodded in agreement, and Scooter left the surface, descending to the ocean floor.

The ocean floor in Cook Inlet consists of mud and silt, so the water is silty and muddy. As soon as the diver leaves the surface, he is unable to see anything and is working only by feel. It's up to the tender to keep him going in the right direction. With the tide changes, while the diver is on the bottom, the diver can lose all sense of direction. When he first dives he uses the tide to keep his direction, but this change happens rapidly, so he must rely on his tender to direct him. Jerry was feeding out hose, while Scooter was descending. The diver's bubbles were visible on the water's surface and, as he went deeper, the bubbles would be traveling down tide from his location. All this had to be taken into consideration when positioning the boat and keeping the propellers away from the diver's air hose.

As the dive progressed I got a better feel for what my responsibilities were. I felt comfortable maneuvering the boat and staying within close proximity of the diver, but not so close as to create a hazard. As Dave communicated with Scooter I listened to the conversation. The tide, on the surface, was almost at a stand-still when Scooter announced he had located the pipeline. He asked Dave which way he should go to start walking the line. Dave told him to go to his right, and as soon as he turned to the right and started moving, it was apparent by his bubbles that he was going in the wrong direction. Dave stopped him and told him to go in the opposite direction. This revelation indicated the tide had already changed on the bottom, and Scooter was facing south when he found the pipeline, instead of north, as we had thought. This is why he had gone in the wrong direction at first. As we moved in a southerly direction, Scooter kept reporting to Dave what he was finding. Dave was keeping notes and would log anything that he felt was noteworthy. A large three foot rock was found lying against the pipeline. A small void under the pipeline was found approximately eight inches deep and a couple feet long, which was also reported and logged. Dave asked Scooter if he felt it was large enough to mark as a hazard to the pipeline, and Scooter told him it was not. As we worked down the pipeline the tide started to pick up. The air hose was getting a little belly in it, and the hose was pulling harder on the diver. The tide was now visibly flooding, and Scooter asked for more hose. The tide was starting to run, and it was decided to mark the line and bring Scooter up. He said if he gave him more hose, it was going to be a problem and would only be taken by the tide. Dave told Jerry to hook a 3/8 inch cable with an orange buoy to the hose, so Scooter could pull it down and mark his stopping point on the pipeline. He then told Scooter what was going on, and Scooter said he'd dig under the line so he would have a place to wrap the cable. After the cable was attached to the air hose with a shackle, Scooter was directed to pull it down. He pulled the air hose down and unhooked the shackle on the end of the cable. He told Dave the hose line was clear, and Jerry was signaled to pull the excess hose back aboard. Scooter wrapped the cable around the pipeline and shackled it to itself. He then announced he was coming up, and he started to ascend.

When a diver starts to ascend, he opens an air valve and inflates the dive suit with air, which acts like a balloon and lifts him off the bottom. The amount of air he puts into the suit dictates how fast he will ascend. Scooter had only been down for thirty five minutes, before the tide became too strong, and the dive had to be ended. The maximum depth of the dive was only ninety-five feet of water, so Scooter wouldn't have to decompress for very long. A scale is used to determine how long a diver has to decompress. The amount of time he was diving and the depth, are the determining factors in figuring the decompression time. On this dive Dave told Scooter he would bring him up to thirty five feet, and he could hang him off for five minutes to decompress. Scooter told him he was warm enough, and that it wouldn't be a problem.

Dave told me that a diver has to decompress to get the nitrogen out of his joints and organs. The nitrogen builds up due to the pressures at different depths. He said there are two options when decompressing. The diver can come up to a certain depth and just stay stationary for whatever length of time the scale dictates, or he can be brought aboard the boat and be put in the decompression chamber. Air pressure can then be added to the chamber, bringing the pressure to match the depth he would have hung off at. Dave said the scales that have been tested and proven over time determine the decompression time. Since Scooter was not cold, he said they chose to let him hang off for five minutes, so the nitrogen bubbles could leave his system. This is a common practice, and Dave said rarely is the decompression chamber utilized. If a diver doesn't decompress, the nitrogen bubbles can create a very serious and life threatening condition, known as the bends. Professional divers, who do deep water dives, often hang off for hours, if their body temperature does not get too low. They wear insulated clothes in the dry suits, but have to be careful not to dress too warmly when they are working hard on a dive. They could get too warm, which is also a problem, if they start to sweat and have to hang off to decompress. They have to figure out what to wear, so they can stay warm, but not overheat due to overexertion.

After Scooter had hung off for five minutes, Jerry started pulling him in. Scooter helped by adding some more air to his dry suit. He came up approximately 50 feet off the bow of the boat, and I kept the boat in neutral while he was brought aboard. After he was aboard the dive ladder was brought aboard, and the air compressor was turned off. While the tenders took care of their gear, I got my radar and loran bearings on the buoy Scooter had attached to the oil line. It was imperative that the buoy could be located, so we could start our next dive on the next tide. As soon as I got my bearings, I headed back to platform Anna.

Dave came in the wheelhouse and told me I'd done a great job handling the boat. It had been a good dive. He hoped the weather would hold and every dive would go as well. He commented that we would get more time in the water on the smaller tides. I found the crew to be very easy to work with.

I called the platform on the radio and told them we were headed back. It took approximately 35 minutes to reach the rig and the man basket was already swung over the side, with the crane operator awaiting our arrival. I pulled under the crane and the man basket was lowered to the deck. The two divers and the four tenders jumped on and were lifted aboard the platform.

Scooter and I had checked the tide book and it was decided our next dive would be on the 0711 hours tide the next morning. It was a 31.1 foot tide, so we would be picking up the crew around 0530 hours. Scooter decided we would not make any night time dives due to the hazards of keeping track of the diver, when visibility was not the best. It was getting light around 0630 hours and getting dark around 2130 hours. With the lights on the deck of the boat, Scooter and I both felt we could land the man basket safely the next morning and then make the morning dive during daylight hours. By doing this we would be loading the crew in twilight hours, but we would avoid diving in the dark.

After the dive crew had been lifted off the boat, I pulled around to the north side of the platform and nosed up to the northeast leg, where a cable for mooring purposes was located. I told James to run the eye of the tie up line through the shackle and back to the cleat on the bow. We would then let out slack until we were a good distance from the platform leg. This would enable us to cut loose, without having to get too close to the leg, in the event the wind came up. We were secured at 1620 hours, and I checked the tide book and found we had to move to the southeast leg of the platform at 1930 hours, so the tide wouldn't push us under the rig after the tide changed. By not diving until the 0711 hours tide, we all would get a good night's sleep and hit it at first light.

After we were secured James went below and shut down the main engines. He checked the oil, checked the bilge and the shaft logs and then filled out his engine room log. I brought the captain's log up to date, giving the dive times, the run times and the tie up times. James fixed a dinner of steaks, a salad and fried potatoes. We ate like kings. James was a pretty good cook, and we really enjoyed the meal. After the 1930 hours platform leg change, we took advantage of the slack time and went to bed.

James and I were out of bed at 0500 hours. By 0520 hours the main engines had been started and warmed up. I called the platform on the radio and told them we were going to pull under the crane to take on the crew. They acknowledged, and said they would convey that to the divers and tenders.

We untied from the leg of the platform, and I pulled under the crane. We only had to wait a few minutes until the crew was lowered onto the deck. It was still dark, but we had the deck lights on, and we were able to land the man basket and crew without any problem. As soon as the crew was aboard and the crane picked up the man basket, I went from the bridge to the wheelhouse to run the boat. I always operated the boat from the bridge, when anything was being done on deck. Visibility was better there, which made everything much safer.

I checked my notes and radar and took a heading in the direction of the buoy we'd attached to the pipeline. As we neared the location I had to adjust my headings from time to time, due to the tide pushing us to the north. At 0615 hours I located the buoy and pulled up to it. The tide was still running too strong for a dive, but we stayed on the buoy and waited for it to slow down. At 0640 hours the tide had slowed enough to put the diver down. The dive ladder was again put over the side, and Jim put on his gear and hard hat and readied himself for the jump. The dive compressor was started, and the fittings were checked for air leaks.

Jim's lead tender, Al, took a position on the bridge beside me and asked if I was ready. After I had the buoy just off the dive ladder, I told Al and he signaled the tender to put Jim in the water. As soon as Jim was in the water and had a grip on the buoy line, I backed the boat off about twenty feet. Jim left the surface and descended to the ocean floor. Jim soon reported he was at the pipeline, and Al told him to stand-by until we could grab the buoy. Al told me to ease up to the buoy, and the tenders readied the boat hook to retrieve it. As soon as they had the buoy aboard, Al told Jim to cut the cable loose. In a couple minutes Jim reported he had unhooked the shackle, and they could pull the cable aboard.

Jim started walking the pipeline feeling for voids under it, rocks, or other hazards that could damage the line. He was making good time walking the line, and reported he'd not found any significant problems that needed addressing at this point. At 0720 hours the tide had changed and was picking up speed. We had gone from a flood tide to an ebb tide in less than an hour, but Al told me this was not bad given the tide was so big. Al asked Jim if he was feeling the tide very much on the bottom. Jim reported he felt it somewhat, but it was not a problem yet. Al told him to locate an area where he could fasten the buoy to the line, and we'd send it to him. Within a couple minutes Jim told Al he was ready for the buoy. Al told Hank to send the buoy down, and he shackled the cable to the air hose. As soon as it was ready, Al told Jim to pull it down to him. Jim pulled the line down and unhooked it from the air hose. Hank pulled the excess hose back aboard. As soon as the cable was again fastened to the pipeline, Jim told Al he was ready to come up. Al told him he'd bring him to thirty feet and hang him off for eight minutes. Al told me to stay clear of the buoy cable and to ease the diver west of it. I moved the boat over and Jim added air to his suit and ascended to a depth of thirty feet. He stopped at that depth and we stood by until the eight minutes had passed, and we could bring him aboard. As soon as Jim was aboard and the ladder was secured, I went below deck to get a radar and loran bearing on the buoy. We then headed back to platform Anna. Al told me he was happy with the dive, and that we covered a good bit of line for the time we were on the bottom. He said at this rate we should be able to walk the entire line in a couple weeks' time, if the weather held. There were many variables, and we didn't know what we would run into.

We arrived back at the oil rig at 0820 hours. The man basket was swinging over the side of the rig awaiting our arrival. Our next dive would be at 1358 hours with a -1.8 foot tide, so we decided we'd pick up the crew at 1215 hours. This would give us time to reach the buoy a good half hour to forty-five minutes prior to low tide. That should be plenty of time to locate it and to get ready for the jump. The crew left the boat, and we tied up to the southeast leg of the platform again. For the next four days this became the routine. We lost a couple tides due to darkness, but we were making good time on each dive. We had walked better than a quarter of the pipeline by the fifth day.

On the 3rd day of May we picked up the crew at 0730 hours. We had a 29.9 foot tide at 0945 hours, and we had to run nearly an hour now to reach the buoy. The weather had been great, and the only dives we'd missed were due to darkness. We really hoped the weather wouldn't change, until we could get more pipeline checked. When we reached the buoy, the tide was still moving very fast, so we stood by waiting for it to slow down. Scooter was diving on this dive, and the tenders checked out all the gear, while we waited on the tide. It was 0915 hours when Scooter entered the water. After reaching the bottom he released the buoy, and it was then pulled aboard the boat. Scooter then started to walk the line, reporting his findings as he advanced. He had been in the water around 25 minutes, when he reported he'd located a void under the pipeline. He estimated the void to be around two feet deep at the starting point, but said it seemed to get deeper as he continued down the line. At one point he said the void was at least four feet deep, if not deeper. It varied up and down in depth, as he continued checking it. Due to everything being done by feel, Scooter could only estimate the length of the void. He guessed the void to continue for 35 to 40 feet. When he reached the point where the pipeline was again supported by the ocean floor, he called for a marker buoy. He said he would mark both ends of the void, and we would have a better idea of how far it actually reached. A marker buoy with a 3/8 inch cable was tied off to the air hose, and Scooter pulled it down to him. As soon as he unhooked the cable from his air hose, Jerry pulled the slack back aboard the boat. Scooter fastened the marker buoy to the pipeline, and then reported he was reversing direction and going back to where the void started. After a time Scooter called for another marker buoy, stating he was at the void's starting point. Dave signaled Jerry to hook another marker buoy to the air hose. The tide was just starting to ebb, and Scooter had plenty of time to get the buoy tied off to the line. Dave told Scooter that he was going to bring him up to 30 feet and let him decompress for 10 minutes. Dave told him the tide was picking up, and even though he could probably work a while longer, he felt it was important that they get back to the rig and call the office to report their findings. Dave said with a void this large the oil company may want to cease diving operations and get the barge on location to secure the pipeline. Scooter agreed, and he was brought up and hung off at 30 feet. While Scooter was hanging off, I eased over by the buoy and got my radar and loran bearings. With the bearings we could be more specific with the office about the location of the void. I wrote the coordinates down and gave them to Dave, so he could pass them on. Dave and I estimated the two buoys to be around 50 feet from one another, making the void approximately 50 feet long.

After Scooter was brought aboard and the equipment secured, I headed back to the platform. Scooter and Dave told me they would be contacting Ted, and/or Roger, and they would let me know what was decided. Both felt the void was so large that it would become a priority, and we would probably be headed to town to rig the barge and load it with sandbags to fix the problem. There was a great propensity for a weld or pipe to break and cause a huge oil spill. They didn't think the oil company would want to waste any time checking more line, until this was corrected. I told

Dave and Scooter that I would not make any plans concerning the next dive, until I heard from them. They agreed a decision would have to come down from the office before we continued. We arrived at the platform, and I pulled up under the crane. The crew left the boat, and we tied up to the southeast leg. James took care of the engine room, and I filled out my captain's log. I had considerably more to add due to locating the void under the pipeline.

We had been hanging off the leg for a couple hours, when I received a call from Scooter via the VHF radio. He said he'd talked with Ted, and it was decided they would ready the SS-18 barge and bring it out filled with sand bags to secure the pipeline. Scooter said Ted wanted me to head to town, since I would be needed to run the tugboat and handle the barge on this job. I told Scooter we would head in on the next flood tide and should be in Anchorage by around midnight. He said he'd call the office back and advise them of our ETA. Low water was at 1655 hours and was a -0.3, so we would get underway at around 1530 hours. We would be bucking tide for a while, but it would be slowing down enough so we would be making some headway. We arrived at the Active Diver's yard at 2135 hours, just before high tide. We secured the boat alongside the SS-12 barge on the north side of the dock, and then James and I went home. It was Friday, and I told James we should probably check in with Gene at around 1300 hours the next day.

I arrived home at around midnight, and Ann was surprised to see me. The next morning Donica also showed her surprise with a big hug. They had made it fine without my being home and the Smiths had provided transportation for them to the store a few times. With them living next door I felt a lot better when I was away from home. Everything seemed to be working out, and we still felt good about our decision to move to Anchorage. I told the girls what we had found, and what we planned to do about it. I told them I'd be gone from home probably more than a week on this trip. I was enjoying the job, and they seemed to enjoy my stories. All was going well with us.

Just before 0900 hours on Saturday morning, Gene called me and asked if I would mind coming in to work. He said due to the void we'd found under the pipeline, the oil company was in quite a hurry to get the

SS-18 barge geared up and on location to make the needed repairs. Gene told me they needed a crane operator and he knew that I had operated cranes before. I told him I would come right in and I drove to the Active Diver's yard. When I arrived, I observed that a couple truckloads of sand had been delivered to the yard. The four yard hands were busy filling sandbags and placing them on pallets.

I went into Gene's office, and he told me he had four pile bucks coming in to rig the SS-18 barge with the anchors and buoys. They would need a crane operator to move the anchors, buoys and cables around for them. He said we would also be loading pallets of sandbags aboard the barge. The oil companies had put a rush on prepping the barge after finding out about the problem with the oil line. They wanted to get on location as soon as possible to avoid an oil spill. The barge worked very well for this kind of job and had been utilized in the past in Cook Inlet to assist the oil companies. Gene said he hoped to be able to have the barge and the tug ready to go by Tuesday or Wednesday of the next week. He also told me I would have to get acquainted with the tug, Fair wind, sometime during the first of the week. It would also have to be rigged up for the job. Gene said they had launched the tug after getting the information about the oil pipeline problem, but nothing more had been done. He said we'd have to take on fuel, groceries, and check all the winches to make sure they were in good working order. But first we needed to get the barge ready to go.

The SS-18 barge is 130 feet long and 32 feet wide. It had an American 60 ton double drum cable crane, located on a pedestal, approximately 30 feet from the bow of the barge. Its location left adequate deck space available for any equipment or freight needed for the variety of contracts the company took on. The barge also had four double drum winches, which were located above deck on each corner. The winches had 400 feet of 1½ inch cable on each of them. Six 1500 pound anchors were also aboard the barge. The winches were operated independently of one another from a seat the operator occupied just behind the controls. Each winch was powered with a 671 GMC diesel engine. The anchoring system on the SS-18 used one anchor off each corner and one anchor amidships off the bow and off the stern. The cables from the winches would be strung through pulleys to facilitate the positioning of the amidships anchors.

Metal buoys were attached to the fluke end of each anchor to mark their location, when the barge was anchored on the job site. The buoys also held the picking cables, which the tug used to pull the anchors when bringing them back aboard the barge or when repositioning them. Living quarters were located below deck on the SS-18 barge. It was equipped with bathroom and shower facilities, a laundry room, a full kitchen, staterooms, which could house up to 32 people. It also had an engine room where the generators, pumps, water system, including fresh water storage, and the fuel storage tanks were located. The barge had been set up well for the work in and around Cook Inlet for the oil companies.

The pile bucks arrived at the yard at 1030 hours. I was already aboard the barge and had the crane warmed up and was ready to assist them. They told me they wanted to hook up the anchors to the winches. I would pick the anchors and place them where they would be ready for setting when the barge got on location. They said they would direct me in everything they needed me to do. I got in the crane and we went to work. I picked each anchor, placing it where it would be located on the barge and could be geared up without any obstructions. It took a couple hours to rig the six anchors, and then we broke for lunch.

After lunch we rigged the metal mooring buoys and moved two diving compressors down to the edge of the dock. I lifted them aboard, positioning them amidships on both sides of the barge. Two air winches, called air tuggers, were swung aboard, as were numerous tools that could be needed on the job. The diver's hoses were lifted aboard on pallets and were placed beside the air compressors. The sandbags on pallets were moved to the edge of the dock with a forklift and with pallet slings I lifted them aboard and stacked them on top of one another just aft of the crane. The yard crew had been filling the sand bags since my arrival to the yard. I was told we would be taking as many as 100 pallets aboard over the next few days. Two welding machines were lifted aboard. I also swung two oxygen and acetylene carts aboard, as well as a rack full of oxygen and acetylene bottles. I spent all afternoon swinging items aboard the barge that would possibly be needed once we were on location. We worked until 1800 hours, and then Gene asked me if I could come in on Sunday morning. He said he knew I'd been away from my family, but they were short-handed and needed to work through the weekend to insure the tug and barge would be ready to go by the middle of the week. I agreed to come in at 0800 hours the next morning, and I headed home.

I arrived back at the yard at 0750 hours on Sunday morning and went into Gene's office. He was busy putting a list together for items that would be needed on the barge. He told me the pile bucks were coming in again today, and I would be running the crane again for them. He said he'd keep the yard crew busy loading sand- bags on pallets and delivering them to the edge of the dock. He also mentioned I would need to get acquainted with the Fair wind, and we needed to stock both the barge and the tug with groceries. He said he had a cook and a bull cook coming on Monday morning, and they would be making up the grocery lists and getting the barge ready for housing the crew. He told me James and Laurence would be my deckhands on the tug when we sailed, and maybe I'd want to touch base with them and get an idea of what groceries we'd want aboard. He told me we would be taking meals aboard the barge when we were alongside, but we still needed to have some food aboard the tug. He said there was still a lot that had to go aboard the barge. We would have a crew totaling 12 men aboard, including the divers and tenders, plus the three of us on the tug. There was a lot to consider when getting a barge ready for a job that could last better than a week. Gene was somewhat overwhelmed with everything that had to be done, and he said he was hoping the crew would pitch in with suggestions, if they had any. I told him we'd do everything we could do to assist him, but this was my first time on this kind of a job, and it was all new to me too. He said he hadn't had a lot of experience either in this area, but with everyone pulling together we'd pull it off.

Laurence and James had arrived to load sandbags, and I approached them and asked them to get together and make a list of supplies they would like on the tug. James told me they would have me a list by evening. The pile bucks arrived and we all went to work. Six pallets of sandbags were already staged at the end of the dock, and we lifted them aboard first thing. Some pad eyes had to be made and welded to the deck of the barge so the crane could be secured before we sailed. Anytime a barge was going out to sea, cranes on board had to be cross chained at the front of the cab and at the counter weight. The boom would also be secured in the cradle with the whip line fastened to one corner of the barge, and the block fastened to the other. Both picking lines would be brought taught when the boom was lowered into the cradle. This would eliminate any movement of the boom. The boom would then be cross chained approximately midway of the deck. Pad eyes also had to be welded to the deck in many different areas to tie down the compressors, the welders, the oxygen/acetylene bottles and all the other gear that could become a problem in heavy seas. There was a lot of work to do and everyone was busy. Much of the day I spent waiting on someone needing crane assistance. It is part of the job but it is certainly boring to just be on standby. I couldn't leave the crane because you never knew when someone would need your assistance.

We again worked until 1800 hours and had made a lot of progress. A day or two more at this pace we'd be ready to head down the Inlet. Gene called me into his office before I went home and gave me a list James and Laurence had given him when they left. He told me to check it over and add anything I might want for the boat. He also said a union operator would be coming in on Monday morning to run the crane, and I would be freed up to get the Fair wind ready to go. He said he'd put James with me, but still needed the other yard hands to keep filling the sandbags. I told Gene I'd take the list home with me, check it out, and get it back to him first thing in the morning. He told me to have a good evening, and he'd see me around 0800 hours the next morning.

Before I left Gene's office I called Ann, and told her I'd take her and Donica out to dinner and not to cook anything. She said she'd already started dinner, but she could save it for another night. I told her I was going to get very busy for the next couple weeks, and I wanted to go out and have a nice dinner and just be with the two of them for the evening. She said that sounded great, and they would get ready. When I arrived home I jumped in the shower and then got dressed. We headed downtown to have an Italian dinner, one of Donica's favorites since she loved pasta. We had a nice dinner and a great time then headed home. It wasn't often that we had an opportunity to go out to dinner to an Italian restaurant and, having lived in Seldovia, it was a treat for all of us.

I arrived at the yard at 0800 hours the next morning. Gene told me to head down to the tug and start checking the winches, engines and the electronics to insure all were functioning properly. He said I should take as much time as I needed to get acquainted with the tug. We could be gone from home for up to a couple weeks, and he wanted us to do everything we could to insure the boat was in good condition. Out on the job is not the place to find out there is a problem. I headed down to the boat and the union operator arrived to run the crane.

The *Fair Wind* was a 58 foot steel hulled tug boat converted to a tug from a landing craft, (LCM). The bow gate had been removed and a rounded bow had been added. What used to be the cargo hold was decked over, creating an upper and lower deck. Heavy railings, built up approximately three feet, surrounded the upper deck and continued around the stern of the vessel. An anchor winch was added on the bow, as was a bow roller with upright chocks. A cabin with a wheelhouse, an open bridge, a galley, and below deck quarters replaced the original cabin. The two 671 GMC diesel engines, which had been the main engines, were replaced with two 871 GMC diesel engines. This created considerably more horsepower, making the tug much more versatile. A tow winch with a capstan had been added directly behind the wheelhouse, and 1000 feet of 2 inch cable was spooled onto the winch for towing purposes. The galley, with a table, booth type seating, and a stove was located on the starboard side, while the refrigerator, the bathroom, the staircase leading below deck and a set of bunk beds were located on the port side of the cabin. The galley was separated from the wheelhouse by a bulkhead with a wooden sliding door. Two more sets of bunk beds were located below the main deck just ahead of the engine room, with one set on the port side and the other on the starboard side. An access door and bulkhead, in the lower deck, separated the forward compartment from the engine room. The quarters were somewhat crowded, since the boat was built to accommodate a four man crew.

Upon arriving on the boat, I first checked all the fire extinguishers and life jackets aboard. We had six survival suits, 10 Coast Guard approved life jackets, 8 fire extinguishers and a 12 man canister life raft. All were up to date on inspections. Further perusal of the tug revealed a large spotlight, ample deck lighting, running lights and electronics, all in good working order. The electronics included two VHF radios, a single side band radio, a loran C, Decca 24 mile radar, a fathometer and a large compass. The boat had hydraulic steering with the hydraulic pumps located on both the upper steering station and the steering station in the wheelhouse.

Since the tide was out, and the boat was high and dry, I couldn't start the main engines. The main engines were cooled with keel coolers and needed water under the boat to insure they did not overheat. The light plant was air cooled, so it could be started and checked. It seemed to work perfectly. The oil looked clean and was at the full mark on the dipstick. The hydraulics were checked and found to be in good working order. Even though the boat was an old boat, which had been converted to a tug, it was evident that a lot of thought had gone into its design.

The anchor winch on the bow was powered by the hydraulic system aboard the boat, and it was rigged with 300 feet of 1 inch cable. This winch was used when positioning anchors for the SS-18 barge. The winch held the anchor on the bow when it was moved and to be set on location, and when it was lifted off the ocean floor for repositioning the barge, or when returning the anchors to the barge. Anchoring the barge was done by dropping the amidships anchor up tide of the location then positioning the barge with the tug to drop each of the corner anchors up tide. The crane operator would hang the other three anchors on the bow of the boat one at a time and the tug would run each of them out to a location chosen by the barge master. When all the anchors were set, there would be one straight off the bow, one straight off the stern, and one off each corner of the barge. This would enable the barge master to change barge locations with the anchor winches, without the aid of the tug. When all the winches were brought up tight, the barge would be held on location and unable to move back and forth. This insured a stable platform for the workers.

At 1430 hours a fuel truck arrived at the yard. The fuel hose was stretched across the deck of the barge to the Fair wind. The tug was topped off with fuel and the truck then left and returned in an hour to top off the fuel tanks on the SS-18 barge.

At 1620 hours I called Gene on the VHF radio from the tug, and asked if he would send James down to the boat. The tide was high enough to float the tug. After I checked the engine oil, I started the main engines. When James came aboard I told him I wanted to turn the tug around and tie off near the bow of the barge. I would tie alongside the barge on its port side, with the tug's bow facing the barge's stern. This would position the tug where the bridle and the tow line could be hooked up the next day. We needed to have the tow line and bridle in place before we left the dock with the barge. This would enable us to go on tow quickly, after pulling away from the Active Diver's yard. The tide would not be right for turning the tug around during working hours. To avoid having to come in early on Thursday morning, or stay late Thursday evening, I decided to turn the tug around before leaving the yard. James released the lines on my order and I eased the boat away from the barge. I moved out into the tide to get the feel of the vessel. This was the first time I had been on the controls of the Fair wind, and I was pleased with the way it responded. After doing a number of different maneuvers, I went alongside the port side of the barge near the bow. In this position we could rig the bridle and tow line without any problems.

The union crane operator had arrived at the start of the shift and ran the crane all day. The stack of sandbag pallets was growing, and 65 to 70 pallets had been stacked on the barge by quitting time. The pile buck crew had worked aboard the barge welding pad eyes in place and tying down all the equipment on board. The yard crew would be finished filling the sandbags the next day, and the rest of the pallets would be put aboard the barge. The dive tenders also had moved a connex down by the dock, and had the crane operator swing it aboard the barge. The pile bucks welded pad eyes in place. It was secured with shackles and chains, so it could not shift in a heavy sea. The connex contained all the dive equipment, including a decompression chamber. The dive tenders had spent most of the day going through the gear and hooking everything up. The dive suits, the diver's brass hard hat helmets, the Kirby gear and numerous fittings and tools were all stowed in the connex. The divers and the tenders would be staying aboard the barge during the job so it was very important everything was aboard in the connex and in good condition. The connex worked well for storing all the dive gear and keeping it all organized in one location. This insured it was readily available when needed.

With everyone working together we were getting close to having everything done. Gene told me the cook and the bullcook would do all the grocery shopping the next morning for both the tug and the barge. We would soon be ready to head down Cook Inlet and address the problem with the pipeline. Gene said it looked like we'd be ready to go on Friday morning's high tide. The tide would be high at 0515 hours and was a 27.7 foot tide. We'd need to come in early and make sure everything was ready to go before high water. The Fair wind was nearly ready. The groceries had to be put aboard, as did the tow line, and a few last minute things that needed checked. For the most part, the tug was ready to sail. The braided nylon tow line we'd be using was to be brought aboard the next day. It was 300 feet long and 2½ inches in diameter and was often used when a barge was being towed short distances, or for only a few hours in the confines of Cook Inlet. It was much easier to handle the soft tow line than the cable on the tow winch. The line could be easily stowed flat on the deck when not being used. We also would be using a braided nylon line for the tow bridle, which would be rigged on the barge sometime on Thursday.

I arrived home to find dinner being put on the table. We had a nice dinner and visited for a while, until it was Donica's bedtime. I tucked her in and then packed a bag with the items I'd need on the tug. I still had tonight and tomorrow night at home, but felt I better not wait until the last minute to get everything ready.

I took my bag with me when I went to work the next morning and put it aboard the tug. Laurence and James were both working with the yard crew to finish filling the sandbags. Gene told me he'd send them down to the tug when they were done. It was close to noon when all the sandbags had been filled and put on pallets. They moved all the pallets down near the barge, and the crane operator was swinging the last of them aboard. James and Laurence were assisting from the shore. When the pallets were all loaded, they came aboard the tug. We decided to take lunch and then rig the tow bridle and tow line when we returned. The tow line and the bridle had been put on pallets and moved to the end of the dock, where the crane could reach them to swing them aboard the Fair wind. After we returned from lunch, the pallets with the lines were swung aboard the tug. The tow line was flaked back and forth on the deck from the stern to the bow, so it would peel off without snarling when we were going on tow with the barge. The bridle was rigged up to the bow of the barge and fastened to the cleats on both the port and starboard sides. The bridle was made in a "Y" configuration, so the tail could be joined with the braided tow line aboard the tug. We shackled the tow line to the bridle and fed it through the stern towing chocks. It was then secured to the upright cleats on the tow winch. This would insure the bridal would not inadvertently be pulled off the deck before we were ready.

I pulled Laurence and James aside to talk about any concerns they had. I told them what I expected of them when they worked aboard the tug. I had already worked with James and knew he was a good hand. It appeared that Laurence was also a hard worker and conscientious. He was a welder and a pipe fitter, but said he was eager to go out and experience other kinds of work.

Gene called me to the office and told me he had someone he wanted me to meet. When I reached his office he introduced me to Lowell. He said Lowell was a cousin to Jack, who had owned the High Tide Marine yard. Lowell was going to be the barge master on the SS-18 on this job. I told Gene that Lowell and I were already acquainted. We had worked together on another barge job in Goodnews Bay. We exchanged pleasantries and Lowell said he'd met Gene through Jack, when they all lived in the states. After Jack started High Tide Marine, he and Gene were called to go to work for him in Anchorage. Lowell said he had been a barge master on a couple jobs in Cook Inlet. He asked what experience I had in the Inlet. I told him about working the season for Jack, running the landing craft, and about the two months I spent as engineer on the tug, Southland. I also mentioned that I'd been running the dive boat this year on the oil pipeline. I told him this would be my first time handling a barge on a job like this, but I felt confident I could do it. I told him that anything he could tell me would be very much appreciated. Lowell invited me into the break room, and we sat down at the table. We talked a little about Goodnews Bay and then he drew out a diagram of how we would be setting the anchors when we arrived on location. He said we would drop the bow anchor off the barge first, and then I would move the barge into location with the tug, and drop the port bow anchor. Next we would place the rest of the anchors with the tug to finish anchoring the barge. He said he'd done it on several occasions and it should not be a problem. He told me after I anchored the barge one time, I would have it down. Lowell said he hoped we'd arrive on site when the tide was still ebbing. That way we wouldn't have to wait for the next ebb tide before we could anchor on location. He said it was imperative we anchored the barge on an ebb tide. After he briefed me on what was to come, he told me he was looking forward to the job. Gene then told me to head home and be with my family. I had to be back by 0400 hours to make sure everything was ready to go so I took off.

The Active Diver's yard had been abuzz all afternoon with people coming to the barge to put their gear aboard. We would be leaving early Friday morning and everyone had to be aboard when we left the dock. The cook and bull cook had been working frantically for two days getting the barge ready for the crew. All the bunks had been made, the supplies stowed, and the decks and the galley had been scrubbed down. The pile bucks and dive tenders had everything ready on the barge and were getting their personal gear aboard, as well. There was no helipad on the barge, so everyone had to be aboard and ride the barge down the Inlet. You also had to be ready to stay aboard, until the job was completed. Although it was dependent on the weather and on how the job went, Gene, Lowell and Ted felt it shouldn't take more than a week to do the repair of the pipeline.

I arrived home at 1600 hours and told my wife and daughter we'd go out for dinner again before I left. I walked next door to the Smiths, and asked Jud if she and the family would like to go out with us to dinner. I told her it was my treat, and that we'd love to have them join us. She said Al would be home in a little while, and she would ask him and let us know. I went back home and around 1730 hours Anita came to the trailer, and told us that they would love to join us for dinner. They would be ready to go in a few minutes. I asked Anita what she liked to eat, and she said tacos. I told her we'd go to a Mexican restaurant, if it was alright with her parents. She left to deliver the message to her mom and dad. The Smiths said they knew a good Mexican restaurant in the Spenard area, and we followed them to Spenard Road near Fireweed Lane. We had a wonderful dinner and a great visit. After dinner we said our goodbyes, and Ann, Donica and I went home.

Donica, soon to be six years old, felt she had outgrown being tucked in, but after she got into her pajamas, I went into her room and we just talked for a half hour or so before I kissed her goodnight. I really enjoyed the times my daughter and I would spend just talking. She told me later in life that those times were very special times for her, as well. I had started this when she was around two years old. It was a time when just she and I would sit on her bed in her room and talk about anything and everything. When these talks took place I told her she could talk about anything she wanted, and she could say anything she wanted with no fear of repercussions. It was a time of sharing between a father and a daughter, and I think the family drew closer together because of these visits. It always seemed to end too quickly. All of a sudden, we were all adults and no longer took the time. I still, to this day, miss those special times with my daughter. I told her I would be gone for a week or so. I had an early morning, and I had to get some sleep, so I kissed her goodnight and went to bed.

I arrived at the Active Diver's yard at 0345 hours and was surprised to see Gene already in his office. He told me he'd just arrived a few minutes before me, and he asked if I had everything ready to go on the tug. I told him I thought it was all covered, but since I'd never handled a barge on a job like this before, there could be some unknowns. However, I was fairly sure all was accounted for. As we visited, Laurence and James arrived at the yard, and we all three went aboard the tug.

The tide was coming in and the Fair wind was floating, so I told James to start the engines and warm them up. I also told him we'd need to start the generator for the deck lights and hydraulics. It was not going to be daylight when we pulled away from the dock. James went to the engine room, and in a few minutes the engines were started. I told Laurence to make sure we had a long stern line and a spring line handy to put the barge on the hip. We would need to have all the lines very taut to be able to control the barge. I wanted to wait until just before we were ready to leave to make up to the barge. We wouldn't want to take a chance of digging into the bottom with our propellers. I turned on the radar and the depth finder, as well as a VHF radio. We would be ready to leave ahead of the tide. I was just hoping nothing would come up to delay our departure. We had a lot of people who had to be aboard the barge, before we could leave. After having talked to Lowell about anchoring the barge on location, I wanted to arrive at the oil pipeline before low water, or at least before the tide change, and it started to flood.

At 0415 hours I told James and Laurence we'd slide the tug back and put the barge on the hip. We'd need to first hook a line to the quarter cleat on the port side of the tug, and then we'd hook up the bow line, using the anchor winch. We'd not tighten the bow line until the other two lines were secured. I told them I'd direct them from the bridge. Two pile bucks were asked to assist us from the barge. The spring line and stern line were put in place. The stern line went from the center chock on the stern of the tug to the starboard bow cleat on the barge. I then backed the tug up, going past the bow of the barge about 25 feet. The stern line and the spring line were secured, and then the bow line was brought up very tight with the bow winch. This tightened all three lines, and the tug now was tied tight enough, so it would seem the tug and barge were as one unit. As soon as we were out in the tide, we'd let go of the three tie up lines and put the barge on tow with the braided tow line that was already made up to the barge. We would only have to feed out line until we had the barge on a short tow. I planned to keep it around 100 feet behind us.

Gene had a man counting heads. When he was satisfied everyone was aboard, Gene told me we could leave any time I was ready. Lowell was on deck with a number of pile bucks and told me to give him the word when I was ready to cut loose from the dock. I told him I was ready any time he was, and he gave the order to cut the barge loose. At 0440 hours we were free of the dock and moving out into the incoming tide.

I swung the barge offshore and continued out into the tide for approximately ½ mile, before I gave the order to cut the tug loose from the barge. The stern line was released first, with the spring line second, and then the bow winch was reversed, and the tug was untied from the barge. I told Laurence and James to continue to feed out tow line, until I told them to stop. After I judged we were 100 feet from the barge, I told them to secure the tow line. They tied it on the amidships stern cleat, and I eased the tug ahead until the tow line became tight. The barge then swung in behind us. I slowly increased the RPM's, until the barge was pulling in a straight line behind us, and the tow line was pulled free of the water. I told James to shut down the generator and to turn off the deck lights. The running lights and the cabin lights were all 12 volt, so the generator was not needed to run them.

The seas were calm with hardly a breeze blowing, and the forecast for the next few days was great. I was very pleased with the way everything had gone up to this point, but I didn't want to jinx myself, so I didn't say anything regarding the weather. After everything seemed to be working, I left the bridge and went to the wheelhouse to operate the tug. I brought both engines up and synchronized them to 2800 RPM on the tachometers. I called Lowell on the VHF radio, and gave him a report that all was well. I told him I would do everything I could to get us on location before slack water. Lowell told me to call him when we were an hour away from the location. He'd have the crew start unlashing the equipment, and we'd be ready to anchor when we arrived. We settled in, heading down Cook Inlet. I brought the captain's log up to date with departure times and a weather report.

The tide had slowed enough, so we were making some headway. We'd speed up more as soon as it slacked completely and then swung around and started the ebb. Running with the tide we should make very good time. All of this was new to Laurence. He was very curious and asked a lot of questions. I didn't mind because I always appreciated someone who wanted to learn. Hopefully I'd know the answers to the questions he would ask. I showed him how the radar worked. He asked about compass headings and how we knew what course to run. As we continued down the Inlet, I schooled Laurence in navigation and things to watch for. He was a very curious student and our visiting helped pass the time. I hoped it would be beneficial to him in his future. I told him one of the most important things to remember on any boat was to always watch the gauges on the control panel. The oil pressure and temperature of both engines had to stay within acceptable limits. I told him we watched constantly for overheating and low oil pressure problems. If he did see something wrong, he immediately had to take action to alleviate the problem, even if that meant shutting down an engine. However, being on tow was not a great time to shut the engines down, so he might want to alert me if that happened on his watch. James made us a hot breakfast, which we enjoyed. I stayed at the wheel and ate in the wheelhouse, while James and Laurence ate in the galley. James was a good cook, and this lifted our spirits and gave all of us a second wind.

The next low tide was at 1152 hours. If we arrived before noon, we should be able to set the barge's anchors before the flood tide became a problem. If we were successful in getting the barge anchored on location on this tide, we would then hopefully be ready to dive on the high tide, which was a 25.7 foot tide at 1730 hours. That was what we would be shooting for, but if we didn't have time to anchor the barge before the tide changed, we would have to wait until we had the next ebb tide. Everything stemmed on our arriving on location by low tide.

At 1005 hours, after having figured the speed and location, I called Lowell on the radio and gave him an estimated time of arrival of 1110 hours. He said he'd get a crew busy unlashing the equipment, and they would get ready to set anchors. He commented on the nice weather we were having, and I told him not to jinx us. He laughed and said if the weather changed now, he'd get the brunt of it. I agreed with him wholeheartedly.

When we were getting near the pipeline repair site, I pulled Laurence and James into the wheelhouse and outlined how we would handle the barge during anchoring. I told them we would have to unhook the tow line from the bridle at the shackle, removing it from the barge, and then we would put the barge on our hip. I told them we would do the same as we did in town. Due to the bow of the barge having to be anchored over the pipeline, we had to put the barge on our hip on our port side, so we would be making up to the starboard stern of the barge. I reminded James that we'd need the generator started for the hydraulics to work. He said to give him the word when I was ready, and he'd start the engine.

At 1120 hours we arrived at the northern buoy, which marked the start of the void under the pipeline. I called Lowell on the VHF and told him I would be cutting loose from the barge to put it on the hip. The barge crew would need to pull the tow bridle aboard and then stand by on the starboard stern to catch our tie up lines. Lowell said they were ready. I moved to the flying bridge to run the boat from the upper steering station. I told James to start the generator and to activate the hydraulics. I stopped the tug, and James and Laurence started pulling in the tow line, as the barge drifted toward us. As soon as they had the tow line aboard, the shackle was taken off, and the barge crew hauled the tow bridle aboard the barge. The tow line was flaked out on the deck and stowed. I pulled the tug around the barge to the starboard stern. The bow line was passed to the barge crew and was thrown over a cleat. The bow line was left with a lot of slack in it for the time being. The spring line was then secured to the starboard stern cleat on board the barge and then to the quarter cleat aboard the tug. A stern line was then stretched across the stern of the barge to the port stern cleat. After the spring and stern lines were brought up snug, I signaled James to pick up on the bow winch, which acted as the bow line. He activated the winch, and the bow line was pulled in tight to the barge. This tightened the spring line and the stern line even more. Within a few minutes we had unhooked from the tow line and put the barge on the hip, where we would have control of it. I called Lowell on the radio and told him I was ready. I needed to know where he wanted the barge located. He told me to head up the Inlet and a little west. As I was moving the barge, Lowell was signaling for the anchor on the port bow of the barge to be hung off the front, so it could be dropped on his command. The mooring buoy was also put overboard and secured to the bow cleat of the barge.

I moved the barge to the location Lowell wanted and he then told me to stop the barge forward movement and hold it in place. I stopped the barge and Lowell had the barge crew drop the port bow anchor and mooring buoy. As he let cable out on that anchor, he directed me to move the barge to the east and a little north to set the amidships anchor. After we had moved approximately a hundred yards, Lowell told me to again stop the barge. The amidships anchor and mooring buoy were then dropped. We then continued to the east, where the starboard bow anchor and mooring buoy were dropped. We had set the three bow anchors in less than a half hour. Lowell then directed me to back the barge toward the south. As I backed down on the barge, the winch operators let out cable, allowing the barge to be moved. The amidships anchor was hung and the buoy was tied off. When we reached the location Lowell wanted, he directed the winch operators to hold the bow anchor winches and for me to stop the barge. He then ordered the amidships stern anchor dropped. I then cut loose from the barge. We would have to set the other two anchors with the tug. Lowell said we would set the port stern anchor first. I told James and Laurence we'd be hanging the anchor off the bow winch cable holding it with the pelican hook, a quick release mechanism. I told them to tie the mooring buoy alongside, by securing it with a soft line to the quarter cleat. I eased the bow up to the barge, and Lowell signaled the crane operator to pick the anchor and hang it on the bow of the tug. Laurence had rigged the pelican hook onto the bow anchor cable. James put a choker through the eye on the anchor's stock and back to the pelican hook on the winch. After the tug had the load of the anchor the crane then picked the mooring buoy and set it in the water alongside the tug. Laurence tied it to the quarter cleat with a soft line. As the winch operator slacked off the winch line, I backed away from the barge and then proceeded to the west pulling the cable of the anchor off as I went. When we were in position, Lowell told me to drop the anchor. James hit the quick release on the pelican hook with a hammer and the anchor was dropped. Laurence then cut the mooring buoy loose, and the port stern anchor was in place. I returned to the starboard stern of the barge and the whole procedure was repeated. The SS-18 barge was on location, anchored up, and all had gone smoothly. I was very happy with my crew and the way things had gone on our first time anchoring a barge on location. We worked like a well-oiled machine, even though none of us on the tug had ever had any experience in anchoring a barge.

I called Lowell and asked permission to come alongside. He told me to lay off the barge until he got all the anchor wires tightened up and was satisfied we were in position to dive on the next tide. We stood by for half an hour before Lowell called and told us to come alongside on the starboard side. While we were standing by, I told Laurence and James that someone would always be aboard the tug, when it was tied off to the barge. That way if anything went wrong, someone would be on board to either deal with it or call for assistance.

Lowell told me the tide was changing, and to consider that when I tied off to the barge. As we were moving in, I told the crew we would have to turn the tug around at every slack tide, so we would always have the tide on the bow and not on our square stern. We tied up with the bow to the south facing the flood tide. As soon as we were secure, I told James to shut down the engines and to check the engine room. He also needed to keep his engine room log book up to date. He said he had been keeping it up, but would get the engine hours and time of shutting the engines down entered. I went into the wheelhouse and brought the captain's log up to date, as well.

Lowell came aboard the tug, and said he was very pleased with the way everything had gone. I thanked him and offered him a cup of coffee. He said he'd drink a cup, and we visited in the wheelhouse of the tug, while he enjoyed his coffee. Lowell shared information about a couple other jobs he'd been the barge master on. He said the crew on the tug on those jobs had handled barges on many jobs and we had done just as well as they had done. This was quite a compliment, but I told Lowell it was all because we had professional guidance and direction. He smiled and then said lunch should be ready aboard the barge now. I told the crew to go with Lowell and get something to eat, and then one of them could relieve me and I'd go over. I didn't ever want to leave the tug unmanned alongside the barge, so I decided to stay aboard while the crew chowed down.

After lunch everyone got busy getting the gear ready for the upcoming dive at high tide. The divers would be diving off the bow of the barge, so the tenders were busy moving the hoses and gear close to the bow. The air hose was connected to the dive compressor and stretched to the bow of the barge. The compressor wouldn't be close by, and the engine noise would not be a problem. The communication equipment was brought out of the connex. The radio box was placed on a stand that was made especially for that purpose. The head tender would be signaling the crane operator, so the communication equipment's location was very important. A dive ladder was moved to the bow area, where it could be hung overboard at any time. The pile bucks were gearing up for moving the sandbags to the diver. The bags would be placed under, on, and around the pipeline. It appeared everything would be ready for the dive. It was readily apparent this was a seasoned crew, who had been on these types of jobs many times before.

A winch, which they referred to as an air tugger, was welded to the deck near the middle of the barge at the bow. The air tugger held 300 feet of ½ inch cable. This cable would be pulled off the winch and taken to the sea floor by the diver and fastened to the pipeline. The pallets of sandbags would then be lowered to the ocean floor by the crane. One side of the pallet slings would have a shackle on it that would be placed around the air tugger cable, which would act as a guide when the pallet was lowered down to the diver. The pallet sling, where the shackle was located, would be tied to the pallet enabling the sandbags to be dumped after the opposite side pallet sling was removed. The crane operator would only have to pick up on load to dump the sandbags. Since the diver couldn't see anything, and everything was done by feel, he had to be very careful not to be in a position where the sandbags would hit him when they were dumped. The lead tender would signal the crane operator, after being directed by the diver, to assure no one was injured.

When the tide had slowed enough to put the diver in the water, the dive tenders lowered the ladder into place off the bow of the barge. Scooter was making the first dive and the tenders assisted, as his weight belt, ankle weights, gloves and diving helmet were put on. After everything was checked and was found to be working properly, Scooter went into the water. Jerry lowered the air tugger cable to him, and Scooter moved to the buoy that had been left to mark the area. After reaching the marker buoy cable, he started to descend. Shortly after he reached the bottom, Scooter told Dave he had secured the air tugger line to the pipeline. He would cut the marker buoy loose, as soon as the crew got its buoy aboard the barge. A boat hook was used to bring the marker buoy aboard. Dave told Scooter to release the marker buoy, and in a couple minutes Scooter told them it was free. The marker buoy and cable were pulled aboard. Scooter told Dave to take the slack out of the air tugger cable and to send a pallet of sandbags down. Dave acknowledged and signaled the crew to tighten up on the air tugger. As soon as it was tight, Dave signaled the crane operator, who had a pallet of sandbags hanging on the block, to lower it to the wire. There it would be attached by a shackle. After the shackle was in place, Dave told

Scooter he was lowering the pallet down to him. Scooter acknowledged, said he was clear, and to let him know when it was on the bottom. As soon as the crane operator felt the pallet weight lessen, he nodded at Dave, who told Scooter the pallet was on the bottom. Scooter told Dave he had reached the pallet and was releasing one side of the pallet sling. When the pallet sling was released, and Scooter was clear, he told Dave to pick up on the pallet and dump the sandbags. Dave signaled the crane operator, and he picked up on the block. The first pallet of sandbags had been dumped on the pipeline. Dave told Scooter the bags were dumped and Scooter told Dave he would be checking the bags to see if he would have to rearrange some of them. Dave reported the pallet was on its way to the surface, and Scooter was clear to check the bags. Scooter checked the bags and reported he was happy where they were placed, and to let him know when the next pallet was on the bottom. Dave acknowledged and, when the empty pallet reached the surface, it was disconnected and another full pallet was picked up and rigged to be lowered to the bottom. From time to time Scooter would ask that the tugger cable be slackened, so he could move it down the pipeline. Lowell would move the barge with the anchors, when it was needed. Scooter would sometimes report that he was relocating some of the sandbags, and would tell Dave when he was clear. Dave would wait for Scooter to tell him he was clear, before he would start another pallet down to him. Before any action was taken the diver's safety was taken into consideration.

This routine was repeated again and again until the tide changed and the diver had to be brought off the bottom. Twelve pallets had been put in place on the first dive, and everyone seemed happy with the progress. Dave told Scooter he should get ready to come up, and that they were sending a marker buoy down to him on the air tugger cable. Dave told him, after he received the marker buoy cable, to release the air tugger cable so it could be brought aboard the barge. Jerry attached the marker buoy cable to the air tugger wire, and Dave told Scooter it was on its way to him. As soon as the marker buoy cable was received and released from the air tugger wire, Scooter secured it to the pipeline. He then released the air tugger wire and it was brought aboard. In a couple minutes Scooter reported he was blowing up his suit to come up. Jerry assisted him by pulling him up with the air hose which he coiled on a pallet. Dave told Scooter to be careful not to come up under the barge and to keep his hands above his head. Scooter managed to stay clear of the barge and when he reached the surface he was pulled over to the ladder. He came aboard and his helmet, weight belt, ankle weights and gloves were quickly removed. Scooter was then taken to the connex, where he quickly got out of his diving suit and entered the decompression chamber. Due to the barge being anchored in a stationary position, and because the tide was picking up speed, Scooter was not able to hang off to decompress, as he had on the dive boat. It was imperative he enter the chamber quickly, where the pressure could be brought to the same pressure, as it would be at a depth where he would have hung off in the water.

As the days passed we were very fortunate to get good weather. We didn't miss any tides, and progress went very well. The divers alternated, with one on stand- by, while the other was on the bottom. It took five days to place the sandbags under, around and on top of the pipeline in the area where it was endangered. Eighty-two pallets of sandbags had been used to repair the pipeline. We finished the dive on a high tide of 32.3 on Thursday at 0930 hours. Because it was high tide, we had to wait through the ebb before we could head to town. We could pull the anchors, but then we would have to buck tide for hours, until the tide changed. Bucking into the tide would prevent any headway, and we'd just be burning fuel.

Lowell told me we'd start pulling anchors around 1500 hours, so we could continue to pull all the anchors without stopping. We could then go on tow, immediately following the last anchor being brought aboard. The tide should have slowed enough by that time, allowing us to make some headway. Low tide was at 16:23 hours and was a -3.8 foot tide. A lot of water would be moving on the flood tide, and we should make good time towing the barge to town. Making it to the Active Diver's yard by high tide at 2200 hours should not be of major concern barring any problems. The tide was a 30.5 foot tide and we should be able to tie up to the face of the dock any time after 2030 hours. I told Laurence and James what was planned, and how we would be pulling the anchors when Lowell was ready. We had not needed to relocate any anchors after we'd anchored on location, so picking the anchors would be new to us. I had it all planned out in my mind, but told the crew I'd direct them as we progressed.

At 1445 hours I told James to start the main engines and the generator and to activate the hydraulics. We would then stand by, until Lowell was ready to pull the anchors. The tide was still ebbing and was moving at approximately 6-7 mph. By the time we had all the anchors pulled, the tide would have slowed considerably. The weather was calm, and the forecast called for it to continue Lowell had the barge crew get everything ready for travel. He had decided not to secure everything to the extreme, as we had before we'd left Anchorage, due to the good conditions. He would secure the crane boom by hooking to the two cleats opposite one another on the stern, but didn't feel it was necessary to cross tie the boom in the middle or on the counterweight.

At 1510 hours Lowell called me on the radio and told me we would start picking the anchors. We cut loose from the barge, and I pulled the bow of the tug up to the port anchor mooring buoy. I had instructed James and Laurence to grab the eye of the cable on top of the buoy and to fasten it to the bow winch, by using the pelican hook that was already shackled to the winch cable. After the eye of the cable was hooked up, I directed them to pick up on the winch. The cable pulled through the buoy, while it stayed floating in the water. As soon as the anchor was lifted off the ocean floor, I called Lowell and told him I was clear of the bottom. He directed the winch operator aboard the barge to pull in the port bow anchor. I placed the tug's engines in slow reverse and held a strain, as we were pulled to the port bow of the barge. As soon as the anchor was brought up out of the water and stopped at the pulley, I signaled the tug crew to reverse the bow winch, while I backed the tug away from the barge. The mooring buoy cable was unhooked from the winch, freeing the buoy. The cranes picking hook was swung over the mooring buoy, and I pulled the boat alongside, where James could hook it to the buoy. The crane operator then lifted it aboard the barge. Lowell then directed us to pick the starboard bow anchor. We pulled up to the starboard bow mooring buoy and followed the same routine for picking that buoy, as we had on the port bow. The three stern anchors were also brought aboard, using the same technique. Each time we were underway to pick another anchor, Lowell would have the crane operator lift the anchor, we had just picked, out of the water and onto the barge.

Following the stern anchors being picked, the amidships bow anchor was the only anchor left securing the barge. Lowell told me to get the tugs tow line hooked up, and he would pull the last anchor with the barge's winch and wouldn't need the assistance of the tug. By doing it this way, I would be ready to go on tow, as soon as he had the bow anchor and mooring buoy aboard the barge. I pulled around to the port bow of the barge and tied alongside with the tug facing the south, toward the stern of the barge. The barge crew handed down the bridle line, and Laurence and James shackled the tow line to it. We were ready to go on tow as soon as Lowell raised the bow anchor and mooring buoy. Lowell signaled the winch operator to come up on the anchor cable, and the barge was pulled up over the anchor. It was then picked off the bottom and brought to the surface with the anchor winch. The crane was then swung around and hooked to the anchor, and was brought aboard the barge. The mooring buoy was then picked and brought aboard. Lowell came on the radio and told me to take them to town. He complimented us over the radio, telling us we did a great job.

I told the tug crew to cut the boat loose from the barge and then stand by to let out the tow line. After I was free of the barge, I swung the boat around and they fed out the tow line, until I told them to tie it off. The barge was approximately 150 feet behind us, and I increased the RPM's bringing the tow line tight. The barge swung in behind the tug, and I added some throttle. When we got underway the tide had nearly come to a standstill. Our timing could not have been better, as the tide was just changing, and we would be riding the flood all the way to Anchorage. I looked at my watch, and it was 1640 hours. I told James to shut down the generator and to check the engine room. I left the bridge and went below to the wheelhouse, where I would run the boat and fill out my captain's log.

When Laurence and James joined me in the wheelhouse, I told them I had never worked with a better crew. They had done everything that had been asked of them, and had done it well, without any complaints. I told them I'd be proud to ship with either of them at any time. They said they had learned a great deal, and that they enjoyed working with me. They complimented me, as well, alluding to the fact that I was the best skipper they had ever had. They failed to mention that I was the only skipper they had ever had.

I checked the gauges, synchronized the engines at 2800 RPM, and checked my heading. I was hoping we would get the barge and crew home without any problems. The way everything had worked out seemed too good to be true. I'm not superstitious, but I couldn't help but worry a little.

At 2050 hours I slowed the tug down and told James and Laurence to stand by to take in the tow line. I told them we would be taking the barge on the hip on the port bow. This would enable us to lay the barge alongside the face of the Active Diver's dock with its stern facing south. I told James to start the generator and to again turn on the hydraulics. As soon as the generator was running, I stopped the tug and backed into the tow line. The crew picked up the slack and secured the tow line loosely to the port stern quarter bit. This would enable me to maneuver the boat without the line interfering, and insured it would not get fouled in a propeller. As soon as this was done, we put the barge on our hip on its port side. Lowell had the crew on deck catching our lines, and we tied off without any problem. I turned the barge toward the Active Diver's yard, and eased it in alongside the face of the dock. Gene was on shore and caught the tie up lines, as the barge crew threw them to him. In a few minutes the barge was secured to the dock, and I told the tug crew to loosen the lines on the tug, but to leave them tied to the barge. I directed James to shut down all the engines and to fill out his engine room log. He headed to the engine room, and I went below to the wheelhouse to bring my captain's log up to date.

After everything was secured on board the boat, Laurence, James and I went ashore. Lowell was talking to Gene, and we stopped to say hi. Gene said he heard everything went very well, and that the oil company would be very happy with the job we'd done. I told Gene I hoped all our future jobs went as well as this one. I told him it was all due to the great leadership Lowell had provided. Lowell smiled and just shook his head. Gene told me Ted had mentioned we would have to go back out next week and start checking the rest of the pipeline south from the repair location. I told Gene we'd left a marker buoy at the south end of the repaired section, so we wouldn't have a problem finding our starting point. He told us to go home, and he would see us at 0800 hours on Monday. We didn't argue and left the yard heading to our homes.

On Tuesday of the next week, James and I were once again headed down the Inlet to check for any additional problems on the oil pipeline. It took the next two and a half weeks to walk the rest of the pipeline, which went ashore near the East Foreland. We didn't find any major problems that endangered the safety of the line.

During the rest of the season, I ran the Active Diver on numerous diving jobs on different pipelines and at a number of the oil platforms. On one job the divers checked the sub-structures and the legs of three of the platforms and found some electrolysis problems. As an experiment, the next season, we built a number of anodes in Active Diver's yard and then placed them completely around one of the platforms, hoping to fight off the electrolysis problems. We hooked up electrical wires between the anodes and kept a 12 volt charge that surrounded the platform. This was done in hopes the electrolysis problems would be drawn to the softer metals of the anodes and not continue damaging the platforms, by eating away at the metal structures. With these and other jobs, James and I were kept very busy during the summer months, and spent a lot of time on the water and away from our families.

Ann and my decision to move to Anchorage was somewhat of a double-edged sword. We were definitely making more money, but it cost us because I was away from home a great deal of the time. We had decided to move to Anchorage to rise above the poverty level, but we also wanted to be together. We soon realized everything has its price, and we would have to endure our being apart to get ahead financially. We both agreed we had made the right decision, and we could continue this way for a couple seasons.

When the weather started to cool off, we pulled the two boats and winterized them. I was kept busy with maintenance on the two barges and the two boats up until December. Pulling maintenance became a forty hour per week job, and I was able to be home every night and every weekend. We made plans for every weekend and spent a lot of quality time with the Smiths. I would be called back to work in March.

Ann and I continued to feel good about our decision to move to Anchorage. Donica liked school and was making new friends every day. We traveled to Seldovia for Christmas to see family and friends and to relieve our homesickness. Life was great at the Anderson home.

The next year I continued to work for Active Diver's, Inc. They eventually sold out to Oceaneering International, a firm out of Texas. I was then hired on with Oceaneering, doing the same jobs I had been doing for Active Divers, but ranging out a little further on a couple occasions. I towed the SS-18 barge to Juneau, where we worked for six weeks in Taku Inlet, burying power cables to -50 feet on the Snadisham power project. I also towed a barge to Valdez for a job.

My life has really been one adventure after another, and I have many more stories that I think you might find interesting. At this point I think I will wait to share them with you in future writings. I hope I've gained your interest enough, so you will want to explore what happened as my exciting life experiences continued.

PRUDHOE BAY

The year was 1977 and I was employed as a heavy equipment operator for Frontier Rock & Sand, located on the North Slope of Alaska near Prudhoe Bay. I'd been employed with them since the spring of 1976 and I was a heavy equipment operator and operated graders, dozers and loaders, depending on what was needed on any given contract. I worked the day shift from 6:00 a.m. to 6:00 p.m., seven days a week. My work schedule was 9 weeks on the North Slope then 2 weeks off for R&R. The company flew me back and forth to and from my home in Anchorage. Frontier's camp was located inland in the Prudhoe Bay area and all the equipment they owned was kept at the main camp until needed to fulfill a contract.

On an early July morning in 1977 Pete Peterson, the foramen for Frontier, called me into his office and told me he wanted me to take a D-7 Caterpillar to the East dock at Prudhoe Bay and meet with Jim Adams of Adams Barge Company. Pete said a large pile of material had been hauled out to Niakuk Island, in the middle of Prudhoe Bay, via an ice road during the winter, and they needed to build a drill pad on the island using that material. The oil company wanted to put a drill rig on the island and drill for oil. Pete said he was sending a D-7 Caterpillar because the machine had to be hauled out to the island and the LCM 6, the landing craft they had to haul it, was too small to haul anything larger. Pete said the gravel would still be frozen and I would have to corner bit it out. This meant I would have to utilize the corner of the blade to break the material out of the pile. He said after the material was broken away from the pile, it would have to be run over with the dozer to break it up enough so it could be used for fill material. Pete told me a driver with a low boy trailer was waiting for me to load the tractor and haul it to the East Dock at Prudhoe Bay. He also told me to take a pickup and follow the low boy so I would have transportation back to camp after I took the Cat to the island. When I asked him how I would be getting fuel for the dozer, he said a tanker truck with 2500 gallons of fuel had also been taken to the island over the ice road, so fueling the Cat shouldn't be a problem. Pete said I would be flying back and forth every day on a helicopter from Prudhoe Bay airstrip and I should plan for the job to take at least three weeks if not a little longer. He said it was hard to figure how long the job would take due to our having to work with the frozen material. I told him I'd get it done and I left his office. I packed a lunch and then located the truck driver who would be hauling the Cat. He had already backed the lowboy up to the loading ramp so I jumped aboard the Cat and loaded it on the trailer. We then secured the load with a number of chains and chain binders. With the load secured we headed for Prudhoe Bay. I followed the load in a company rig.

Jim Adams, of Adams Barge Company, was waiting for us at the East Dock when we arrived. I introduced both myself and the truck driver to him and Jim shook our hands. I found Jim to be very outgoing and friendly and was very likeable right from the start. He was jovial, with a great sense of humor and a great attitude.

Jim told me he had the landing craft ready to load and that it was pulled up to the beach, near the Dock, with the gate down. I ask him about the stage of the tide and he said the tide really wasn't a big factor this far north and that the wind pretty much dictated the water's depth. The West wind increased the water's depth while the East wind sucked the water out of the Bay. At present the wind was calm but Jim said there was enough water to get pretty near the Island. He said the deepest point in

Prudhoe Bay was around nine (9) feet. He also shared that we couldn't get all the way to the Island but he'd ease the boat ahead as far as he could and when the boat went aground I'd have to walk the Cat off the boat ramp and then through the water the rest of the way to the Island. Because there was no way of knowing the depth of the water, from where the boat went aground and the Island, Jim said he would put a couple of his guys in a skiff ahead of the Cat so they could keep checking the depth as I walked the tractor through the water to the Island.

We unhooked the chains we'd used to secure the dozer and I jumped aboard and backed it off the lowboy. The driver was already in position after having backed the lowboy up to the off-loading ramp. I walked the dozer off the lowboy and down to the landing craft. The truck driver headed back to Frontier's base camp with the tractor/trailer after the dozer had been offloaded.

After turning it around, I backed the Cat up the ramp and aboard the boat. One of Jim's deckhand jumped up on the canopy of the Cat with a short line tied to a buoy, and tied the line to the picking eye on top of the Cat's canopy. Everyone was laughing when Jim said they didn't want to lose a tractor if the water got too deep but operators were a dime a dozen. Everyone got a big kick out of this and I again found myself enjoying Jim's sense of humor.

After backing off the beach with the landing craft and getting underway to Niakuk Island, Jim and I got better acquainted. I told him of my previous sailing experiences including my salmon and crab fishing, tug and dive boat operations in, and around, Cook Inlet and the two barges I had towed to Juneau and Valdez. Jim said he was always looking for a good skipper and if something came up did I think I would be interested in running a boat for him? I told him it was all dependent on what I had going at the time. We exchanged contact information and promised we would stay in touch with one another.

We continued moving slowly toward Niakuk Island knowing the landing craft would run aground at any moment. When we did touch bottom with the boat, Jim told me that was as far as he could go and it was time for me to walk the dozer off the boat and through the water to the Island. He cautioned me saying I shouldn't hesitate once I started of the ramp of the boat because the angle created by offloading would most probably dip my radiator fan under water which, in turn, would throw water everywhere. He said the quicker I get off the ramp the sooner the Cat would level out and the fan would come out of the water, stopping the shower I would be getting. He did comment something about a shower most likely wouldn't hurt anyway. Jim was a character and spontaneous and it seemed he rarely missed an opportunity if he could say something humorous.

I got ready to walk the tractor off the boat while Jim's crew lowered the bow ramp. Jim then told his two crew members to take the skiff and stay ahead of the Cat, checking the depth of the water ever few feet. He said we didn't want to walk the Cat into a deeper hole than it could handle. He again referenced the buoy on top of he Cat and said at least if it happened they would be able to salvage the tractor if not it's driver. Again, there were laughs all around.

I started walking the Cat off the ramp of the boat and as soon as it broke over the bow the radiator fan did dip under water and it looked as if a geyser had erupted off the front of the Cat. I gave the dozer more throttle, which only increased the spraying water, but, by doing so, I quickly walked the tractor ahead, which brought the Cat back to a level plane, stopping the unwanted shower.

The dozer's tracks were now invisible under water and I found it really strange to be walking the Cat to the Island without being able to see the tracks or the terrain that lay ahead. I couldn't tell if I was about to get into deeper water or not. I was very alert to any angle changes in the position of the Caterpillar as I eased my way forward toward the Island. The two deckhands were staying ahead of me and were checking the depth of the water every few feet with an oar. They had been directed to make me aware of any increase in the depth. This did give me some comfort but I was definitely experiencing some anxiety, not being able to see my tracks or the ground ahead of me. I had never been in any circumstance like this before and I can't say I really was enjoying it too much.

Even though it took approximately 20 minutes to reach the Island, it seemed like forever. That was one of the longest 20 minutes of my entire life. Fortunately, we were able to get to the Island without any problems.

After I made it to the Island, I parked the dozer and shut it down. I then joined the two deckhands in the skiff and we returned to the landing craft. Since the dozer was no longer weighing the boat down, it was floating high again and Jim had eased ahead within a hundred yards of the Island.

The two deckhands and I boarded the landing craft after tying the skiff to the stern and we then got underway back to the East Dock. Jim and I visited some more and got better acquainted on our return trip. He said he owned a couple other boats and worked mostly in the Artic. He said he was serious about possibly needing a skipper sometime and I again told him it all depended on what I was doing when he called but I did tell him I was very happy at Frontier Rock & Sand. They had treated me well and I was making good money. Jim said he also paid quite well but never really knew year to year how busy he'd be because everything was done under a contract, following the bid process. I told him to call if something came up and we'd talk and he told me not to be surprised if I heard from him.

We arrived at the East Dock and Jim invited me to lunch at a diner nearby. We enjoyed a lunch together and continued getting better acquainted. I really enjoyed his company. I found him to be a sincere, hard-working man with a great sense of humor with, what I defined as an honest and sincere approach. I felt I would really enjoy working for him.

For the next three and one-half weeks I flew back and forth to Niakuk Island in a helicopter and built a pad for the oil company. There were a number of days the weather would keep us from landing on the Island and we would have to return to the airport and then try again in a couple hours. A few of those flights became harrowing experiences and, on a couple occasions, I felt the helicopter should never have left the ground. Fortunately we never did have any mishaps.

The gravel they had stock piled was thawed approximately one foot down and then was frozen solid making it very difficult to cut out using the corner bit of the Caterpillar blade. After I was able to corner bit it out, I did find it pretty easily broken up when I ran over it with the dozer. Little by little the pad did take shape but I think Pete Peterson was wondering if I was ever going to finish the job. On four or five occasions representatives from the oil company flew in to check on my progress.

They took into consideration the frozen material and they realized it was no easy task bringing the pad up to grade. Upon completion Pete Peterson and the oil company representatives did an inspection and everyone was satisfied with the job I'd done.

After finishing the job Pete told me to leave the D-7 Caterpillar on the Island and said they would haul it off over an ice road that would be built during the winter. I had no argument with that, not wanting to have to walk the dozer back through the water and aboard the landing craft again. I can only imagine the geyser I would create trying to back the tractor up the landing craft ramp.

I continued to work through the winter and into the spring for Frontier Rock & Sand. I ran a grader for a few weeks when we were building an ice road and operated loaders and Caterpillars on a couple road jobs and then again, when we were building two on-shore oil pads. I was kept to the 9 weeks on and 2 weeks off schedule.

In the second week of May of 1978, while I was home on my two-week R&R, that Jim Adams called me and told me he had been given a contract for the summer months which consisted of his tug boat working out of Prudhoe Bay with a seismic crew from Texas. He said he needed a captain for the summer months to run his boat, the Point Barrow. He said the tug would be catering to and, more or less babysitting, a 6-man seismograph crew for a couple months, or until the ice conditions ran them off the water. The job would include cooking one meal a day for the crew and escorting then from Prudhoe Bay and then back to Prudhoe Bay on a daily basis. The tug would be accompanying their seismograph boat to many different locations where they would be doing seismograph work. The seismic crew would be operating a catamaran type vessel named the Seisjet. Jim said it was a 58-foot aluminum boat powered with twin 871 GMC diesels and it had two 8" jet units for propulsion, instead of shafts and propellers. The boat had been built in Anchorage, he said, in four sections, then hauled on tractor trailer trucks to Prudhoe Bay where the boat was then offloaded and assembly had gotten underway. They had to have the boat ready for the upcoming season. Jim said the Seisjet had never been tested, because it had never been completely assembled before. They had partially assembled it in Anchorage when building it but it was never assembled to the point where it could be launched. They would have to wait until the ice left Prudhoe Bay before they could launch it and do the necessary sea trials. Jim said he had to be totally honest with me and said no one on board the Seisjet would have any previous sailing experience. He said he needed someone to skipper the Point Barrow who could look out for the Texas crew. He said he'd put a cook/deckhand/engineer combination on board the Point Barrow with me and I would only be responsible for running the boat and doing what was necessary to assist the crew on the Seisjet. He did say I would possibly need to assist in some light maintenance to the Point Barrow from time to time but, after the tug was launched, that would only consist of minimal maintenance when the engineer needed assistance. We discussed wages and Jim made me a very attractive offer. I asked when I would be needed and he said we would need to get to Prudhoe Bay around the end of May or the first week in June, so we could have the tug ready for launching when the ice went out. He said the boat was up on dry dock at this time and needed the hull prepped and painted and zincs welded on. It also needed some light mechanical work done but Jim said that work would be done by a diesel mechanic. I told him I'd talk it over with my wife and we'd decide and I'd get back to him in a couple days. Jim said he really needed to know as soon as possible so he would know what he would have to do to man the tug. I agreed to call him back within two days with an answer. He said that would be fine and he'd be waiting for my call but really hoped I'd be interested in taking the job. He said he thought we'd work great together.

After getting off the phone with Jim, I told my wife, Ann, about his offer and the fact that, if I took the job, I'd be gone most all of the summer months. She said I was away 9 weeks anyway and then only home for 2 weeks so this wouldn't be all that much different. The money was quite a bit better than I'd been making at Frontier and it was only for the summer, she said. She assured me she and our daughter, Donica, had been making our okay with me gone and this increase in pay could help us tremendously. She said we could possibly even pay off the mobile home we were buying. I was surprised that she wasn't fighting the idea of my taking the job because she often voiced that she was tired of me being gone and wished I could find a job close by so I could stay home. At the same time, even though surprised, I felt proud that she was taking such a lead role in making this decision. It was really out of context for her to take such a stance when making such an important decision as this. Always before, when an important family decision was discussed, she would always say she'd go along with what ever I decided so; I was totally shocked by her response. With her input, and her logic, it was decided I would take the job for the summer. I mentioned I'd have to call Pete Peterson with Frontier and tell him I wanted to take the summer off and hopefully he'd have a job for me come winter. Ann, always the eternal optimist, told me if not at Frontier Rock & Sand, I'd find work somewhere. I was pleased she had so much faith in me but I still was concerned about future employment and I really didn't share her optimism.

I called Pete Peterson and told him I had a job opportunity that would last only for the summer months and would like to take that time off and possibly come back to work for Frontier the next winter. Pete told me he couldn't promise me a job later if I did quit but said, if he had an opening, he would put me back to work. I told him I would probably be touching base with him in the fall and I thanked him and told him I had enjoyed working for him and we then said our goodbyes.

After getting off the phone with Pete I called Jim Adams and told him I would like to take the job as skipper on the Point Barrow, if it was still open. He said he was very pleased to hear this and told me he'd be in touch with me in a week or so to let me know when we'd be heading to Prudhoe Bay and what I would need to take with me. He told me it'd most probably be near the end of the month, or the first of June, before we left for the North Slope. He said he had a number of loose ends he had to take care of but would get back to me as soon as he could put together a schedule.

I told Ann we had until around the end of the month before I would be headed back to the Slope so we should go to Seldovia for a quick visit before I left for the summer. Her eyes lit up and I knew she was all for that so she started getting together what we'd need for the trip. Donica had just finished her school year and was off for summer vacation so the timing couldn't have been better.

After we decided we would take a short trip to Seldovia I called Jim Adams back and told him of our plans and gave him a telephone number in Seldovia where I could be reached. He told me I would have at least a couple weeks, if not a little longer, so I should go and enjoy myself while I had time.

We loaded the pickup and the next morning we were on the road to Homer. We would fly to Seldovia from Homer on Cook Inlet Airlines. My wife and daughter were both tickled we were going back home for a short visit. Ann's mother, two sisters and her extended family all lived in, or around, Seldovia. Ann had lived her entire life in Seldovia until I moved her and Donica to Anchorage in 1974. Donica had Aunts, Uncles, cousins and lots of friends in Seldovia so she could hardly wait to get back, to what she called, home. We had moved to Anchorage when she was 5 years old so, as far as she was concerned, Seldovia was home.

We stayed in Seldovia for two weeks and had a wonderful visit but I felt it was time we headed back to Anchorage even though I had not heard from Jim Adams.

We were back in Anchorage for three days before I received a call from Jim and he told me we'd leave for Prudhoe Bay around June 5th, which was still better than a week away. He said I should bring warm clothes, rain gear, a good sleeping bag, a warm coat and whatever I would need for toiletries. He said we'd be taking showers at a bathhouse near Prudhoe Bay's East Dock and all towels and wash cloths would be provided but if I needed a certain shampoo or soap I should bring it with me. Jim said we'd be living aboard the Point Barrow while we worked on it getting it ready to launch. He said he'd get back to me with a departure time from Anchorage as soon as he had it confirmed. I thanked him and told him I'd get everything together and would be ready to go when he called. Jim said he looked forward to the summer and to working with me. Before he then hung up he told me he'd be calling when he was sure of the departure time. After I got off the phone, I shared the information with Ann.

We started packing everything we thought I'd need for the summer. We went shopping and I picked up a warm work coat and some new blue jeans. Donica kept trying to persuade us to buy a number of items that I wouldn't need but she, like her mother, loved to shop and she was really enjoying it. If memory serves, I think she may have come out pretty well on that shopping trip.

Jim called me on the 29th day of May and told me we were confirmed on the 1:00 p.m. flight on Alaska Airlines to Prudhoe Bay on June 5th. I told him I'd meet him at the airport around 11:30 a.m. if that would work for him. He said that would be fine.

For the next week I took Ann and Donica out to movies, a couple dinners and out to lunch on a number of occasions. I think I felt a little guilty leaving them for the summer but hopefully it would pay off in the end and we'll benefit from being apart.

On the morning of June 5th, I took a cab to the airport and met Jim near the Alaska Airlines ticket counter. He had taken care of all the arrangements and had a ticket ready for me. I checked my bags and Jim and I walked to the departure gate.

When we reached Prudhoe Bay the sun was shinning and if felt warm out. We didn't have a thermometer so we didn't know what the temperature really was but Jim guessed it to be around 40 degrees. Jim introduced me to a man named Bob, who was waiting for us when we arrived. After getting out luggage we loaded our gear into a Ford pickup and drove to the East Dock at Prudhoe Bay where the Point Barrow was up on dry dock.

Jim had described the tug to me on the flight up from Anchorage so I wasn't too surprised when I observed a landing craft which had been converted to a tug boat. The boat was 58 feet long what a flat bottom. Two shafts and propellers were in half tunnels with the rudders directly behind them. The boat's steel hull was in rough condition and definitely needed cleaned up and painted. It appeared it had been years since it had been touched. I could see why we needed to come up early. It was going to take a great deal of time to get the boat ready to launch.

Further inspection of the tug revealed the forward cargo hold had been decked over and living quarters had been built below deck. Above deck a galley with all the necessary appliances was in pretty good shape inside the cabin. It had a table with bench seats which would work well feeding the seismic crew. A ladder in the starboard corner of the galley accessed the wheelhouse and a ladder in the port side of the galley accessed the lower deck, where the engine room and living quarters were located. A lot of thought had gone into the planning when the boat was converted from a landing craft to a tug. Two 671 GMC diesels powered the boat and the engine room was accessed through a hatch on the bulkhead that separated the engine room from the living quarters.

I checked out the wheelhouse and found a 32-mile Decca radar with an insulated cover over it. Two VHF radios, and a depth finder, where found packed in insulated boxes. I installed the radios and the depth finder in their respective brackets left in place when the instruments were stored. An amidships steering wheel, with a large compass located just ahead of the helm, was observed. This far north a compass is, more or less, just added weight because we were too close to the North Pole for it to be anywhere close to accurate. Dual clutch and throttle controls were to the right of the steering wheel. There was a single bunk attached to the back wall of the wheelhouse.

On the front deck a winch had been added for anchoring purposes and a below deck water tank had been added, in the bow. This would be used as a ballast tank when we needed to raise the propellers and rudders a little higher off the bottom. By adding weight to the bow of a boat the stern can be raised a matter of inches which, in shallow areas, could mean the difference of whether you could navigate the area or not. The boat had been built very well when it was transformed from a landing craft into a tug.

Jim came to the wheelhouse and asked me if I thought I could handle the boat. I told him if we can keep it running I could handle the boat. I told him I didn't see any problem at this point. He said he certainly hadn't lost any sleep worrying about that.

It was nearly 6:00 p.m. when Jim told Bob and I it was dinnertime. We went to a small diner located near the East Dock where we had a nice home cooked meal of beef roast, potatoes and vegetables. For desert some cherry cheese cake hit the spot.

We returned to the Point Barrow and made up our bunks and got settled in. Jim said we'd start work the following morning grinding the rust off the hull and getting it ready for paint and zinc plates.

Jim started an air-cooled Lister diesel engine which ran a 4 KW generator. The boat was set up with electric heat and Jim said we'd run the generator when we needed heat or lighting. In the lower deck of the tug it was dark and lighting was definitely needed.

We visited for a couple hours and then headed for our bunks. Morning would come early and we had a lot of work to do. Jim told me he'd talked to Bob, the man who picked us up at the airport, and he had agreed to work on the tug for the summer as the deckhand/engineer/cook combination. He said Bob was a good hand and that he had worked for Jim on previous contracts and was very capable of covering all three aspects of the job.

The next morning, we rolled out at 5:00 a.m. and went for breakfast at the diner where we'd had dinner the previous evening. We would get to know the owners of the diner very well before the summer was over. We would take many of our meals at the diner when we were moored at the East Dock.

For the next 10 days we were working on the boat. We were cleaning the boat inside as well as grinding, sanding and prepping the hull for painting. We were working 10 to 12-hour days. The hull of the tug was in pretty tough shape when we started on it. When it was ready for paint Jim called a man asking that he come and weld the zincs on the hull prior to us painting it. A mechanic had been working in the engine room and the stuffing boxes, the gear reductions and the engines had all been gone through to insure they were ready for the upcoming season. The mechanic told Jim everything looked good and he didn't foresee any major problems. Jim was happy to get the positive report. The mechanic said he'd changed oil and oil filters, as well as fuel filters, on all the engines, which included the light plant.

The crew assembling the Seisjet was getting close to having the boat ready to launch and were busy checking the boat over to make sure they hadn't overlooked anything. They were anxious for the ice to go out of Prudhoe Bay so they could launch the boat and do some sea trials. Jim told us, if these temperatures held, the waterways most probably would be free of ice and navigable within a week or so. The seismic crew from Texas had not yet arrived at Prudhoe Bay but was due to arrive any day now. They too had to get all their gear and equipment ready by the time the ice went out. They needed to be able to start collecting data as soon as possible, due to the short season, the large area they had to cover and before the ice again made navigating these waters impossible.

I asked Jim what the Seisjet was contracted to do this summer. He said they were hired to record seismic readings in areas pre-selected by the oil companies. He said the Seisjet crew would be towing a mile-long cable, which would be stored on a spool on the deck of the boat, and they would be detonating explosive charges over the pre-selected areas. He said the cable housed a number of different sensors throughout its span which would send signals to instruments aboard the Seisjet which the cable would be connected to aboard the Seisjet. Those instruments would record the information generated by the shock wave from the blast, and print out its findings on a graft. The shock waves reached deep below the earth's surface and scientist could determine, through the printouts, the different types and configurations of the rock and soil materials at all different depths. They could then determine, from the rock configurations and other data recorded on the grafts, where oil could most likely be located. This sounded very interesting to me and I was anxious to see the operation in action.

The next morning a man towing a welder arrived bright and early to weld the zinc plates on the hull of the tug. It took him most of the morning to weld all the zincs in place. The zincs would greatly reduce and damage caused by electrolysis, which is generated when a metal hull moves through salt water. The zincs keep the electrolysis from eating up the metal hull of the boat. With the zinc plates being the softer of the two metals, the electrolysis would be drawn to them instead of the boat's hull.

After the welder had finished welding the zincs on the hull, we started applying a primer coat of paint. We had the primer coat on the boat's hull before we quit working that evening. We were applying it with paint rollers and the paint went on quickly. We hoped to have the finish coat on the hill by the evening of the next day. Good weather had held and we weren't having to deal with any rain or cold temperatures that would keep us from painting.

The next morning, we got up early and got breakfast out of the way then went to work applying the black finish coat of paint on the hull. We had the finish coat completed by 3:30 p.m. and Jim said he was pleased with the way the paint job had turned out. I asked if it was too early in our relationship to ask for a bonus. He smiled and, shaking his head, he affirmed it was way too early for that. After inspecting the paint job, Jim decided to apply a second coat of paint on the hull. He said it could use the paint and he had enough to cover a second coat, so, with no time frame limitations, he decided we'd roll another coat on.

The Point Barrow was nearly ready to launch and Jim said the ice had receded enough that we had sufficient water to launch without any problem but he thought we should wait a few days to make sure the temperature didn't drop and to let the paint set up. He said the Seisjet crew wasn't even here yet and they had a lot of work to do to ready their vessel so we weren't in a big hurry. Jim said it felt good to be ahead of the game, for a change, and not have to always be playing catch-up.

For the next few days, we painted and tinkered with the boat, fixing little things and doing some general cleanup. On the second day, after we had finished painting the Point Barrow's hull, he Seisjet crew finally arrived from Texas. They immediately went to work readying the Seisjet for launching. With the boat assembly crew, and the Texas seismograph crew working together to ready it for launching, it wouldn't take too long to have the Seisjet up and ready. From our perspective it appeared the two crews were in one another's way, but the work continued. Even though they were not organized they seemed to be making great progress and it appeared they would be ready to launch within a couple days.

The weather had continued to stay above freezing and the west wind started to blow, causing the ice in Prudhoe Bay to recede more and more. Jim told us this was a good sign and we should be free of ice by the end of June. We would be able to get in a good couple month of work before we would have to deal with any icing conditions again, he said.

Jim told us he was scheduling a time to launch the Point Barrow the next day. He said he wanted to get the tug in the water to insure we would not interfere with the Seisjet's plans and he wanted to have the Point Barrow ready and waiting when the Seisjet was ready to go to work. Jim said enough ice had left the Bay so we could launch the boat and do out sea trials without any problems. I could see Jim was one to thoroughly cover all angles and he wanted nothing left to chance. With the Point Barrow setting for months on dry dock, he wanted to be sure there were no unforeseen problems that would surface and hold up the job once the Seisjet was ready to go.

The following morning, at 10:00 a.m. the crane operator and a rigger arrived to launch the Point Barrow. We had everything ready to go and the crane was walked over next to the tug. A spreader bar, with four rigging slings, was attached to two 12" wide nylon straps. The nylon straps would be placed under the Point Barrow's hull, one in the bow and one in the stern. The crane operator will then lift the boat and, holding it in the air, will walk it down near the dock and set it in the water. One end of both nylon straps would then be released and the crane operator would lift the rigging clear of the boat.

Everything went as planned and the Point Barrow was launched without incident and appeared to be floating high. The nylon straps on the boat's starboard side were released and the rigging was lifted and the crane operator walked the crane back up near the Seisjet.

As soon as the tug was lowered into the water it was tied to the boat float. Bob and I went below deck to make sure there were no leaks. We checked the bilge, the stuffing boxes on both engines, both rudder shafts and the lazarette. No leaks were found and, thus far, everything seemed to be going as planned.

Jim came aboard and asked if I wanted to get the feel of the boat. I said sure and Jim told Bob to start both main engines. Jim said he wanted me to run the boat for a couple hours to get the feel of it and to check it for any problems that we may have overlooked. After the engines had been started and were up to temperature, I told Bob to throw off the mooring lines. The ice had receded to the point where it would not be an obstacle during the sea trials.

Jim, Bob and I took the boat out in the middle of Prudhoe Bay and I put it through a number of maneuvers, checking the steering and the engines. I found the boat handled well but reacted a little slower to the helm than most of the boats I'd operated in the past. It was not a problem but would take some getting used to. I turned on the two VHF radios, the depth finder and the radar. One by one I checked each of the electronics and found all to be in good working order. It appeared the Point Barrow was ready to go to work. All we needed to do was take on fuel, fresh water and stock up with whatever groceries would be needed to feed the Texas crew and ourselves.

The next morning, we took on fuel and supplies and then were left anxiously waiting for the Seisjet to be launched and get her sea trials out of the way. The west wind continued to blow and, with the mild temperatures, the ice was leaving the Bay rapidly. Jim said we could navigate the Bay without a problem now but we still would most likely have to dodge ice bergs when traveling outside Prudhoe Bay where the Seisjet would be collecting their data.

Jim took out a chart and showed me the large area where the Texas crew would be working throughout the summer. The location of the on-shore oil drill rigs, surrounding the area, had been drawn onto the chart. Jim told me the land mass was so flat the radar could not get a return signal so we would have to use the radar signals off the oil drill rigs as our reference points. They were high enough off the ground to send a return signal back to the radar. This was great information for me in that I had never been in a terrain that didn't bounce back a return signal when I was navigating utilizing a radar. The way Jim explained it, while referencing the chart, made navigating the area quite simple. He did caution me however, saying I should always know my direction of travel in case the radar failed. With no radar readings, and the compass not functional this far north, knowing your direction of travel may play a huge role in your getting back into Prudhoe Bay from off shore. On some of the trips we most likely will be too far out to be able to see the land mass, because of its low profile, and also possibly too far offshore to get a radar reading off an oil rig. But, Jim said, if you are sure of the direction you need to go you can close the distance and the land mass, or radar readings, will come into view after a time. He said I should use the wind direction, and any other references I might have, when determining the direction we would need to travel to get back to Prudhoe Bay, or close enough to get a radar reading. Jim said he hoped we didn't have any situations like this but it had happened to him in the past and he thought it was worth mentioning. I thanked him telling him this is certainly different from where I had learned about navigating.

It was another two days before the Seisjet was ready to be launched. The same crane operator responded who had launched the tug, and he launched the Seisjet without incident. The boat was put in the water and the crane was again moved back away from the waterfront.

The Seisjet crew checked the boat for leaks and, before long, we heard them start the two main engines. With the boat being powered with jet units instead of props and rudders, and with the engine exhausts being routed through the jet unit, the boat was quite noisy. It was more readily noticed where you were positioned behind the vessel. The Point Barrow was tied directly behind the Seisjet and we quickly noticed how loud the two 871 GMC diesel engines were.

For the next two days the Seisjet was busy doing sea trials around Prudhoe Bay. Everything they would be using to collect data had to be tested to insure they could fulfill their contract with the oil companies. This included the two main engines being checked out, as well. They were new and had to go through a break-in period. The assembly crew was still aboard in case of a mechanical failure or a malfunction of any of the equipment aboard. They would be leaving as soon as everyone was satisfied the boat and equipment were working properly.

While the Seisjet crew was busy checking out their boat and equipment, Jim, Bob and I were busy marking the channel that led out of Prudhoe Bay. Because the Bay is so shallow it was important that reference buoys be put in place so we could stay within the channel when leaving and returning. The buoys were always removed after the season each year, due to the icing conditions, so it was an annual task to replace them and again mark the channel.

We utilized the depth finder and the radar aboard the Point Barrow to ascertain the channel's location. Buoys were then placed on both sides of the channel so we would only have to be concerned with staying inside the buoys. Without the reference points we would have to utilize the depth finder and radar every time we exited or entered the Bay. This would be very time consuming and, because the channel was so narrow, we could find ourselves running aground which could substantially delay the entire operation.

The west wind was still blowing 5–15 mph and the ice was nearly gone from Prudhoe Bay. Jim said the ice outside of Prudhoe Bay would also have receded enough by now to allow navigation to the areas the Seisjet needed to access. He again reiterated that it was important to get to work on the project as soon as possible because the season was short and unpredictable. Sometimes the ice started building earlier than in prior years so anyone depending on working the open waters had no time to waste. Jim said the Texas crew had a lot of data to gather from quite a large area so it was important they get started as soon as they were ready and as soon as the waterway was navigable. He said our job aboard the Point Barrow was to cater to the Seisjet crew but it was their responsibility to fulfill the contract. Jim wanted to insure we were ready and in no way delayed the project. He was very happy with the way things had gone up to this point, he said, and he had a good feeling about this season.

On the second day of sea trials for the Seisjet, a man who introduced himself as Tom, came aboard and told us he would be the skipper on the Seisjet this summer and he confided that he had never operated any boat larger than a 27-footer. He also said he had never operated a boat with twin motors, or what is commonly referred to as a twin-screw vessel. He wondered if it would be over-stepping for him to ask for a few pointers. Jim told him he was not at all overstepping and we were there to assist them in any way possible. Jim told me to go back to the Seisjet with Tom and help him out with anything he needed. I told Tom I had never operated a jet powered vessel before but I could show him how a conventional powered boat operated. I told him there shouldn't be too much difference between the two. He said he had been having problems docking the boat and ask if I could teach him how to dock and maybe give him some pointers on how to best maneuver the boat, as well. He said they were going out on another sea trial in a little while and asked if I could accompany them. I told him I'd be more than happy to go along.

Tom and I walked back to the Seisjet and went aboard. The assembly crew was offloading their equipment and would be leaving. They were satisfied with the operations of the boat and equipment and were anxious to go home. Tom introduced me to the Texas crew and told them why I was aboard. He introduced me to Larry, who he said was a deckhand, and then Rueben was introduced as a deckhand/engineer combination, with Clint, Marlin and JB being introduced as the Technical team, or commonly known as the Techs. The Techs would be responsible for the care and maintenance of all the data collection aboard as well as any maintenance on the cable. They also maintained the instruments on board. As I was introduced I shook each of their hands and everyone seemed very friendly. My initial opinion was that we would all work well together and we'd have a great summer.

After the boat assembly crew had their gear ashore and were on their way, Rueben started the engines to let them warm up. I explained to Tom the proper way to get the best response out of a twin-engine boat. I drew a diagram on paper explaining, what I call, the push/pull method utilized when operating a twin-screw vessel. I told him anytime the starboard engine is in forward gear it is pushing on the starboard bow and when it is in reverse it is pulling on the starboard bow. The same principle applies to the port side. If you place a boat in forward gear on the starboard side and leave the port engine in neutral, the boat will start to turn to the left, or, in nautical terms, to the port. If you put both the engines in forward gear, at the same RPM, with the rudder amidships, the boat will travel in a straight line because both engines are pushing on the bow, one on the port side and one on the starboard side, thus canceling out the starboard or port turn that would be happening if only one engine were in use. If you consider only the bow of the vessel and you have control of it, the stern and the rest of the boat will follow. When you need to turn sharply port or starboard, you can put one engine ahead and the other in reverse, dependent on the direction you wish to turn. You can augment your turn by turning the rudder, or steering wheel, in the direction of your turn, as well. Example: When turning hard starboard you would want your rudder to be turned hard to right, or starboard. Your port engine would be in forward gear, (pushing the bow to the starboard), and the starboard engine would be in reverse, (pulling the bow to the starboard). You can then add or reduce power to the engines to get the desired speed of the turn. The opposite is used to turn to the port. This concept can be learned quickly if you only consider pulling or pushing on the bow and controlling your speed by utilizing the throttles. I told Tom to continually consider what is taking place at the bow of the vessel when maneuvering. I added that he had to be conscious of where the stern is only when there is another boat, or object, that could interfere with its direction of travel. To sum up, I told him if you wanted to turn hard to the starboard you can enhance the turn by turning your steering wheel hard to the starboard and reversing the starboard engine while the port engine is in forward gear. The port engine is pushing the bow of the boat to the starboard while the starboard engine, in reverse, is pulling the bow to the starboard, thus my definition of the push/pull method.

I informed Tom there were a lot of variations he needed to learn but I could see he had the interest and I had no doubt he would master the operation of the boat in no time.

I told him it does take some practice and getting used to but, if he can visualize the concept, he can operate any twin-screw vessel. I also encouraged him to start slow and not to get in any hurry.

Tom told me he thought he was starting to understand the concept but he wanted me to show him by taking the helm when we pulled off the dock. I agreed to take the boat out from the dock if he would agree to dock it when we returned. He agreed and I took over the helm.

As we got ready to pull away from the dock I explained every move I was making to Tom. I explained that the rudder should be turned to the starboard. I would put the starboard engine in reverse and the port engine ahead. I showed him how to use the throttles to kick the stern of the vessel out from the dock, and at the same time, hold the boat from moving fore or aft by using the throttles. As soon as the stern had swung out away from the dock, I put the starboard engine in neutral and reversed the port engine. At the same time, I brought the rudder indicator to the center position. I showed Tom the maneuver and told him this would pull the bow away from the dock and the boat would back pretty much straight out, clearing the dock or any other boat tied directly behind it. I showed him how he could adjust the speed of the bow swing by using his throttles and going ahead or astern with the engines. Tom seemed impressed after finding the method actually worked the way I had explained it. He said

I made it look so easy and I told him it was easy once you had mastered the push/pull method of running a twin-screw vessel. I told him I had a lot of experience running dive boats with diver's in the water and you had to know what your boat was doing at all times and how it would react when you were attempting a maneuver. I also cautioned Tom with regards to running a boat in a wind or fast tide. The only way to learn is through experience. I said you have to be able to react to whatever the environment throws at you but I assured him, with practice, he should not have any major problems.

I did notice running a boat with jet units is quite different than running a boat with props and rudders in that the jet boat is slower to respond to your commands and you need to think ahead a little further than on a conventional boat. I warned Tom that he should always be thinking ahead regarding any maneuvers he would be undertaking and mentally plan them out. Even though the Seisjet reacted differently than the Point Barrow, Tom was learning on a jet boat so he wouldn't be influenced by having run a conventional boat in the past. There was little doubt he would even know the difference, at this point.

We continued out into the middle of Prudhoe Bay and I told Tom to take over the helm. Then, standing beside him, I coached him on how to make a number of different maneuvers by utilizing the push/pull method. Tom caught on quickly and in no time was making port and starboard turns smoothly and was getting more and more comfortable operating the boat. It was a real joy for me to watch how quickly Tom caught on. After a couple hours we headed back to the float and I stood beside Tome and coached him when he docked the boat. I told him the most important thing when docking was to be going slow enough you could correct any mistakes you might make before they became major problems. With coaching, Tom docked the boat like an old pro. He took direction very well and learned quickly. I had no doubt he would make an excellent boat handler with time and practice.

When I went back aboard the Point Barrow Jim asked me how Tom had done and I told him I felt Tom would make an excellent skipper, in time. Jim said that was good to hear because the actual collecting of data was scheduled to start the next morning. He had met with the project engineer who came to check to see if the Point Barrow was ready. Jim said he told him we were ready and awaiting their directions. The project engineer told Jim everything seemed to be ready aboard the Seisjet and they wanted to take off early the next morning, if possible. Jim told him we would be ready and eager to get started. Arrangements were made and we planned to leave the East Dock at 0600 hours. Jim pulled out the chart of the area and showed me where he'd been told they would be starting their data collection. He said it was up to me to see they reached the right area. He reminded me that no one aboard the Seisjet had any sailing experience and, even though they would be taking data readings from specific areas, none of them knew how to get to those areas. To the Texas crew the data collection consisted only of a series of numbers and it was likely that no one aboard would have any idea where they actually were at any given time, or any clue of how to access those areas. I told Jim I would have to be updated daily with the latitude and longitude to determine where they wanted to go next. Jim told me I should be kept informed every evening after returning to Prudhoe Bay and that was the responsibility of the Seisjet crew.

The next morning, we rolled out of bed at 0500 hours and ate a light breakfast then warmed up the main engines. We didn't want to take any chances that we would hold up the operation in any way. I called the Seisjet on the VHF radio on channel 10, the working frequency we would use, and told Tom to call us when they were ready to sail. He told me it would be a few minutes and that he would let us know. After approximately ten minutes Tom called and said they were ready to go. I told him to pull in behind me when we were going out the channel and not to vary port or starboard because the channel was very narrow and they could go aground if went outside the marker buoys. Tom said he understood and I told Bob to cut us loose.

We eased out away from the float and proceeded out of the Bay, watching closely not to get outside the buoy markers. The Seisjet didn't have any problems navigating the channel and, after exiting Prudhoe Bay, I kicked the RPM's up to 2800 on both my main engines. We traveled at around 10 mph with the Point Barrow and the Seisjet could probably go 18 mph so, they had to throttle back to keep from leaving us behind.

Because they did not know how to reach the area where they wanted to start collecting data, they had to travel with us. Tom did ask if the speed we were traveling was as fast as we could go and I told him it was. He was disappointed but had to accept the speed or go on ahead. For various reasons this did not happen.

We were underway for an hour and twenty minutes when we arrived at the general area where I'd been told the data recording would start. I called Tom on the radio and notified him we were near to the area where I was told they were to start the project. Tom thanked me and cut back on his throttles. I moved off to the Seisjet's port side, approximately 300 feet, and held that position. I was anxious to see how the operation was going to go.

Tom called me and said they had taken a reading from their Loran C instrument on board, and was happy to report I had led them to within a hundred yards of where they would start collecting data. With the Loran C, which they had aboard, they could tell when they were on location. The Longitude and Latitude readings, which were taken from the Loran C, must coincide with the locations on the nautical chart the oil companies had provided. The oil company representatives had marked all the areas on the chart they wanted checked and, upon checking the chart, the technicians found them to be near the location where they were to start.

Larry, Rueben and Mike came out on the deck of the Seisjet and were busy readying the cable and moving items around. It appeared Clint and JB were responsible for the instruments inside the wheelhouse, as well as the collection of the data. Within a few minutes a buoy, which was tied to the end of the data collection cable, was thrown over the stern of the boat and Tom put the Seisjet in gear and headed in a northeasterly direction. As the boat slowly moved ahead the men on deck fed the cable out, off the stern.

The cable was only a couple inches in diameter with a number of sensors and wires encased inside. It was waterproof and I was told it was imperative the outer covering of the cable be protected at all cost to avoid any contamination that salt water could cause. The outer covering was made of a very resilient material which, hopefully, would prevent it from sustaining any damage.

As the Seisjet crew continued laying the cable out, I kept pace with them but stayed a couple hundred yards away. It took nearly an hour and twenty minutes for the cable to be completely stretched out behind their boat. Tom called me on the VHF and told me they were preparing to set, and detonate, a charge and requested I hold my position and not move any closer to them. I acknowledged and within a few minutes the charge was in place, and after Tom announced "Fire in the hole" on the radio, the charge was detonated. Bob and I felt the concussion aboard the Point Barrow but, due to the depth of the charge, only ripples were observed on the surface of the water. Shortly after the charge was set, and after Clint and BJ had gathered some data from the detonation, Tom called and said I would have to move further away. He said they were receiving data readings off the steel hull of the Point Barrow. No one was aware this would happen but, in the future, we would need to make sure we were far enough away so our hull would not interfere with their data collecting. Tom suggested we stay a minimum of one mile away from them when they were setting charges. Bob suggested, since we had to kill some time, that we take a closer look at a couple of the floating ice bergs. I agreed and we moved off to the north west in the direction of a number of ice bergs that could be seen on the horizon.

Bob and I spent the rest of the day checking out ice bergs and watching the seagulls and the different species of birds that migrated to the area. I was surprised to see so many different species. I had no idea what kind of birds most of them were but we found it very enjoyable to watch them.

As we traveled we observed a number of floating ice bergs. They were of all different sizes and configurations. The largest one we observed was approximately 200 yards wide by 300 yards deep. Toward the outer edges the ice was much thicker and stood higher out of the water than in the center. On one of the ice bergs we observed what appeared to be a small lake, being very deep blue in color and approximately 150 yards long by 50 – 75 yards wide. I later learned the blue lake was actually a fresh water lake that had been formed from melting snow and rain water. A number of the ice bergs we saw had smaller fresh water lakes, or ponds, on them. The ones with the lakes on them were beautiful but hazardous at the same time. After we were informed the blue water was actually fresh water trapped in the ice bergs, we would use our stand by time to search for an ice berg with a lake on it and then we would take on fresh water aboard the tug. This occurred a number of different occasions throughout the summer. We would use a 2" gasoline powered water pump, which we kept aboard the boat in case of an emergency. We had enough fire hose aboard to reach the boat from the lakes or ponds. I would nose up to the ice berg and Bob would get the hose and pump set up and we would take on fresh water. Taking on water off an ice berg negated our having to contact someone and arrange a schedule to take water at the East Dock. We had found taking on water at the East Dock to be somewhat of a hassle every time we needed water. The water off the ice tasted fine and, even though one would think you would taste some salt in it, we didn't find that to be the case.

It was 1650 hours when I received a call from Tom on the Seisjet reporting they were pulling in the cable and would be ready to head back to Prudhoe Bay within ½ hour. He said we could start their direction without interfering with any data collection now. I ask how their first day of data collection had gone and Tom said they had a few bugs to work out of the system and it hadn't gone as well as they had hoped. He said he felt tomorrow would be a much better day. When I inquired if they would be returning to the same location where they had finished today, Tom said they would and that he would get the Loran C coordinates to me at dinner. When I got within a hundred feet of the Seisjet I took radar bearings off three separate oil rigs to insure I would have no difficulty leading them back to this location the next morning. This became normal operations for me. When we would be notified they were ready to return to Prudhoe Bay I would get near them and take radar bearings. It worked very well throughout the entire season and we never failed leading them to the correct locations.

During the time we were on standby, and checking out ice bergs, Bob had put a lasagna together for dinner and said he would put it in the oven when we were getting near Prudhoe Bay. This would be the first day we would actually be feeding the Seisjet crew. They had been taking all their meals at the diner near the East Dock while we were in port. Bob now would be cooking all their dinners until the project was finished. This included he make sure all the needed supplies were ordered and delivered to the boat. He would order the supplies via telephone after we reached the East Dock and a time for delivery would be scheduled. This became standard procedure and worked very well.

I had found Bob to be an all-around good hand. He was a good deckhand, a good engineer and an excellent cook. He had prepared a number of meals for Jim and I when we were working to ready the tug while waiting for the Seisjet crew to get their boat ready. Along with being able to do anything you asked of him, he was also a very nice guy and very easy to talk to. It was a pleasure to work with Bob. He was always asking what needed to be done and always ready and eager to do whatever was asked of him. Bob was very eager to learn and was always asking questions about navigation and about my past sailing experience. We became very good friends during that summer. We still keep in touch with one another to this day.

Upon arriving at the East Dock in Prudhoe Bay, Bob told me to let the Seisjet crew know dinner would be ready in an hour. Due to limited space aboard the tug, we were forced to feed half the crew at one setting and then, after the first four had finished, Bob and I would join the other two Seisjet crew members and have our dinner. The lasagna turned out great and the meal, along with the garlic bread Bob had made, generated a number of compliments from the Seisjet crew. Ice cream was served to top off the meal. Everyone was in a great mood and we all visited for a while following dinner.

Plans for the next day were discussed and it was decided we would leave the East Dock at 0600 hours. JB said they were pleased with the limited data collection they had gotten today but, like with any new equipment, some bugs had to be worked out. They will still have to deal with some small problems but felt they had the major problems behind them, he said. JB said he hoped to get twice the data tomorrow than they had gotten today. Even though they had a very large area to work, if everything held together and the weather participated, JB felt they should have no problem in finishing the contract before freeze up.

At 0600 hours the following morning we were again underway to the location where the Seisjet had ended operations the day before. Again, Tom called me on the VHF and asked if this was as fast as the Point Barrow could go. I, again, told him yes it was but if he wanted to go on ahead we'd catch up. He said we'd travel together and, chuckling, said he didn't want to take the chance of my getting lost. In reality Jim, nor anyone else aboard the Seisjet for that matter, didn't know how to find the location so they were forced to stay close to me.

When we arrived on location the Seisjet started stringing out cable right away. Bob and I took the Point Barrow a little over a mile off and stood by in case we were needed.

This was the way the summer progressed. In all honesty, the job we were doing left us standing by much more than actually working, which made for extremely long days. We would lead the Seisjet to their coordinates everyday and then would guide them back to Prudhoe Bay every evening. The data collection was going very well and it seemed the problems the Seisjet crew had been experiencing at first had been corrected and they were very pleased with the way things were going now. There had only been two days that the weather had kept us from working. The wind had blown too hard to take a chance of stringing out the cable and possibly damaging it. On those two days any maintenance items that were needed aboard the Seisjet were taken care of. This worked out well in that we didn't experience any down time due to mechanical or instrument failures aboard either vessel.

During mid-July, through the first week in August, the "Sea Lift" would be busy at the West Dock offloading equipment, building modules and supplies for the Prudhoe Bay oil field. The "Sea Lift" was made up of a number of ocean-going tugs and barges delivering needed supplies from the states, or other locations, to Prudhoe Bay on the North Slope. The modules were, in fact, large multi-story buildings that were constructed and then put on barges to be delivered to the Prudhoe Bay field by ocean-going tug boats. Some of the buildings were pump stations or housing units. Due to the waters being so shallow in and around the West Dock, smaller push tugs would go out into deeper water and take the barges from the ocean-going vessels and bring them to the West Dock for offloading.

Because the season was so short, and it took a great deal of time to offload the large buildings and other equipment, the ocean-going tugs feared being caught in the ice when the freeze came. They had to be out of the North before the big freeze. Because of this all mariner rules of the road were suspended for the "Sea Lift" and, regardless of the circumstances, all boats not associated with the "Sea Lift", had to yield the right of way to any of the boats working the job. There were no exceptions and the activity at the West Dock went on 24 hours a day until the barges were offloaded. I was told the tugs never got caught in the heavy ice but some had to push their way through some ice that was building so they hadn't left any too soon.

On September 22nd we made our last trip to the data collecting grounds. The weather was turning cold, with some freezing temperatures in the mornings, and the wind was becoming more prevalent. Some thin ice was forming but it wouldn't be long before the temperatures dropped and winter ice started to build in Prudhoe Bay. I was told the ice built rapidly when the Bay did start freeing over. We had some snow on three occasions but it never stuck and was gone within a day or so. It seemed as if someone had flipped a switch, with regards to the weather changing, and the cold was being felt more and more with each day that passed.

On the afternoon of September 22nd Tom called me on the VHF and told me they were pulling in the cable for the last time this season as they had satisfied their contract. The areas the oil companies had designated for data collection had all been covered, he said. I moved into within a couple hundred feet of the Seisjet and, even though he said they had finished the job, I took coordinate readings with my radar just in case anything had been overlooked. One never knows what to expect and I wanted to be ready for anything.

After the cable was aboard, and on the spool, we headed for Prudhoe Bay. I was running the same RPM's I had used all summer but today I was pulling away from the Seisjet. I called Tom on the VHF and asked if they had a problem. He told me he didn't understand what was going on but, even with added RPM's, he was unable to keep up with the Point Barrow. He said he noticed the difference in the boat's speed within the last week but didn't know what to attribute it to. I jokingly told him I'd kicked in the after burners on the tug and was having trouble controlling it. Tom chuckled and told me he didn't know the problem but he'd noticed a difference in the Seisjet speed the last few trips and, even though he added RPM's, he was not able to out run the Point Barrow. I reduced the throttles on the tug so we could travel together to the East Dock.

Tom called via radio again and told me to convey to Bob that he didn't need to cook dinner tonight. He said they wanted to take Bob and I out to dinner at the diner by the East Dock. Bob said he hadn't started dinner so that would work for him. I told Tom we'd be looking forward to it and added that now I really did wish he had a faster boat so it wouldn't take so long to get fed. He chuckled but I got the distinct impression he didn't really share the humor of my statement.

After we arrived at the East Dock a mechanic was summoned to look into the problem on the Seisjet. We were later told the mechanic found that, due to the shallow water in Prudhoe Bay, and with the Bay's bottom being made up of a fine sand, the Seisjet's salt water intake pumps had pumped a good amount of sand through the jet units, wearing the impellers out due to the sandpaper effect. No matter what RPM's the engines would be turning, the amount of water being pumped through the jet units would be considerably diminished. The volume of water that is pumped through its jet units determines the speed of a jet boat. With the impellers being so worn down they could not pump a sufficient volume of water through the jet units to sustain the speed as they had during most of the season.

Dinner at the diner tuned out great and everyone had a good time. A lot of laughing and storytelling took place and everyone present seemed to really enjoy our time together. The diner went all out, as well, and served New York steaks with all the trimmings. Apple pie alamode was served for desert. It was a perfect meal ending a great season working with a bunch of great guys.

Borrowing the phone at the diner, I called Jim Adams and told him we had finished the contract and further that the Seisjet crew was happy with the job we had done. Jim was in Anchorage and said he would be coming to Prudhoe Bay in a couple days. Jim told me Bob and I should pull the buoys we'd set in the channel in Prudhoe Bay and then we could start gathering all the items together which would be taking off the Point Barrow. He said we should pump off any excess water, including the water in the forward ballast tanks. He said he really didn't want to take a chance of anything freezing aboard the tug. He also said we could empty most of the drinking water and keep only what we would need for cleaning and cooking. He said we could empty the rest of the water when we were on dry dock before we left the boat.

The next morning the Seisjet crew got busy dismantling their equipment and getting their boat ready to winterize. They had considerably more gear on board than we did but, with their whole crew pitching in, it wouldn't take long before they would have it all packed up and ready to be offloaded. Tom told us they had met with the oil company representatives earlier in the day and had given them the rest of the data they had collected. He said they seemed pleased to see the project come to an end. He also said they were hinting about possibly having the Seisjet back to gather more data the next year but it was all contingent on what leases they let out for bid and the results of this year's findings from the collected data. Tom did say it had been a long summer and he was a long way from home and didn't know if he'd want to again be part of a project like this. He said he had a wife and two children at home and he really missed them. I told him he was an experienced skipper now so he could write his own ticket. He smiled and said it was blatantly apparent I hadn't worked for the company he was employed with.

Bob and I got busy reading the Point Barrow for dry dock. We went out and retrieved all the buoy markers we had put in the channel and then we pumped the forward ballast tanks dry. The fresh water tank was also pumped down, leaving approximately 50 gallons of water aboard for living purposes. We collected all the items we would be offloading and boxed up everything that we wouldn't need. The electronics in the wheelhouse were disconnected and stored in boxes, with the exception of one VHF radio we would still be using. We boxed them up so they could be put in warm, dry storage. After the boat was pulled from the water and on dry dock, we would be pulling the four big D cell batteries from the engine room and storing them in warm, dry storage, as well. If the batteries were not removed they, most likely, would have to be replaced the next year, or whenever the boat was again made ready for use. When I had talked to Jim on the phone, he told me we could take our meals at the diner for the rest of our stay in Prudhoe Bay, if we wanted to. Bob had no argument with that at all. He said it would be nice to have someone cooking for him again, for a change, instead of his having to cook for everyone else. All summer Bob had not only deck handed and engineered the boat, he had cooked the meals and kept up with seeing to the orders for all the groceries that were needed. The cooking responsibilities were no easy chore but Bob seemed to pull it off without a problem even with his deckhand/engineer duties. He was certainly an all-around hand. Bob's only saving grace was that we were on stand by most days, which gave him a lot of time to get everything done. He told me he really liked his job and that all his responsibility kept him busy during the standby times. I guess it was somewhat of a longer season for me than for Bob. I was, more or less, glued to the wheelhouse and the radio in case the Seisjet crew needed us. At least Bob was kept busy while I monitored the radio and ran the boat. I certainly would never hesitate to have Bob as a co-worker on any job I was on in the future. He certainly proved himself this season.

Jim arrived at Prudhoe Bay two days later in mid-afternoon and told us he was very happy with the way the season had gone and the Seisjet crew had nothing but good reports about the Point Barrow.

Jim said before he came to the boat he had contacted the crane company to schedule a time we could pull the tug out of the water and he was told it would be October 2nd before they would have time to do it. The Seisjet was scheduled to come out of the water in the morning of October 2nd and we would be pulled in the afternoon, or immediately following the Seisjet being pulled. That was better than a week off and Bob and I had nearly everything already packed so we were in for a long boring week. Jim jokingly said we could rest up from our long hard summer. I told him we've been resting up most of the season with the job we were given. He laughed and said we'd find something to pass the time until they pulled the boat.

It was a long week but October 2nd finally did come around and the crane crew arrived mid-morning to pull the Seisjet. It took nearly two hours to get the boat on dry dock so the crane operator and his crew had lunch before pulling the Point Barrow. The Point Barrow was rigged and brought out of the water without incident. The boat was set on cribbing and the crane's rigging was unhooked and the crane crew left.

Bob and I got busy pulling the huge batteries out of the engine room following our pumping off the rest of the fresh water. Jim had a heated storage unit leased near the airport and we had transferred most everything from the tug to that location during the past week so we didn't have a lot to do to finish winterizing the boat. We were all anxious to finish the season and get back home.

The Seisjet crew were also anxious to leave and they were busy taking care of last-minute duties on their boat. Clint, Mike and JB had already flown home, after the seismic gear was all packed and ready to be taken off the vessel. Tom, Reuben and Larry must have drawn the short straws and had to stay until the Seisjet was on dry dock and see to all the equipment and gear being stored on shore.

The Point Barrow was winterized and all the gear was stored within a day of it being brought out of the water and Jim, Bob and I were on an airplane to Anchorage the next day. It had been a long, but good, season and we were all anxious to see our families. Jim was very pleased and gave both Bob and I a bonus for the job we'd done for him.

I kept in touch with Jim for many years, up until his death a number of years later, and I can honestly say, I have never worked for a more honest and fairer employer in my life. To this day I miss our phone calls, our visits, Jim's humor and a good man who I called friend.

When I arrived home, I spent the next couple weeks figuring out what I would do next. I stayed at home just enjoying my wife and daughter but, I had to be thinking about going back to work. I didn't really want to go back to the North Slope with Frontier & Sand, working nine weeks on with two weeks off so I had to come up with something. We were able to pay off the mobile home we were buying from my sumer earnings. and we had a little left for a rainy day but it wouldn't last and I had to find work. After much thought, more discussion with Ann, I went to the DMV in Anchorage and applied for, and obtained my chauffer's license. I jumped through the necessary hoops and I leased a Yellow Cab, working nights. I found it was not something I would want as a career but, for the winter, it would keep me home with the family and I would be making a living.

In the spring Ann and I sold the mobile home, packed up all our belongings, and moved back to Seldovia. Donica and Ann were both nearly ecstatic when I decided to move out of Anchorage. Ann confided in me that she and Donica were very pleased to be moving back and that they were never really comfortable in Anchorage and were afraid a lot of the time that I was away from home. I ask Ann why she hadn't said something and she told me she did not want to put any added stress on me knowing that I was doing what I had to do and that I really didn't want to be away either. She said everything turned out well and we had been able to get ahead a little bit. This was just one more reason I loved this lady so much.

After moving back to Seldovia, my brother-in-law and I traveled to Chinita Bay, across Cook Inlet from Seldovia, to gillnet for herring for the next six seeks. Following that season, I returned to Seldovia where I fished halibut out of my skiff, pulling by hand while Ann ran the outboard. We never made a lot of money but we did keep the wolf away but I was able to stay home with my family.

In August of 1979 my prayers were answered, relating to my finding employment where I would be home with my family every day. The City Manager. for the City of Seldovia, offered me a temporary position as Chief of Police for the City, telling me they needed someone for six weeks, or until they could find someone to fill the permanent position. After discussing it with my wife, we decided I should take the position in that it would provide employment for me until they did find someone permanent. Besides, I would be home working and would not have to leave to find work, for at least the next six weeks. So, I met with the City Manager and I was sworn in as Chief of Police for the City of Seldovia, a career lasting for the next nearly 32 years. Although I knew nothing about being a Cop when I started, I did continue to learn throughout the years with considerable help through the Alaska State Troopers and the Homer Police Department.

I was finally able to stay home with my family and make a living which would support us. At present I hold the record for being the longest serving Chief of Police for any City in Alaska's history. My Police career was very educational, as well as an interesting and exciting one, but, as they say, that's another story. Watch for my next book entitled *Alaska Bush Cop,* which I hope to have in the book stores near you in the spring of 2019.

www.ingramcontent.com/pod-product-compliance
Lightning Source LLC
Chambersburg PA
CBHW052041090426
42739CB00010B/2000